Modern Italy's Founding Fathers

The Making of a Postwar Republic

Steven F. White

BLOOMSBURY ACADEMIC
LONDON • NEW YORK • OXFORD • NEW DELHI • SYDNEY

BLOOMSBURY ACADEMIC
Bloomsbury Publishing Plc
50 Bedford Square, London, WC1B 3DP, UK
1385 Broadway, New York, NY 10018, USA
29 Earlsfort Terrace, Dublin 2, Ireland

BLOOMSBURY, BLOOMSBURY ACADEMIC and the Diana logo are
trademarks of Bloomsbury Publishing Plc

First published in Great Britain 2020
This paperback edition published 2022

Copyright © Steven F. White, 2020

Steven F. White has asserted his right under the Copyright, Designs and
Patents Act, 1988, to be identified as Author of this work.

For legal purposes the Acknowledgments on p.x constitute an
extension of this copyright page.

Cover design by Tjaša Krivec
Cover image: Communist Palmiro Togliatti speaking
to the crowd during election campaign (1948) (© Walter Sanders /
The LIFE Picture Collection / Getty Images)

All rights reserved. No part of this publication may be reproduced or
transmitted in any form or by any means, electronic or mechanical, including
photocopying, recording, or any information storage or retrieval system,
without prior permission in writing from the publishers.

Bloomsbury Publishing Plc does not have any control over, or responsibility for,
any third-party websites referred to or in this book. All internet addresses given
in this book were correct at the time of going to press. The author and publisher regret
any inconvenience caused if addresses have changed or sites have ceased to exist,
but can accept no responsibility for any such changes.

Every effort has been made to trace copyright holders and to obtain their
permissions for the use of copyright material. The publisher apologizes for any
errors or omissions and would be grateful if notified of any corrections that
should be incorporated in future reprints or editions of this book.

A catalogue record for this book is available from the British Library.

A catalog record for this book is available from the Library of Congress.

Library of Congress Cataloging-in-Publication Data

Names: White, Steven F., 1950- author.
Title: Modern Italy's founding fathers: the making of a postwar republic/by Steven F. White.
Description: London; New York: Bloomsbury Academic, 2020. |
Includes bibliographical references and index. |
Identifiers: LCCN 2020005762 (print) | LCCN 2020005763 (ebook) |
ISBN 9781474215497 (hb) | ISBN 9781474215503 (ePDF) | ISBN 9781474215510 (eBook) |
Subjects: LCSH: Statesmen–Italy–Biography. | De Gasperi, Alcide,1881-1954. |
Nenni, Pietro, 1891-1980. | Togliatti, Palmiro, 1893-1964. | Italy–Politics and
government–1945-1976. | Partito della democrazia cristiana–Biography. |
Partito socialista italiano–Biography. |
Partito comunista italiano–Biography. | Cold War. | Fascism–Italy–History–20th century.
Classification: LCC DG578.W48 2020 (print) | LCC DG578 (ebook) | DDC 945.092092/2–dc23
LC record available at https://lccn.loc.gov/2020005762
LC ebook record available at https://lccn.loc.gov/2020005763

ISBN: HB: 978-1-4742-1549-7
PB: 978-1-3503-3862-3
ePDF: 978-1-4742-1550-3
eBook: 978-1-4742-1551-0

Typeset by Integra Software Services Pvt. Ltd.

To find out more about our authors and books visit www.bloomsbury.com
and sign up for our newsletters.

To David Roberts and, in memoriam, to Hans Schmitt and Pietro Scoppola

Contents

List of Illustrations	ix
Acknowledgments	x
Introduction	1
Why Italy?	2
Biography and History	9
1 Three Founding Fathers	19
Political Friendship	20
Alcide De Gasperi	23
Palmiro Togliatti	28
Pietro Nenni	34
2 A Daunting Prospect	45
Allied Occupation	46
The Schools	51
The Church	58
The Monarchy	60
Miseria	61
3 From Resistance to Restoration	71
The Resistance and the Anti-Fascist Parties	72
False Dawn	78
Underground Once More	79
The Salerno Turn	82
Problems with the Purge	85
Uomo Qualunque	87
From Parri to De Gasperi	88
4 Monarchy or Republic?	99
De Gasperi's First Government	99
The Administrative Elections of Spring 1946	103
June 2: The Republic Is Born	108

5	The Constitution and the Peace Treaty	129
	The Constitutional Compromise	129
	A Punitive Peace	139
6	Toward April 18, 1948	147
	The Demise of the Anti-Fascist Alliance	148
	Togliatti versus De Gasperi	152
	The American Connection: Round I	155
	Pius XII, Gedda, and the Civic Committees	158
7	Cold War Stasis, 1948–1954	169
	An Ambiguous Mandate	171
	The Shadow of the Vatican	173
	The Sturzo Operation	175
	The "Swindle Law"	182
	The American Connection: Round II	185
	The Fall of De Gasperi	188
8	Aftermath	197
	1954–1964	197
	1964–1980	203
	1980–1994	208
Chronology of Events		217
Bibliography		222
Index		243

Illustrations

1	Alcide De Gasperi, January 31, 1950	120
2	Palmiro Togliatti, December 1, 1944	121
3	Pietro Nenni, December 1, 1944	122
4	Victor Emmanuel III, King of Italy	123
5	Alcide De Gasperi countersigning the constitution, December 27, 1947	124
6	Pietro Nenni giving a speech	125
7	Luigi Einaudi talks with Mario Scelba and Palmiro Togliatti, June 2, 1952	126
8	Palmiro Togliatti casting vote, June 7, 1953	127
9	Alcide De Gasperi, August 1, 1948	128
10	Façade of Montecitorio palace	128

Acknowledgments

The origins of this book date back to my years of graduate study at the University of Virginia. In the course of my studies in Charlottesville, I developed a strong interest in Italy's transition from Fascist dictatorship to democracy following the Second World War. My doctoral dissertation focused on Italian educational reconstruction, first under Allied auspices and then under Christian Democratic supervision. Despite the efforts of progressive, Deweyan reformers guiding the Allies' Education Sub-commission, indigenous Catholic authorities took control of educational reconstruction during Italy's *secondo dopoguerra* (1945–1955). After completing my dissertation and first book, my scholarly interests shifted from educational to political reconstruction.

What was it, I asked, that empowered the Christian Democrats to garner the mantle of political leadership? And how was it that the bitter Cold War rivalry which ensued between the Christian Democrats and Italy's powerful Communists and Socialists did not degenerate into civil war? Seeking answers to these historical questions, I have come to focus on the intersection of leadership, ideology, and outside pressures emanating from the Vatican, the United States, and the USSR.

Three historians provided me with valuable instruction, advice, and encouragement during my formative years as an historian. Under David Roberts' mentorship, I wrote my master's thesis on Antonio Gramsci's early understanding of the Bolshevik Revolution and its bearing on hegemonic project of Italian Communist Party. Roberts' use of intellectual and cultural developments to illuminate broader trends in twentieth-century European history has lastingly informed my own pedagogy and scholarship. Hans Schmitt's steady guidance through the long process of researching and writing my dissertation was invaluable. I am grateful too for Hans' and his wife Florence's lasting friendship with all of the members of my family. Over the course of several research trips to Rome, I had the good fortune to meet the progressive Catholic historian Pietro Scoppola. As a scholar and a public figure, Scoppola embodied the best of Italy's civic humanistic tradition, appealing, in Abraham Lincoln's words, to "the better angels of our nature."

While conducting research for this book, I had the opportunity to interview Alcide De Gasperi's daughter Maria Romana De Gasperi, De Gasperi's former undersecretary Francesco Bartellota, and former OSS officer and historian H. Stuart Hughes. I thank the following scholars who shared their critical judgment and expertise with me: James Miller, Roy Domenico, Rhiannon Evangelista, Spencer Di Scala, Mark Gilbert, Sara Lorenzini, Leopoldo Nuti, Federico Romero, Paolo Pombeni, Maurizio Cau, Rosario Forlenza, Augusto D'Angelo, Francesco Malgeri, Eric Terzuolo, Umberto Gentiloni Silveri, and Paolo Acanfora. I am indebted to the US State Department for sponsoring my 2004 lecture tour to the Istituto Luigi Sturzo, the Università degli Studi di Roma III, the Suor Orsola in Benincasa Università di Napoli, and the Università degli Studi di Trento.

I would also like to acknowledge the expertise and consideration afforded to me by archivists, librarians, and others at the Istituto Luigi Sturzo, the European University Institute Historical Archives, the New York Public Library, the US National Archives and Records Administration, the Library of Congress, the State Department's Foreign Service Institute, Mount St. Mary's University, the Fondazione Trentina Alcide De Gasperi, the Fondazione Pietro Nenni, the Istituto Gramsci, the Archives of the Italian Senate, and the Archivio Centrale dello Stato. Particular thanks go to Ana Ulrich and Charlie Gallagher of Mount St. Mary's University's Phillips Library for their assistance with what must have seemed like an endless stream of inter-library requests.

The inter-disciplinary and comparative approach adopted in this work owes a great deal to my many years of teaching within Mount St. Mary's National Endowment for the Humanities sponsored core curriculum. Among the colleagues with whom I shared the challenges, insights, and satisfactions of contributing to this curriculum, a special thank you to Curt Johnson, Indrani Mitra, Sue Goliber, Carol Hinds, Teresa Rupp, Andrew Rosenfeld, Kurt Blaugher, Bill Collinge, Greg Murry, David Rehm, Carmen Schmersahl, Bill Portier, Robert Ducharme, and John Donovan.

I am deeply grateful for the support and understanding of family and friends. From the outset, Alicia White offered invaluable aid and encouragement. Thanks as well to Dan White, Sara Van Meerbeke, Peter Eberhart, Bill Prudden, Jane and Martin Malone, and Stephen Whitman.

Rhodri Mogford and Dan Hutchins at Bloomsbury Academic Press have generously offered their time and counsel at every stage of this endeavor. Lisa Rowe and Samantha Rice gave essential help with copyediting. A special word of thanks to my dear friend and partner Lynn Diviak for all of her assistance as we shepherded this scholarly work to conclusion.

Needless to say, I take full responsibility for any errors of fact or interpretation in the work.

Introduction

On July 14, 1948, Italian Communist Party (Partito Communista Italiano—PCI for short) leader Palmiro Togliatti was shot and gravely wounded by a right-wing extremist as he left Italy's Chamber of Deputies. Rushed to a nearby hospital, the Communist leader underwent emergency surgery for wounds in his neck and lung. The operation was successful, but it would be a week before Togliatti could be considered out of danger. In the interim, Italy teetered on the brink of civil war. The left-leaning Italian Confederation of Labor proclaimed a general strike, accusing Christian Democratic Party (Democrazia Cristiana—DC for short) Alcide De Gasperi's centrist government of fostering a climate of anti-democratic violence. Agitation in Genoa and other northern cities reached insurrectionary proportions. Hardnosed Interior Minister Mario Scelba responded by deploying the country's 180,000 police and Carabinieri, and threatened to call up military units to restore law and order.[1] Togliatti's ally Pietro Nenni, head of the Italian Socialist Party (Partito Socialista Italiano—PSI for short), confirmed in a journal entry that the country now faced extreme danger.[2]

Confronted by this volatile state of events, Togliatti, De Gasperi, and Nenni each sought to mitigate the crisis. Prior to losing consciousness in the hospital, the Communist leader begged the comrades who had rushed to his side "[Be] calm, do not lose your heads!" Shaken by the prospect of a mass uprising should Togliatti die, De Gasperi visited the stricken leader in the hospital, remaining in Togliatti's room for some time in silence.[3] Speaking the next day in the Chamber of Deputies, Nenni reiterated pleas he had made throughout the previous year, urging De Gasperi not to draw his country into the same spiral of violence that had brought Austrian dictator Engelbert Dolfuss to power in the 1930s. Nenni noted that he had couched his words in "human terms," and that this had "made a deep impression on [the prime minister]."[4] For several days Italy's civil peace hung in the balance, but then tensions began to ease.

These individual actions were taken against the backdrop of the Cold War animosities that had worsened markedly in Italy, as they had internationally, over the preceding several years. Economic recovery following the war, such as it was, advantaged the country's bourgeoisie, including its industrial and landed elites, at the expense of workers and peasants. Italians' chronic distrust in the State[5] resurfaced across the peninsula, assuming particularly alarming proportions in the *Mezzogiorno* (southern Italy). Italy's independence and national identity were called into question. While Communists and Socialists idealized Stalin's Soviet Union, most other Italians looked to America for salvation. Pius XII's Church proclaimed an all-out crusade against "atheistic Marxism."

Why Italy?

Unlike Spain during the late 1930s, Greece in the 1940s, or the countries situated behind the Iron Curtain, Italy's ideological rivals forsook all-out violence for enduring, if surly, coexistence. What made it possible for Italy to navigate between the Charybdis of Communist subversion and the Scylla of integralist Catholic and monarchical authoritarianism? How, in other words, are we to account for the Italian Cold War exception?

In seeking answers to these questions, I have focused my attention on De Gasperi, Nenni, and Togliatti as the Italian republic's three central founding fathers. The book centers on these statesmen's complementary personal attributes, aspirations, and accomplishments. Collectively, this trio of leaders played indispensable roles in fashioning the political values and practices which would shape Italian parliamentary life through the next half century. While each of these figures has been the subject of individual biographies, no Italian or Anglophone study to date has systematically looked at the three men as an ensemble.

As Italy's prime minister from late 1945 until mid-1953, De Gasperi's calm, clear-eyed, and resolute style of leadership proved vital as the nation set about righting itself from the twin disasters of Fascist dictatorship and world war. Head of eight successive coalition governments, he drew support from both the Vatican and the United States while retaining a measure of autonomy from both. For his part, the coolly cerebral, tough-minded Togliatti offered a political vision—at times critical and at times inspirational—which provided a necessary counterpoint to the hegemonic pressures exerted by political Catholicism between 1948 and the mid-1950s. Neither De Gasperi nor Togliatti was charismatic in the conventional sense[6]—arguably a virtue in the eyes of Italians exhausted by two decades of Mussolinian self-aggrandizement and hyperbole. A brilliant orator, Nenni lacked Togliatti's ideological rigor or De Gasperi's political savvy. Publicly Nenni was an unstinting tribune for the common man and for republicanism; privately, he served as intermediary and sometime broker between his two mutually diffident peers.

Each man had suffered at the hands of Mussolini's regime. Between the wars, Togliatti and Nenni were in exile in Moscow and Paris respectively, while De Gasperi was imprisoned for sixteen months before experiencing a form of "inner exile" as a ward of the Vatican. These congruent experiences fostered a measure of trust between the three. Drawing on a common fund of anti-Fascist language, they began to fashion a new political order as the Second World War ended.

Following the war, the three leaders shepherded Italy through a hotly contested institutional referendum (which deposed the House of Savoy in favor of a republic), contributed to the drafting of a new constitution, and headlined the nation's first democratic, multi-party elections. While imperfect—as we will see in this book's final chapters—the Italian republic's constitutional order endures to the present. De Gasperi, Togliatti, and Nenni were equally remarkable for what they refrained from doing. As minister for justice, in April 1946 Togliatti issued a broad amnesty decree for many Italians associated with one degree or another with the Fascist regime; though controversial, this decision helped to unify the nation as it moved into the postwar era. Unceremoniously dropped by De Gasperi from his governing coalition in May 1947, Togliatti and Nenni shifted to angry but constitutional opposition. In Togliatti's phrasing, the two Marxist parties had been "excluded from the Government but not from the State." In turn, as the decade drew to a close, De Gasperi bucked intense pressure from the United States and from the Vatican to outlaw the Italian Communist Party (as in fact happened in West Germany). The Christian Democratic leader pointed to the broad support (some 25 percent of the electorate) that Togliatti's party then commanded. Despite the deep Cold War cleavages separating Marxists from non-Marxists at the time, both within Italy and beyond it, De Gasperi continued to believe that parliamentary engagement represented the best way to contain, and in the long run domesticate, his Communist and Socialist adversaries. Even as a political foe of De Gasperi's, Nenni never gave up on the possibility that, in time, he and his Christian Democratic counterpart would resume the fruitful political dialogue they began while sheltered underground in late 1943 and early 1944 during the Nazi occupation of Rome.

Viewed in retrospect, the chiliastic ideologies[7] of the Cold War era have come to appear less determinative of Italian political decisions and outcomes than they once did. Even during the highly polarized years of the *secondo dopoguerra* (roughly spanning the decade 1945–1955), contrasting Cold War doctrines mattered less—and the discretion of key leaders mattered more—than was perceived by contemporaries.

To substantiate this interpretive thesis, I draw especially heavily on the political addresses and writings of the three leaders, examining that evidentiary corpus through the lenses of discourse analysis, political context, and historical contingency. Further supporting this study's multi-perspectival treatment of the three founding fathers are correspondence, interviews, memoirs, and commentaries left by family members, friends, governmental and party colleagues, journalists, and intellectuals of the day—figures ranging from Togliatti's consort Senator Nilde Iotti and De Gasperi's daughter Maria Romana to journalist Indro Montanelli and Action Party leader Leo Valiani. The testimonies of many of these contemporaries are cited in extant biographies of one or another founder, though no work to date has gathered as wide an array of accounts as I have done in this group biography. The judgments of American diplomats, policymakers, reporters, and columnists writing on both sides of the Atlantic have also found their place here, offering their own perceptions (some quite insightful, other less so!) of Italy's political luminaries.

During the Cold War, the paramount question in the minds of politicians and policymakers on both sides of the Atlantic centered on the intentions of the Italian Communist Party and its leader. What were the Communists' "true" intentions? Were they to prevail electorally in a dreaded "Hour X," would they continue to honor democratic parliamentary governance? Having spent nearly two interwar decades in Stalin's Moscow, could, or would, Togliatti and company resist the temptation to install a Soviet-style dictatorship? Disbelief in the PCI's bona fides ran as deep in Italian conservative circles as it did in Washington. In the parlance of the day, Togliatti and his party were accused of pursuing a policy of *doppio binario* ("proceeding on two tracks," e.g., playing a double game—in Italian *doppio gioco*), for example, of speaking reassuringly and reasonably in formal, institutional settings while simultaneously whipping up anti-governmental anger in the piazza. Certainly such games were played (and not just by the PCI). We should take care not to read too much into this, or to focus unduly on would happen next, as opposed to what in fact did take place. Assessing underlying intentions is no simple task, especially if presumed insurrectionary aims are not acted upon.

As lead political actor during the *secondo dopoguerra*, it is De Gasperi's objectives and actions, rather than Togliatti's, that most require exploration. Plainspoken and reliable though he appeared in the eyes of most Italians, De Gasperi was arguably the most inscrutable of the early Republic's political luminaries. The Christian Democratic leader managed to combine starkly dissimilar qualities. He demonstrated an exceptional measure of political *virtù*[8] manifested in his knack for reading persons and political situations, his sense of timing, and in his capacity for compromise. Yet his private and familial life was marked by a simplicity and steadiness grounded in deep Christian piety. The task of reconciling these two sides of De Gasperi continues to challenge biographers and historians.

His ethical transparency contributed greatly to his personal stature, but could not simply be translated into policy commitments or actions. The prime minister's absorption in the day-to-day affairs of governance, and in the accompanying tactical jockeying with both allies and opposition, sometimes obscured his longer-term vision for his country. Several Italian scholars have questioned whether he even had an ideology, while others have suggested that his Christian faith functioned in lieu of a conventional political creed.[9] All of this helps to account for Socialist leader Pietro Nenni's characterization of his partner-turned-rival De Gasperi as a "sphinx." Similarly, historian John Harper has described De Gasperi as the most "enigmatic" of the republic's founding fathers.[10]

The burst of scholarship in Italy which followed upon the sesquicentennial of the Christian Democratic leader's death has amply enriched our understanding of this man's life and work, without fully resolving the challenges alluded to above.[11] In her introduction to the three-volume official biography of De Gasperi, published between 2006 and 2009, the statesman's eldest daughter Maria Romana conceded that it remained difficult "to integrate the different facets of her father, or to convey the wholeness (*discrivere nella sua interezza*) of the man." De Gasperi did not wear his feelings on his sleeves, nor did he keep a proper diary. Even his personal papers, finally transferred a decade ago by Maria Romana to the Historical Archives of the European University Institute in Florence, provide the researcher but glances of—again citing Maria Romana's phrasing—"De Gasperi's inner dynamic (*spinta interiore*) and way of being (*modo di essere*)."[12]

In view of De Gasperi's prudence, and his sometimes frustrating focus on pressing, immediate matters, it makes sense to contextualize him as amply as possible with his two prime political peers. In his study of the American

Revolution entitled *Founding Brothers: The Revolutionary Generation*, Joseph Ellis has offered a description which applies equally well to the protagonists of my study: "the achievement of the founding generation was a collective enterprise that succeeded because of the diversity of personalities and ideologies present in the mix."[13] Like the American republican constitution, the constitution of the Italian Republic embodied a compromise between divergent ideological orientations. Catholics, secular progressives (referred to in Italian as *laici/progressisti*), secular moderates, and Marxists each harbored their own notion of the "true" meaning of the peninsula's constitution.

Also informing my work is the multi-perspectival approach employed by Doris Kearns Goodwin in her celebrated study *Team of Rivals: The Political Genius of Abraham Lincoln*. Goodwin addresses the president in the following manner: "Just as a hologram is created through the interference of light from separate sources, so the lives and impressions of those who companioned Lincoln give us a clearer and more dimensional picture of the president himself."[14] Much the same may be said of the central figure in this work—the indispensable, but enigmatic De Gasperi.

For American historians such as myself, the crucial and pervasive role of political parties in the genesis of the Italian republic stands in sharp contrast to our own founding fathers' dread of "faction"—the functional equivalent of the party structures which nevertheless emerged within the first decade of the American republic. How did De Gasperi, Togliatti, and Nenni themselves envision the contribution which their three mass parties would make to the postwar genesis of Italian democracy? How firm was their grip on those political forces? De Gasperi and Togliatti were able to exercise near-undisputed leadership over their respective parties during the *secondo dopoguerra*. Nenni's prestige among his Socialist peers—great though it was in the mid-1940s—began to falter thereafter. The potency of each man's leadership within their respective parties afforded them valuable autonomy and flexibility of action both within and beyond governmental circles. As Pietro Scoppola has persuasively argued, Italy's pluralistic party system served an indispensable function in linking the Italian people with their nascent republican state.[15]

Also undergirding Italy's success in tempering the wider, transnational predominance of Cold War dogma was a resilient tradition of political humanism dating back many, many centuries in Europe and across the Mediterranean world. Drawing on rhetorical conventions and interactive customs already present in antiquity,[16] and developed further since the Renaissance, modern Italian politicians engaged directly and personally with one another, debating and dueling not with swords but with words.[17] In May 1947, De Gasperi confided to Nenni that he "would rather argue with you than agree with Togliatti."[18] De Gasperi's candid remark conveyed not only his aversion to Togliatti, but his determination to preserve discursive space for the two Marxist leaders and their parties within Italy's parliamentary arena. Volume one of Nenni's celebrated diaries (spanning the years 1943–1956) is replete with particularly colorful comments on his relationship with his Christian Democratic counterpart. As he was to muse in an entry written shortly after De Gasperi's passing, "he [De Gasperi] always had his foot on the brake, mine on the accelerator."[19] At least the two were driving the same vehicle.

In writing this biography, I have sought to not overestimate my three protagonists' ability to control events, as over and against the determinative role of larger historical forces. As my high school American history teacher Jim Martin was fond of asking, "Does the man make the times or do the times make the man?" Related to this question is the distinction to be made, within a given leader's life, between persisting personal values and political commitments and more contingent, tactical elaborations and adaptations to changing circumstances on the other.

This book's first two chapters deal respectively with each man's formative experiences up through the interwar years, and with the daunting, many-faceted societal crisis which followed in the mid-1940s. Chapters 3 through 7 trace the thoughts and actions of each man as events unfolded between the fall of Mussolini in July 1943 and De Gasperi's death in August 1954. Each chapter focuses on selected pivotal events, the better to delineate the counterpoint in each between individual initiative and contextual influence. The book's final chapter reviews the three leaders' posthumous legacies, set against watershed moments in Italy's history between the mid-1950s and the close of the twentieth century.

While recognizing the fruitful aspects of the republican constitution, the book also attends to its weaknesses, both formal and substantive. From the outset, the constitution's authority was hobbled by an awkward disjunction between, on the one hand, its sweeping, opening proclamation of fundamental principles and its delineation of citizens' rights and duties and, on the other, its staid delineation of the new state's organization. Over time, this weakness perpetuated Italy's all-too-familiar cleavage between the nation's *paese legale* (the State and its officials) and its *paese reale* (the lived experience of ordinary Italians).

Between mid-1944 and mid-1947, the anti-Fascist ideology and rhetoric enunciated by De Gasperi, Togliatti, and Nenni had converged effectively, empowering the Italian people to inform the nation's course via party affiliation, free participation in elections, and the pivotal June 1946 institutional referendum. But after the May 1947 collapse of the anti-Fascist coalition, and still more during the coldest Cold War period of 1948 to 1954, the political slogans, speeches, and writings of De Gasperi on the one hand and Togliatti and Nenni on the other calcified. Escalating vituperation on both sides obscured, rather than explicating, pragmatic, ongoing parliamentary jockeying for advantage. Particularly unfortunate was the erosion of Prime Minister De Gasperi's stature and statesmanship as he scrambled to cobble together successive coalition governments even as his Christian Democratic Party, now destined to rule for decades to come, disguised its squabbles over perks and patronage behind a convenient façade of boilerplate anti-communism.

I have written this book with three audiences in mind. The first is composed of Italianist scholars working on both sides of the Atlantic. In the second place, I have endeavored to deepen university students' (both at the undergraduate and graduate levels) understanding of modern Italy. More broadly, the work aims to reach a general public interested in Italian politics, history, and biography. Over the last several decades, the single leader widely recognized beyond Italian shores has been Silvio Berlusconi. His self-aggrandizing prominence between the mid-1990s and mid-2010s has all too often prompted patronizing, dismissive foreign assessments of the Italian polity. The present volume invites readers to take a second look, offering three alternative, more edifying faces for Italy's Republic. Unlike Berlusconi, the Italian republic's founding fathers forged principled, yet practicable, compromises to advance the country's common good. For American and British readers disheartened by the intolerance and disharmony presently crippling those nations' public life, the Italian example of resourceful compromise and positive action, even after twenty years of numbing dictatorship and war-spawned socio-economic devastation, should offer encouragement.

What lessons might we draw from that republic's first years? What political practices and civic customs from that time and place invite us to rethink our own? De Gasperi, Togliatti, and Nenni fortified their political parties as indispensable conduits of democratic deliberation and cohesion—rejecting a politics of personality which, all too recently, had led the nation terribly astray. Boisterous though they were, Italy's Chamber of Deputies and Senate constituted "talking shops" of the nation—not echo chambers of disconnected peroration. Party organs, independent journals, and newspapers flourished, alive with discourse and debate. The republic's founders looked forward, not backward, in charting a new political course for their nation, resolved to avoid the missteps which had opened the door to Fascism.[20]

Biography and History

In the United States and Great Britain, domestic political biography has long occupied a prominent place within the wider pantheon of historical writing—especially that aimed at broad domestic audiences. As regards Italy, Anglophone biographers have contributed amply to our understanding of the Risorgimento, and, more recently, of Fascist dictatorship. Yet English language studies of twentieth-century Italian leaders have lagged.[21] As of 2000, no full-length Anglophone studies of major statesmen—De Gasperi, Togliatti, and Nenni included—had yet appeared.[22] Also neglected were Giovanni Giolitti[23], Vittorio Emmanuele Orlando, Amintore Fanfani, Giulio Andreotti, Enrico Berlinguer, and Bettino Craxi.[24]

In 2010 Italian scholar Alfred Canavero's brief synthesis *Alcide De Gasperi: Christian, Democrat European* appeared in English translation. Two thoroughly documented, yet contrasting English language monographs on Togliatti have been published. Aldo Agosti's sympathetic *Palmiro Togliatti: A Biography*—published first in Italian in 1996, and then in English in 2008—comprehensively charts of the entirety of the Communist leader's life and career. Drawing extensively on recently available Russian sources, Elena Agarossi and Victor Zaslavsky's *Stalin and Togliatti: Italy and the Origins of the Cold War*—published in Italy in 1997 and in English translation in 2011—stresses Togliatti's subservience to Stalin and persistent opportunism.[25] Nenni still awaits a comprehensive Anglophone biography.

The evolution of political biography composed in Italian by native scholars has been a mercurial one. Historian Caudio Pavone and journalist and writer Sergio Romano have identified a series of distinct and sharply contrasting stages in that developmental process.[26] Over the past several centuries in Italy, studies of that nation's eminent leaders have served a colorful variety of needs—pedagogical, intellectual, and propagandistic.[27] This observation merits elaboration here, reminiscent as it is of eighteenth-century philosopher Giambattista Vico's theory of history. For Vico, history develops as a series of *ricorsi*—spirals which recapitulate and extend prior epochs. This model fits the evolution of Italian politics over the centuries, as succeeding generations of leaders engage with precedents set by their forerunners. In an intriguing piece appearing in the pages of the Roman daily *Il Messaggero*, journalist Mario Ajello asked a cross-section of leading Italian politicians to identify a figure from Italy's past whose values and actions informed their own political praxis. Prominent among historical mentors mentioned were Niccolo Machiavelli, Thomas More, and Camillo De Cavour.[28]

Each in their own way, De Gasperi, Togliatti, and Nenni shared in the humanistic intellectual and cultural ethos memorably evoked by Benedetto Croce in his celebrated 1925 "counter manifesto" against Fascism. "We do not feel the need," Croce wrote,

> to abandon our ancient faith, the faith that for the least two centuries and a half has been the soul of the Italy... This faith was composed of the love of truth, desire for justice, generous human and civil sense, fervor for intellectual and modern education, readiness for liberty that is the strength and guarantor of all growth. We turn our eyes to the images of men of the Risorgimento, those who worked, suffered and died for Italy; and it seems as if we see their offended and disturbed faces as they hear the words uttered and the acts carried out by our Italian adversaries. We almost see them turn to us to keep high their flag.[29]

Italy's preeminent philosopher of his time, Croce viewed historical reality as a continuing and cumulative process of cultural growth and enrichment. Christian humanism constituted another vital strand within this ineluctable historical process. In his 1942 essay "Why We Cannot but Call Ourselves 'Christian,'" Croce tempered his longstanding anti-clericalism. Even if the Church's presence should wane in Italian society, he argued, "we carry [Christianity] with us, rather than cut ourselves off from it."[30]

With this in mind, a summary follows of the evolution of biography in Italy, as it has informed the present study. Until well into the nineteenth century, Italian and other Western elites groomed themselves for societal eminence via the study of Plutarch's noble ancient Greeks and Romans as moral paragons. In the nineteenth century, a similar function came to be filled in France, Great Britain, and the United States by what Romano has called "national popular biographies." Commemorating the lives of eminent statesmen, these works strengthened national identity and simultaneously elevated the prestige and popularity of the biographical form.

In Italy, the single most popular figure in the pantheon of the Risorgimento has not been the prosaic political insider, Cavour, nor the puritanical Mazzini, but the insurgent guerilla Garibaldi, whose exploits in Italy only transpired during the second half of his storied military career—hence his nickname "The Hero of Two Worlds." It is Garibaldi who has most fully captured the imagination of succeeding generations of Italians.[31] Still, it took the full triumvirate of Mazzini, Garibaldi, and Cavour to realize Italy's founding in the nineteenth century, and it would take all three of this study's three protagonists to reincarnate the Italian nation as a post-Second World War republic. De Gasperi and Togliatti each bear comparison with Cavour as practitioners of calculated, and at times opportunistic, forms of political praxis. Nenni's exuberant republicanism echoed that of Mazzini. The most deserving inheritors of Garibaldi's mantle were the anti-Fascist partisans, whose largest and most effective group called themselves the "Garibaldi Brigades."

The status of political biography in Italy fluctuated dramatically during the half-century lasting roughly from 1890 to 1940. For figures like Croce, Italy's preeminent late nineteenth- and early twentieth-century thinker, political leaders mattered less than cultural luminaries. It fell chiefly to intellectuals like himself to sustain the humanistic creed cited above. By the interwar years, some of Croce's anti-Fascist peers faulted this position, arguing that the philosopher harbored a passive and acquiescent attitude toward history that seemed to exclude human agency and ratify the status quo. Not surprisingly, Croce shied away from biographical writing. Meanwhile, the "Great Man" interpretation of history returned with a vengeance under the willful autocracy of the Duce. The numerous biographies of Mussolini published in the peninsula were predictably effusive, while equally fervent denunciations were penned by anti-Fascist exiles.[32]

The exaggerated voluntarism of Mussolinian hagiography prompted a historiographical backlash during the first several postwar decades. The single Italian figure who continued to benefit from a full-blown cult of personality was Pope Pius XII, although his charisma was arguably less personal than institutional.[33] Such hagiography notwithstanding, postwar political Catholicism—like Italy's Marxist and lay/progressive subcultures—downplayed the role of charismatic leadership in promoting or explaining political change. In accordance with the Church's doctrine of subsidiarity, Catholic writers and statesmen championed the interests and influence of intermediate social institutions such as families, local communities, and church organizations. For their part, Marxist and lay-progressive historians proffered socio-economic causational interpretations, focused on class interests and material conditions, while turning their backs on biographical approaches as elitist.[34]

Also marginalizing political biography were postwar intellectual trends informed by the social sciences, many arriving from outside the peninsula.[35] This scholarly tide was composed of four major waves. Influential in the first decades following the war was the work of analysts such as Norman Kogan and Muriel Grindrod, authors of institutionally focused surveys of the first decades of the Republic.[36] These studies cast light upon the "public" side of the Republic's founding fathers' catalyzing roles, both within their respective parties and within the ministerial and parliamentary arenas in which they found themselves. In the 1970s and 1980s, Paul Ginsborg and Martin Clark produced fuller histories of the Republic which rooted political developments in the dramatic and discontinuous evolution of the modern Italian economy and modern Italian society.[37] According to these British scholars, the country's broader socio-economic context largely dictated the policies championed by party leaders such as De Gasperi, Nenni, and Togliatti. Useful though they are, these broad-brush surveys are less nuanced than studies such as that of Italian scholar Agostino Giovagnoli, notably in his *Cultura democristiana*.[38] More recently, political scientists as Carolyn Warner and Stathis Kalyvas have moved in a very different direction, focusing on political parties' material interests and their patronage relationships rather than their putative ideologies and rhetoric.[39] Their revisionist approach, stimulating though it is, is more relevant to the *partitocrazia* (the partitioning of political power and patronage among parties) of the 1960s, 1970s, and 1980s than it is to the immediate postwar years. A fourth influential scholarly tide has been the French *annaliste* school.[40]

The present study largely departs from such materialist and anti-elitist historiographical approaches, focusing as it does on political leadership and political culture. At the same time, I have attempted to avoid the rather lopsided cultural determinism and essentialism of Joseph LaPalombara's *Democracy Italian Style* and Robert Putnam's *The Civic Culture*.[41] The highly fluid period between the collapse of Fascism in mid-1943 and the launching of the country's republican constitutional order at the end of 1947 offered wide latitude for the decisions and actions of a transformed political elite. It was only as the Christian Democratic Party consolidated its near-monopoly of power following the 1948 parliamentary elections that material interests, class privilege, and (for a period) institutional clericalism more manifestly delimited political initiative. The "heroic youth" of the republic, fleeting as it was, had passed. As expressed in Marxist terminology, "super-structural" causative forces may be said to have predominated between 1943 and 1947, and "structural" forces gained greater salience thereafter.

This work's reading of the *secondo dopoguerra* owes much to Pietro Scoppola's path-breaking book *La proposta politica di De Gasperi* (1978)—a work which compellingly elucidates its subject's fruitful and forward-looking first years of post-Fascist national prominence, in contrast to the conservative retrenchment which followed. Scoppola's book, along with Ernesto Raggioneri's *Palmiro Togliatti: per una biografia politica e intellettuale di Palmiro Togliatti* (1976), Giuseppe Tamburrano's *Pietro Nenni* (1986—part of the series *Il pensiero dei padri costituenti*), and Enzo Santarelli's *Pietro Nenni* (Turin: UTET, 1988), heralded the reemergence of rigorous political biography to the front rank of Italian historiography, after the backseat the genre took during the preceding three decades.[42]

Each of these scholars thoughtfully engaged with a perennial problematic for historians: that of balancing scholarly equanimity with their engagements in the political agendas of the day. During the Cold War, entrenched partisanship did taint domestic studies of the early republic and its founding fathers. But in works like those of Scoppola, Raggioneri, Santarelli, and Tamburrano we see revived a resilient brand of civic humanism which can be dated back to the Renaissance, and indeed to Roman antiquity. Already under the Roman republic, intellectuals recognized that just as political commitment can fruitfully inform historical scholarship, so too can historical writing serve the public good. During the late republic, Sallust embraced the cross-pollination of political engagement and historical inquiry, arguing that history is "in fact a form of public service: it excites men to political glory in the same way as do the busts of the ancestors in the atria of the great noble families."[43] Reaffirmed during the Renaissance by Machiavelli, this activist creed was echoed by twentieth-century historian Gaetano Salvemini, for whom "historical interpretation requires 'ethical judgments,' the necessity of which justifies the scholar's political advocacy of his ideas. Ultimately, both the historian and social scientist should be judged by a utilitarian standard: Did their work offer the community greater opportunity for justice, well-being, and happiness?"[44]

Broadly shaping Salvemini's methodology and epistemology—and indeed that of generations of fellow Italians—was Benedetto Croce's assertion that "all history is contemporary history." In his seminal study *Benedetto Croce and the Uses of Historicism*, David Roberts notes that the Neapolitan sage recognized "the gap between the historian and the past individual whose responses he seeks to understand." But Croce "always minimized the significance of that gap for historical understanding—essentially by taking over the dictum of Vico that we human beings can know what we have made." Thus, the past's meaning is indissolubly linked to the historian's own unfolding life experiences and outlooks. History recurs in the historians narrating of it; in this sense, the past is never past. "Understanding the historical other is not qualitatively different from understanding the present other, whose situation is also different from mine."[45]

I concur with the proposition that engagement with present concerns need not be an obstacle to genuine historical insight (what late nineteenth-century German historian Wilhelm Dilthey termed *verstehen*[46]), and indeed can enrich it, so long as the writer acknowledges such commitments, and makes a good faith effort to bracket those concerns. As John Davis has persuasively argued in an essay on nineteenth- and twentieth-century British historiography on Italy, even the most perceptive historians, whether foreign or indigenous, inevitably frame their investigation of the past in terms of present concerns.[47] The fundamentally sympathetic assessment which my book brings to its protagonists derives in no small measure from my frustration at the impotence of contemporary political discourse in the United States.

Notes

1. Aldo Agosti, *Palmiro Togliatti: A Biography* (London: I.B. Tauris, 2008), 198; Pasquale Iuso, ed. *Lezioni sul secondo dopoguerra (1945–1960)* (Rome: Gangemi, 1993), 158; H. Stuart Hughes, *The United States and Italy* (Cambridge: Harvard University Press, 1979), 157.
2. Pietro Nenni, *Tempo di Guerra Fredda. Diari 1943–1956* (Milan: SugarCo, 1981), 445.
3. A relieved but exasperated De Gasperi subsequently took Togliatti to task for leaving Montecitorio without his usual complement of bodyguards.
4. Nenni, *Tempo di Guerra Fredda*, 445.
5. In Italian scholarship, it is the custom to capitalize the terms State, and also Republic.
6. Marzia Marsili, "De Gasperi and Togliatti: Political Leadership and Personality Cults in Postwar Italy," *Modern Italy* 3:2 (1998), 249–262.
7. As Michael Freeden cogently argues, "The school of ideology as dogma, as a closed and abstract 'ism', is wishful thinking, a streamlined generalization which is itself highly ideological product of the Cold War. Even the so-called closed ideologies on which it concentrates are far more elaborate, more concrete and more historically situated, than their portrayal by the pragmatist suggests." Freeden goes on to caution against the unwarranted Cold War assumption that "concrete ideologies consist of mutually exclusive systems of ideas." The challenge facing the scholar "is to establish synchronic balance between the self-definition of an individual professing to adhere to an ideological family, the understandings of other contemporaries concerning that individual's place in the family, and the interpretation by the scholar both of the concrete evidence and of the diachronic tradition currently held to constitute that family. This threefold interplay is essential

to determine the nature of any individual ideology." Michael Freeden, *Ideology and Political Theory: A Conceptual Approach* (Oxford: Clarendon Press, 1996), 23.
8 As used by Machiavelli in *The Prince*. Norton Critical Edition (New York: Norton, 1992), this term implies initiative, political finesse, shrewdness.
9 See editor Giovanni Capua's introduction to *Processo a De Gasperi* (Rome: EBE, 1976).
10 John Harper, *America and the Reconstruction of Italy, 1943–1948* (Cambridge: Cambridge University Press, 1986), 58.
11 Steven White, "In Search of Alcide De Gasperi: Innovations in Italian Scholarship since 2003," *Journal of Modern Italian Studies* 15:3 (2010), 462–470.
12 Maria Romana De Gasperi, introduction to Pier Luigi Ballini et al., *Alcide De Gasperi*, vol. 1 (Soveria Mannelli: Rubbettino, 2009), xiii, xxi.
13 Joseph Ellis, *Founding Brothers: The Revolutionary Generation* (New York: Knopf, 2000), 17.
14 Doris Kearns Goodwin, *Team of Rivals. The Political Genius of Abraham Lincoln* (New York: Simon and Schuster, 2005), xv.
15 The central thesis of Scoppola's work *La repubblica dei partiti. Profilo storico della democrazia in Italia (1945–1990)* (Bologna: Il Mulino, 1991).
16 In his *Rhetoric in the European Tradition* (White Plains, NY: Longman, 1990), Thomas Conley traces the rhetorical strategies employed by politicians to inform, encourage, persuade, dissuade, or alarm public audiences, beginning in fifth-century BC Athens and continuing to modern times.
17 Steven White, "Italy's Odd Couple: Alcide De Gasperi and Pietro Nenni as Founders of the Italian Republic," paper delivered at the Society of Italian Historical Studies Annual Meeting (January 7, 2018), Washington, DC, as well as Michael Pakaluk, "Political Friendship," in Leroy S. Rouner, ed., *The Changing Face of Friendship* (Notre Dame: Notre Dame University Press, 1994), 197–213. Also pertinent is Rhiannon Evangelista's work on the postwar fate of prominent ex-Fascists. As Evangelista has documented, ties of family and friendship—ideological legacies notwithstanding—proved crucial in the public rehabilitation of such figures as Giuseppe Bottai (Minister of Corporations, 1929–1932, Minister of National Education, 1936–1943), and Dino Alfieri (Minister of Popular Culture, 1936–1939). In this process of rehabilitation, prior Fascist pronouncements and actions by these men mattered less to postwar Italian contemporaries than more intimate, and to some extent apolitical linkages, including *racommandazioni* as well as other forms of patronage. Rhiannon Evangelista, "The Particular Kindness of Friends: Ex-Fascists, Clientage and the Transition to Democracy in Italy, 1945–1960," *Modern Italy* 20:4, 411–425.
18 Recounted in Enzo Biagi, *Io c'ero: un grande giornalista racconta l'Italia del dopoguerra* (Milan: Rizzoli, 2008), 69. De Gasperi made the statement shortly after deciding to exclude both Socialists and Communists from his governing coalition—a dramatic political watershed detailed more fully in Chapter 4.

19 Nenni, *Guerra Fredda,* 634.
20 As students of history and as citizens, there is merit in recalling Benedetto Croce's insight that "we choose our past ... as we choose our future by responding creatively to the present moment," to cite David Roberts' felicitous paraphrase in his book *Benedetto Croce and the Uses of Historicism* (Berkeley: University of California Press, 1987), 155.
21 As an academic specialty for American historians of contemporary Europe, Germany, France, and Great Britain have, since the middle of the twentieth century, attracted much more attention than "lesser powers," including Italy. Victoria De Grazia, "Dagli Stati Uniti D'America," in Filippo Mazzonis, ed., *L'Italia contemporanea e la storiografia internazionale* (Venice: Marsilio, 1995), 284–287.
22 Elisa Carrillo's concise 1972 work *Alcide De Gasperi: The Long Apprenticeship* curtailed its treatment of its subject's career in 1943.
23 In 2000 Alexander De Grand published *The Hunchback's Tailor: Giovanni Giolitti and Liberal Italy from the Challenge of Mass Politics to the Rise of Fascism, 1882–1922* (Westport: Greenwood, 2000).
24 Mark Gilbert, "Biography in Modern Italian Studies. A Conversation with Carole Angier, Richard Bosworth and Christopher Duggan," *Modern Italy* 8:2 (November 2003), 226.
25 Elena Agarossi and Victor Zaslavsky's much more critical *Stalin and Togliatti: Italy and the Origins of the Cold War* (Washington, DC: Woodrow Wilson Center Press, 2011) touches only marginally on the Communist leader's formation and domestic actions.
26 Claudio Pavone, "Italy: Trends and Problems," *Journal of Contemporary History* 2:1 (January 1967), 49–77; Sergio Romano, "Considerazioni sulla biografia storica," *Storia della storiografia* 3 (1983), 113–116. See also Bianca Valota, "Storia e Biografia," *Storia della storiografia* 1 (1982), 89.
27 Romano, "Considerazioni sulla biografia storica," 113–116.
28 *Il Messaggero,* June 5, 1995. Responding from the Center-Left, Massimo D'Alema cited Cavour as a political influence. From the right, Catholic integralist Rocco Buttiglione spoke appreciatively of Machiavelli, while Silvio Berlusconi invoked Thomas More (the Church's patron saint of politicians). Economist and centrist politician Lamberto Dini recalled Plutarch's dictum that "one should reconcile oneself with one's enemy."
29 Cited in David Ward, *Anti-Fascisms: Cultural Politics in Italy, 1943–1946* (Teaneck: Fairleigh Dickinson University Press, 1996), 55.
30 Roberts, *Benedetto Croce and the Uses of Historicism,* 312.
31 For Anglophone readers, three key resources focusing on Garibaldi are Clara Lovett, *Giuseppe Garibaldi, 1805–1882. A Biographical Essay and a Selective List of Reading Materials* (Washington: The Library of Congress, 1982); Jasper Ridley,

Garibaldi (Stanford: Hoover Institution Press, 1974); and Lucy Riall, *Garibaldi: Invention of a Hero* (New Haven: Yale University Press, 2007).

32 In Italy a dispassionate assessment of the Duce remains a daunting biographical assignment to this day. See in this regard Richard Bosworth, *The Italian Dictatorship: Problems and Perspectives in the Interpretation of Mussolini and Fascism* (London: Arnold, 1998).

33 Oliver Logan, "Pius XII; *romanità*, Prophesy and Charisma," *Modern Italy* 3:2 (1998), 237–247.

34 Gilbert, "Biography in Modern Italian Studies," 226.

35 On Italian historiographical trends since 1945, including increased receptivity to social science approaches and renewed attention to biography, see Claudio Pavone, "Italy: Trends and Problems," 51–68, and Stefano Cavazza, "Suspicious Brothers: Reflections on Political History and Social Sciences," *Ricerche di Storia Politica* (Special Issue 2017), 53.

36 Muriel Grindrod, *The Rebuilding of Italy. Politics and Economics, 1945–1955* (Westwood: Greenwood Press, 1977); Norman Kogan, *A Political History of Postwar Italy* (New York: Praeger, 1966).

37 Paul Ginsborg, *A History of Contemporary Italy: Society and Politics 1943–1988* (London: Penguin, 1990); Martin Clark, *Modern Italy, 1871–1982* (London: Longman, 1984).

38 Agostino Giovagnoli, *La cultura democristiana: fra Chiesa cattolica e identità italiana* (Bari: Laterza, 1991).

39 Carolyn Warner, *Confessions of an Interest Group. The Catholic Church and Political Parties in Europe* (Princeton: Princeton University Press, 2000); Stathis Kalyvas, *The Rise of Christian Democracy in Europe* (Ithaca: Cornell University Press, 1996).

40 See Victoria De Grazia's and John Davis' essays, dealing respectively with American and British scholarship, in Filippo Mazzonis, ed., *L'Italia contemporanea*. Also see S. J. Woolf, ed. *L'Italia repubblicana vista da fuori* (Bologna: Il Mulino, 2007), and, more broadly, Lucy Riall, "The Shallow End of History? The Substance and Future of Political Biography," *Journal of Interdisciplinary History* XL:3 (Winter 2010), 375–397.

41 Joseph LaPalombara, *Democracy, Italian Style* (New Haven: Yale University Press, 1987); Robert Putnam, *Making Democracy Work: Civic Traditions in Modern Italy* (Princeton: Princeton University Press, 1993). See as well Victoria De Grazia's comments on essentialist readings of Italian culture and society. De Grazia, "Dagli Stati Uniti D'America," 290–291.

42 Valota, "Storia e Biografia," *Storia e storiografia* 1 (1982), 89. At an October 1981 Milan seminar on biography and historiography, Alceo Riosa noted the relative scarcity of contemporary critical reflection on biographical methodology. *Biografia e storiografia* (Milan: Franco Angeli, 1983).

43 Donald Earl, *The Moral and Political Tradition of Rome* (London: Thames and Hudson, 1976), 23–24.
44 Charles Killinger, *Gaetano Salvemini* (Westport: Praeger, 2002), 259.
45 Roberts, *Benedetto Croce and the Uses of Historicism,* 276–277. See further Benedetto Croce, *Filosofia e storiografia. Saggi* (Bari: Laterza, 1947). A moving illustration of this whole approach, drawn from the field of contemporary German history and grounded in that author's own family experience, is Hans Schmitt's *Quakers and Nazis: The Inner Light in the Outer Darkness* (Columbia: University of Missouri Press, 1997).
46 A fully rounded, empathetic connection with historical persons and events.
47 Davis, "Dalla Gran Bretagna, 93–114.

1

Three Founding Fathers

In a 1984 newspaper interview, Togliatti's long-time companion Nilde Iotti asserted that Togliatti and De Gasperi had been *carissimi nemici* (literally "dearest enemies").[1] Journalist Vittorio Gorresio, the press's most respected observer of the Italian Communist Party, entitled a 1977 study with the same phrase. When, and to what degree, could Togliatti and De Gasperi be characterized as *amici-nemici*—to use a closely related term of Italian political discourse?[2] And what of the affable Nenni? The three leaders' anti-Fascism initially bound them together as friendly rivals. Their rivalry turned to enmity with the onset of the Cold War. Even as friendly enemies, Nenni's and De Gasperi 's public animosity never eclipsed a measure of private sympathy. Never amicable in a personal sense, Togliatti and De Gasperi's calculated alliance of convenience endured until mid-1947. All-out antagonists thereafter, they continued to count on one another as formidable opponents and polemical foils.

American historian and former OSS officer H. Stuart Hughes has left the following characterization of the interaction between the Communist and Christian Democratic leaders:

> Similar in mental agility and even in physical appearance, the leaders of the two great parties faced each other—like two Jesuits, as one of their colleagues put it—with quiet deadliness across the ministerial council table.[3]

In another evocative passage, Hughes found in the Christian Democratic leader

> something sacerdotal ... in that sense he appeared a fitting leader for a Catholic party. Looking far younger than his years—when he first came to power he was sixty four—with a lean and wiry physique, he was able to survive repeated bouts of illness and political crises until he had either driven his rivals from the field or brought them into service as allies.[4]

Friendship, both personal and political, occupies a central place in the analysis that follows. Here I take exception to the tendency in many studies of modern, ostensibly bureaucratic, rationalized state structures[5] to under-emphasize the role of relational dynamics such as political friendship. In the case of Italy, as in other Mediterranean societies, social bonds and networks of all kinds, formal and informal, continue to offer essential keys for unlocking broader political developments.[6] Here we will employ a framework for understanding political friendship first articulated by Aristotle and Cicero, and further developed by such modern thinkers as Hannah Arendt and William Rawlins.[7]

Given De Gasperi's pivotal role in the genesis of the postwar republic, it makes sense to apply our model of political friendship first to the Trentine (a native of Trento province) statesman's modes of association (both personal and political) with others. The balance of the present chapter traces the social and political formation of each founder in turn, beginning in their early years and continuing up until the Second World War. Disparate as the three men's socialization and educational experiences were, all three inherited a humanistic tradition focused on expressive cultivation, social awareness, and civic engagement. Each discovered mentors, past and present, who assisted them in consolidating their political vocations. Each entered politics within a particular geo-political context—for De Gasperi the Trentino under the Austrian Empire, for Togliatti Turin in the throes of rapid industrialization, and for Nenni the intensely anti-clerical Romagna—and these contexts distinctively conditioned their respective political credos.

Political Friendship

The root of friendship, according to Aristotle, lay in the ethical qualities of the two friends. Seven centuries later, Cicero in like manner asserted that friendship "can only exist between good men."[8] By "good men," Cicero intended "those whose actions and lives are ... free from greed, lust or violence; and who have the courage of their convictions." In the eyes of their contemporaries, De Gasperi, Nenni, and Togliatti[9] met this definition.

Aristotle and Cicero regarded friendship as a public as well as a personal good. The kinds of mutual regard and encouragement which link friends are also needed in a proper community, or city-state.[10] Such an extension of interpersonal friendship into the public realm is, in modern parlance, encompassed by the category of "political friendship." Aristotle viewed the community as a *koinonia*—literally a "sharing." Such sharing involves both friendship and justice, which Aristotle asserted "by nature increase together."[11] What's more, as extended friendships informed by justice, communities are "sustained by a "scheme of cooperation"—a kind of constitution.[12] Central to the argument which I advance in this work is the conjunction of personal and political friendship in the genesis of Italy's republican order.

Applying Aristotle schemata to the specific socio-political context of the late Roman Republic, Cicero developed a more nuanced analysis, tying together personal character, interpersonal ties, alliance building, and political efficacy.[13] In the words of classicist Donald Earl, the "politics of the Roman Republic were social and personal." In their political propaganda, Roman statesmen employed class and partisan terms, taking sides in power struggles pitting "Optimates against Populares, Senate and Businessmen, Senate and People, Caesarians and Pompeians." Yet there is little evidence that "the average noble Roman politician subscribed to a consistent political philosophy in the sense that a modern might... Romans did not distinguish morality sharply from politics or economics" but looked at affairs largely in ethical terms, "reflecting the personal and social nature of political life itself."[14]

The leadership exercised by our three founding fathers also depended on their capacity to frame political imperatives in ethical terms. Unlike their ancient forebears, however, and as leaders of modern mass parties, De Gasperi, Togliatti, and Nenni anchored their ethical concerns in political ideologies which tied them to their constituents.

Cicero identified *fides* (trust—*fiducia* in Italian) as the fundamental prerequisite for friendship.[15] As a conservative, Cicero was not describing elements of an idealized polis, but articulating practical principles of governance in a society necessarily composed of unequal social orders. Based on his own experience, the patrician Cicero regarded political friendships with prominent peers as valuable but also vulnerable to shifts in political winds as well as the vagaries of personal sentiment. More robust for the late republic were asymmetrical ties between patrician patrons and lesser clients.[16] De Gasperi too was a conservative—though a moderate one. He remained comfortable with a class society, so long as it was leavened by Christian compassion.

Let us take a moment here to articulate three concentric circles of amicable ties posited by Aristotle—friendships of virtue, of pleasure, and of utility[17]—as these manifested themselves in De Gasperi's relationships with others. Located in the first category—"friendships of virtue"—were De Gasperi's closest friends. These close friends comprised a *cordata*—a mountain climbing team, bound by one rope. An avid climber himself in his younger years, De Gasperi treasured the absolute trust and confidence in each other's skill and the commitment of all members which typified the *cordata*.[18] But besides the Roman lawyer and party organizer Giuseppe

Spataro[19] and Emilio Bonomelli,[20] manager of the papal countryside estate at Castel Gandolfo, there were few political colleagues who De Gasperi trusted so implicitly during the post-Second World War phase of his political career.

The ancient Greeks and Romans dismissed the possibility of full-fledged friendship between man and wife (and more broadly men and women). De Gasperi's experience in this respect could not have been more different. Alcide's ties with his wife Francesca powerfully sustained him through thick and thin. Emotional equals, the two forged an exceptional, enduring bond—an indispensable, intimate foundation for De Gasperi's lengthy political career. Francesca was unquestionably Alcide's best friend.[21]

Yet as several biographers have noted, De Gasperi was not inclined to romanticism in his relationships with women.[22] Deeply involved in Italian politics, he hesitated to court Francesca, even at age forty. A year before their 1922 betrothal, he wrote her, asking:

> Do you think that I shall ever have a respite from this public service that sometimes seems to be my cross and is instead my mission or destiny? And that a man in my position has the right to ask another person to adapt herself to this tyranny that will continue to impose itself inexorably? [23]

He did soften his tone in the subsequent portion of the letter, inviting Francesca to "come, live with me, to be drawn to that same attraction, as toward an abyss of light."[24] This last passage reveals how tightly spirituality and sentimentality were intertwined for De Gasperi. Interestingly, Francesca Romano's family was said to be among the wealthiest in the Trento region. For Alcide, this consideration may have reassured him that his wife and eventual family would be provided for should his political entanglements complicate his ability in that regard.

At the second level—"friendships of pleasure"[25]—De Gasperi did build significant relationships with younger Christian Democratic Party colleagues. A representative figure here is Giulio Andreotti, who served as undersecretary and then secretary to the Council of Ministers from 1947 to 1954. There were elements of both mentoring and patronage in this friendship, but I would stress even more its quasi-paternal nature. De Gasperi had four daughters but no sons. Might Andreotti and several other up and coming party members been substitutes for the sons he never had?

> Andreotti felt orphaned after losing his father—when he was only two—and his mother when he was still a young man. He recalls that when he learned of De Gasperi's death in mid-August 1954, the news hit him as only the passing of his mother had.[26]

Doubtless Cicero would have understood such a bond. In Aristotelian terms, again, these were friendships of pleasure.

Most of De Gasperi's political ties however took the form of alliances—in Aristotelian terminology "friendships of utility"—the third and most inclusive category in the Greek philosopher's analytical framework. This level of friendship implies, at least provisionally, that the self-interest of each partner correlates with their partner's. A great asset of De Gasperi's in forming such ties was the fact that, in Elisa Carrillo's words, "he learned to accept men as they are, not as they seemed or wished to be."[27] Similarly, in weighing candidates for lesser governmental positions, the prime minister inquired first about their temperament and work experience, paying less attention to their political inclinations.

The modern reader may well find that Aristotle's approach to political friendship over-emphasizes cooperation at the expense of rivalry. Hannah Arendt offers a sterner conception, defining "politics as the proper sphere of social antagonism." Particularly in "dark times" (a term of Hannah Arendt's[28] which certainly applies to Italy during and immediately after the Second World War), the public sphere is inevitably a contentious arena. In the view of L. J. Disch, the public sphere calls for "articulated solidarity." Building on Arendt's ideas, she explains:

> We now need to assess *how* we are implicated in a worldly [e.g. public] event. This is the task of articulating solidarity: constructing the 'facts' of a contingent situation in a way that makes possible a coordinate response to a plurality of actors who—apart from that contingency—may have more differences than affinities.[29]

Alcide De Gasperi

Alcide De Gasperi was born in 1881 in the village of Pieve Tesino, situated in the Valsugana valley east of Trento, and reared in a devout middle-class family. Subjects of Austria-Hungary, his forefathers balanced pride in their Italian heritage with deference to the Hapsburg crown—an appropriate hybrid identity since Alcide's father served as a gendarme in the Austrian imperial service.

Already, as an adolescent, Alcide embraced a Catholic middle position in contra-distinction to the two dominant ideologies of the day in the Trentino—liberalism on the one hand and socialism on the other. As a student in the Bishopric of Trento's *ginnasio* (an elite middle school preparing its pupils for entry into the upper secondary *liceo*, the lyceum) his *lettere* (literally "Letters," a composite humanities course encompassing Italian, Latin, history, and geography) instructor introduced him to the modernist writings of Romolo Murri and Antonio Fogazzaro and also the dour orthodoxy of monsignor Ernst Krommer. He was deeply impressed by the Catholic "golden mean" set forth in Pope Leo XIII's path-breaking encyclical *Rerum Novarum*. Heading to Vienna in 1900 to begin his university studies, De Gasperi held progressive views on "the social question" while remaining staunchly dogmatic in his theology.[30] In his temperament, the young De Gasperi combined caution and skepticism with an inner self-confidence and ambition bordering on arrogance; traits which would serve him well through the many ups and downs of his adult life—not least in the challenges he encountered as an independent-minded Catholic politician.

Alcide was especially close to his younger brother and future priest, Luigi Mario. The latter's death in 1906 devastated his older brother. Luigi Mario's absence was one that De Gasperi would feel for the rest of his life, perhaps helping to explain the distance which even close colleagues often sensed in his presence. At the same time, the personal fulfillment that De Gasperi had once felt in mentoring his younger brother may have informed the "formational" side of his political career. A recurrent preoccupation of his was to educate his constituency, whether the Catholics of the Trentino or, three decades later, the electoral base—and rising leadership—of the Christian Democratic Party in the give-and-take inherent in modern parliamentary governance.[31]

While De Gasperi never entirely outgrew his rural Dolomite heritage, he nevertheless aspired to elevate himself socially and educationally. His family's financial circumstances permitted him only to attend the *collegio arcivescovile* until the last year of secondary school, when a scholarship permitted him to transfer to the more prestigious imperial gymnasium of Trento. Finding himself on the defensive socially and politically there, he developed a reflexive pridefulness, which would endure henceforth. As a gymnasium student, and even more energetically between 1900 and 1905 as a university student at the University of Vienna (in the Faculty of Philology), De Gasperi threw himself into Catholic youth activity and student politics.

Meanwhile, De Gasperi's journalistic involvement (his *mestieraccio*, as he fondly referred to it[32]), was getting underway. In 1905, two months after his graduation from university, De Gasperi assumed the editorship of the Trentine newspaper *La Voce Cattolica*. The following year the newspaper, with De Gasperi still at the helm, was rechristened *Il Trentino*. The crusading journalist displayed a noteworthy ability to situate the controversies of the day within broader rhetorical-ideological and historical frameworks. De Gasperi was, in this sense, a thoughtful writer and thus a Catholic intellectual.[33] By the eve of the First World War, De Gasperi had matured as a centrist politician and coalition builder. As a local, provincial, and, eventually, a national parliamentary representative, he did much to fashion a more robust and self-aware Catholic Trentine identity. On the one hand, he drew upon longstanding populist tropes when he extolled "religion of the fathers" and contrasted the urban bourgeoisie (the *siori*, e.g., *signori*) with the inhabitants of the Dolomite valleys (the *montanari*). While the latter might be "simple people, they nevertheless possessed deeper values than the city folk."[34] On the other hand, De Gasperi reached out more effectively to elements of the urban bourgeoisie, calling for an Italian exit from the "Habsburg nexus." Here we see the roots of the Trentine statesman's subsequent desire to construct a broad-based Italian national culture rooted in the "cultural Catholicism" of much of the Italian people. The absence of such a strong societal bond, he came to believe, would leave his countrymen vulnerable to demagogies arising from either Left or Right.

The annexation of Trentino-Alto Adige to Italy following the First World War opened the arena of national politics to De Gasperi. As Don Luigi Sturzo's political lieutenant, he assisted in the 1921 founding of the Italian Popular Party and figured prominently in the short life of the party. Over the next five years, he came to accept the cut and thrust of parliamentary debate as a norm of the democratic process. What he did not count on, however, was the rapprochement which began to develop in the mid-1920s between the Church and the Fascist Regime. In 1926, the Popular Party was abandoned by Vatican diktat, and then disbanded—along with all other non-Fascist parties—in November 1926. In March 1927, De Gasperi was arrested; he would spend the next four months imprisoned in *Regina Coeli* Prison in Rome, followed by almost a year of hospitalization.

Barred from public life, De Gasperi took solace in the hope that his fidelity to his political creed—and even his ability to bear up under the degradation and (often petty) oppression of prison life—might give heart to kindred spirits on the outside. De Gasperi's prison meditations, expressed in letters to a few faithful friends or to his wife Francesca, reveal the statesman's dawning sense that his own seemingly star-crossed political vocation (including the travails of the present) was in some way inscribed within a larger historical frame. Now, it seemed, he was undergoing a gradual but decisive inner transition. As he wrote to Francesca in June 1928, "previously everything—God, family, friends—had revolved around myself. Then slowly, painstakingly, arising from the pressure of experience, the center shifted. Now God stood at the center and I had moved to the periphery, along with the rest of the world."[35]

Two enduring tenets of his political credo now began to crystallize: the championship of liberty as the method (and indispensable precondition) of democracy and Christianity as an essential ethical leaven for Italian democracy.[36] Italian historian Angelo Braschi has gone so far as to characterize the Christian Democratic leader's life as "echoing the trial-strewn curriculum of the Apostle of Peoples (Jesus Christ)."[37] Apropos of Braschi's metaphor, De Gasperi would recall in an article penned for the Christian Democratic newspaper *Il Popolo*:

> It was for democracy that I had withdrawn onto the Aventine and for democracy's sake had made common cause, after Matteotti's murder, with socialists, masons and liberals...only to wind up imprisoned and then marginalized in the political life of the nation. Finally, it had been for democracy that I suffered and risked during the Nazi occupation, organizing our renewal with all, communists included.[38]

Following his release from the prison hospital in July 1928, he struggled for several years in political limbo and economic penury. The signing of the Lateran Accords between the Vatican and the Fascist Regime in February 1929 filled De Gasperi with misgivings. Even so, he recognized that the accords had finally freed the Church from the cul-de-sac of defensiveness and suspiciousness of the State in which it had languished since the founding of the Kingdom of Italy. Yet the resolutely anti-Fascist De Gasperi expressed deep concerns about the Concordat, which was widely interpreted as a vindication of the clerico-Fascist position within the Church, not to mention an invaluable endorsement of the regime itself. His prison letters make clear how hard it was for him to accept the comfortable station then enjoyed by opportunistic fellow Catholics or by convinced clerico-Fascists. Following his release from prison, this proud but impoverished man continued to be mortified by the condescension—or downright avoidance—he experienced as a tainted *ex-popolare*.

De Gasperi personally benefitted from the "honeymoon" between the Fascist Regime and the Church: in early 1929, the ex-leader of the Popular Party was hired as a cataloger in the Vatican Library, with no complaint from Mussolini's regime. As provider for his family, he was of course grateful for Pius XI's intercession, even if his new, rather obscure, lowly paying job certainly represented a letdown for someone with his background and would seem to have been humiliating too. Fortunately, he was able to supplement his cataloguer's salary by preparing translations of German-language scholarly works and by writing occasional articles under a pseudonym.[39]

During the decade that De Gasperi worked as a Vatican librarian, he was never received by Pius XI—doubtless a source of disappointment and even discouragement. Yet the pope's reticence may not have distressed him as much as it would have had he been more "clerical" in orientation. In his writings, De Gasperi referred often to Christian values such as compassion and justice—but rarely of the institutional prerogatives of the Church and its hierarchy. In the words of biographer Elisa Carrillo:

> [T]he party man remained linked with his spiritual mother, the Church, and consequently his public as well as his private actions were bound to be affected by his Christian conscience. De Gasperi's own convictions were inseparable from his Christian heritage, even though his religion was essentially a private matter. Profoundly spiritual in the inner depths of his being, he had an instinctive aversion for people who say their prayers on street corners, who boast of their orthodoxy and religious intransigence.[40]

As prime minister, he attended services almost daily, accompanied by his political acolyte Giulio Andreotti. As one colleague mischievously quipped however, Andreotti promptly sought out a priest, while De Gasperi prayed directly to God. In times of adversity, he was wont to turn to scripture, finding solace particularly in passages from Psalms.[41] Such tendencies may strike some readers as bordering on Protestantism—an ironic association, since De Gasperi's religious identity took shape while a student in Trento, a sixteenth-century stronghold of the Counter-Reformation. Following the Second World War, De Gasperi resisted integralist dreams of "redeeming" a prostrate Italy through a restoration of a Catholic Christendom, fearing that it would provoke anti-clerical responses and, in any event, regarding it as impractical for a modern society. In the words of Italian historian Silvio Lanaro, of all of the Christian Democratic leaders, De Gasperi could most credibly deal with non-Catholics in the secular, "neutral" language of liberal parliamentarism: to secular "eyes, or better noses, De Gasperi was uniquely free of the odor of incense and the sacristy."[42]

During the latter 1930s, Alcide and Francesca De Gasperi hosted gatherings of youthful Catholic activists in their apartment, at which De Gasperi led discussions. These discussions traced the evolution of Catholic social teaching and examined Catholic's political experience beyond the Alps, especially in France, Belgium, and Germany. As Guido Gonella recalled of these sessions, the few friends present were more listeners than anything else.[43]

De Gasperi's homespun expository style would resonate deeply with much of the Italian electorate, but it also exposed him to the reproof of other leaders. Pope Pius XII privately ridiculed the Christian Democratic leader's use of the French language. On one occasion recorded by Cardinal Domenico Tardini, the pope noticed: "De Gasperi had said to foreign press correspondents '*Nous esperons super les difficultes.*'" Pius XII then remarked that the verb, which should have been used, was "*surmonter.*"[44] Even within his own party, De Gasperi was vulnerable to criticism by colleagues such as the silver-tongued Giovanni Gronchi at the plainness of his language. Reinforcing this characterization is journalist Indro Montanelli's wry note that: "About De Gasperi, one did not retell anecdotes, episodes, made up definitions ... he did not inspire anything nor did he resemble anything—nothing, that is, save barebones reality and common sense."[45]

De Gasperi justified his expressive style in this manner:

> I remember quite clearly how at a certain point in my political youth ... horrified by the disastrous effects of excessive rhetoric, I resolved to speak and write simply and concretely, aiming to convince rather than entrance, to persuade rather than receive applause.

De Gasperi acknowledged that his words could be "fragmentary and nervous" and indeed "asyntactic at times." But this was a language which an "attentive public accepted and understood."[46]

Palmiro Togliatti

In their own ways, both De Gasperi and Togliatti rejected the florid rhetorical style used by many of their parliamentary peers. Togliatti's communist colleague and journalist Miriam Mafai credited him with introducing a new style of political oratory to *Montecitorio* (the Chamber of Deputies)—one which avoided conventional tropes in favor of a "professorial," cogent, confident, form of declamation. Togliatti effectively clothed Marxist rhetorical and ideological categories with direct, concise references to the realities of the day.[47] He typically spoke in a reassuring voice, presenting himself as a respectable person, similar to the people to whom he appealed.[48] Known in party circles as *Il Migliore* (The Best), a reference to his intelligence and competitiveness, Togliatti possessed a steely self-confidence, which many found reassuring, but which could also come across as supercilious. His studied reserve in controversial situations, even when colleagues were brave enough to speak their minds, represents another uncongenial side of his character. In the words of historian Eric Terzuolo, one "could say he was a scoundrel at times ... one who knows the most but cares the least." A phrase first used to describe Niccolo Machiavelli, this definition can be applied to Togliatti as well as a person whose "cold-blooded insight into harsh realities" led him consistently to "follow the most expedient course."[49]

Palmiro Togliatti was born in Genoa in 1893. He was named "Palmiro" by his observant Roman Catholic parents because he was born on Palm Sunday. His father was a civil accountant and his mother a schoolteacher; both were lonely non-conformists determined that their children better themselves through single-minded dedication to their schooling. When Palmiro was still quite young, the family relocated to Sardinia. The Togliattis maintained a modest bourgeois lifestyle, scrimping by on the two parents' meager salaries. The young Palmiro devoted himself assiduously to his studies and won a coveted royal scholarship to continue his secondary schooling. He attended a prestigious classical lyceum in Sassari, where he was recognized as the best student in the school.[50] An inspirational teacher figure for the young Togliatti was Mose' Niccolini, described by Palmiro's sister Maria Cristina "as one of those who lacked a precise ideology, but for whom a mere gesture, a smile or a brief remark awakened his students to the reality that behind the idols and sacred institutions of proper society there were ordinary men with whom one needed to establish a connection."[51]

As a student at the University of Turin, Togliatti immersed himself deeply in the humanistic disciplines. His fascination for literature and the arts would stay within for the rest of his life. An exceptionally diligent student, he dutifully attended all of his required courses, and audited many outside of his faculty. He passed all of his courses with the maximum possible 30/30 mark, even though he was not particularly enthusiastic about studying law. More important to his continuing formation was the vibrant intellectual milieu of the university at a time when "the cult of science and of severe philological discipline linked to positivism" prevailed. Like his new university acquaintance and fellow Sardinian Antonio Gramsci, he embraced "precision of thought, a taste for exactness of information, even moral repugnance ... for improvisation and superficiality."[52] Gramsci and Togliatti first met in October 1911 when each competed (successfully) for a Carlo Alberto university scholarship. At the university a habitual dialogue grew between them, rooted in their common provenance and direct knowledge of Sardinia, as well as their similar condition of economic difficulty bordering on extreme poverty, unusual among university students."[53]

Gradually, over the next several years Togliatti also became aware of the plight of the Turinese proletariat—an exposure that coincided with his attendance along with Gramsci at meetings of a young socialist group. Then, in January 1921, the two young men played leading roles in the foundation of the Italian Communist Party. Over the next several years, Togliatti seconded Gramsci's elaboration of a "hegemonic"[54] path to communism uniquely fitted to Italy's history and culture.[55]

Five years later the Fascists outlawed the PCI along with all other non-Fascist parties; Gramsci was arrested and sent to prison, while Togliatti began a difficult, almost two-decade-long exile in Moscow. He headed the Italian delegation to the Communist International (Comintern)'s sixth plenum in February 1926 and was elected to the International's Executive Committee. He was still in Moscow at the time of then-Italian party leader Gramsci's arrest in November 1926, and when the party went underground, Togliatti was put in charge of its foreign headquarters, in essence taking over leadership of the party. Togliatti and his family lived in Moscow's Hotel Lux, which:

> For many Communists of the 1920s and 1930s...was a mythical place. For others, it represented stories of untold horrors and cruelty. It was the housing complex for the International Comintern—the 10 Gorki Street residence for the most renowned and historical figures of communist history. Ho Chi Minh, Tito, Dimitrov, and Rakosi all lived at the Hotel Lux during what was the most difficult period of "world communism."[56]

Once in Moscow he rose to become a top Comintern figure, while retaining his role as PCI secretary general. He confronted the challenge of retaining his mercurial Soviet patron's confidence without losing sight of the eventual prospect of pursuing the gradualist path to hegemony which he and Gramsci had charted for their native land. A consummate political survivor, he persevered through the harshest years of Stalinist capriciousness and brutality, but at a heavy moral cost. Confronted with the choice of distancing himself (albeit with little prospect of influence) from the seemingly endless intra-party purges taking place around him or adapting himself to Stalin's steady ascendancy over Trotsky and other Soviet rivals, he chose the latter course. In so doing, he distanced himself from the anguished concerns of Gramsci, which were expressed in an October 1926 letter to the Soviet Central Committee. Gramsci warned the Soviet leaders that:

> [T]he road on which you are traveling could fall into an abyss. Friends, over the last nine years, you have been the organizing element and propulsion of the revolutionary forces in all countries. But today you are destroying your

work, you are degenerating and running the risk of annulling the driving function, which Russia won through Lenin; we think that you are losing the international element to your vision because of the violent tendencies of the Russian question.[57]

In Gianni Corbi's judgment, the decision to join the "Stalinist camp probably made him suffer much more and was more complicated than most people admit."[58] Certainly, it pained him to break with his erstwhile Sardinian friend and mentor. Nevertheless, by 1934 Togliatti became "Stalin's megaphone." In fiery articles written in the offices of the Comintern, he directed and supervised Stalin's "propaganda campaign set up to tell the world that the 'traitors' and 'assassins' had been unmasked."[59] From 1936 to 1939, he was the senior Comintern representative in Spain, escaping upon Franco's victory in the civil war. He then remained in Moscow until early 1944, half a year after the Italian armistice of September 1943.

Comrade "Ercole," as Togliatti was known to the Italian communist faithful, made his way to his homeland via a circuitous route, which took him through Baku, Teheran, and Cairo. He docked at Naples on March 27, 1944. Four days later, in an address to the Neapolitan federation of the PCI, he pronounced the *Svolta di Salerno* ("Salerno Turn")—a stunning reversal of the party line, for the first time since the 1920s acknowledging the legitimacy of the House of Savoy.

The Communist leader had a healthy respect for the staying power of established institutions in his native Italy (this in part explains the Salerno Turn). The same can be said for his frequently reiterated respect for the historical and cultural value of the Church. Ever the prudent realist, he cautioned his more intemperate followers against launching a revolution prematurely, acknowledging that Italy lay in the capitalist West's sphere of control—a reality which Stalin himself clearly understood. Such moderation was of a piece with Togliatti's pragmatic courting not merely of Nenni's socialists, but—more importantly— De Gasperi's Christian Democrats, both of which were also part of the recently established, anti-Fascist and anti-Nazi Committee of National Liberation.

The scope of Togliatti's intellectual and artistic cultivation was wider than De Gasperi's, a fact which the Communist leader was not above noting. Of the two, Togliatti was the superior speaker, adroitly adjusting his vocabulary and delivery to his audience. Yet the Communist statesman's schoolmasterly, even fastidious manner and fluctuating, occasionally nasal voice put off some listeners. Even his ally Nenni was sometimes taken aback by Togliatti's glacial manner.[60] Togliatti in turn mocked what he viewed as "socialist sentimentalism," writing in the interwar period:

I want to praise the cynical, praise the cerebral, praise the heartless... Because, you see, I am one of those. I am all brain... and this my brain is a machine which never quits—tic, tac, tic, tac—to advance, cold, implacable, as if an inner spring—cast in iron—moves it forward. This is my brain and heart—don't look for my heart, because in its place you will find a void, or perhaps, you will find the sum of my "theories," a book arid and cold: the Statutes of the Third Internationale.[61]

Allowing even for its hyperbole, this is a striking self-portrait.

Following the war, De Gasperi's lieutenant Giulio Andreotti noted, somewhat maliciously, that in comparison with his fellow politicians, Togliatti could seem "cold" and "proper"—qualities which Andreotti attributed at least in part to the difficulties the PCI leader experienced "readopting Italian manners" following his Muscovite exile.[62]

On the other hand, his personal coldness notwithstanding, Togliatti's cultural sophistication attracted a wide range of Italian intellectuals. In British historian Tony Judt's words,

In the decades following World War II, the [Communist] Party openly welcomed intellectuals—as members and as allies—and took care to tone down those elements of the Party's rhetoric likely to put them off. Indeed, Togliatti consciously tailored Communism's appeal to intellectuals with a formula of his own devising: "half Croce, and half Stalin."[63]

In this context, it is interesting in turn to note Stalin's 1946 assessment of his Italian counterpart: Togliatti, he acknowledged, was an able "theoretician and journalist," who "can write a good article, a good comrade, but to gather people and 'guide' them—this he cannot do; he has difficult circumstances there."[64]

Stalin's remark says more about the Soviet dictator than it does Togliatti. In fact, the Italian leader was idolized by his party's rank and file, in no small measure, ironically, because of his identification with *Il Baffone* ("Big Mustache"), Stalin's affectionate wartime epithet. The Italian leader's charisma was in part institutional, linked to the almost mythical Stalin, on the one hand, and to the "saintly" Antonio Gramsci, on the other. Togliatti dressed tastefully, often sporting a double-breasted suit. He urged his followers to dress respectfully as well. A cult of personality did come to surround the Communist boss; in the eyes of many party militants, he was a powerful authority figure in his own right, "sometimes too strict, occasionally friendly, and always paternal."[65] Still, when crossed, Togliatti was capable of chilling denunciations of party colleagues.[66]

Togliatti's familial relationships were more problematic than were his Christian Democratic and Socialist counterparts. His marriage in 1924 to fellow Communist activist Rita Montagnana began auspiciously. In 1925 their son Aldo was born. Palmiro and Rita shared unshakable Marxist convictions; their marriage was the consummation of a bond which had matured over time, reinforced by political passion and by the sense of belonging to an organ (the Communist Party) whose aims transcended individual destinies. It was a bond between two strong personalities.[67]

By 1934, when the Togliattis were living and working in Moscow, their nine-year-old son Aldo had begun to suffer from mental illness. His affliction was probably exacerbated by the material and psychological hardships of life then in the Soviet capital. Palmiro began an extended affair with Elena Lebedeva, a young secretary in the Comintern organization (where, ironically, Rita also worked). Over the ensuing years, as his parents' relationship deteriorated, Aldo struggled unsuccessfully to establish a normal life. Togliatti tried, intermittently, to help his son, but wound up withdrawing further and further from both son and spouse. The marriage would end in separation in 1946; the last straw was the passionate, life-long affair which Palmiro had with Nilde Iotti, the smart, poised, feminist and parliamentarian at the war's end.[68]

In Iotti's company, the severe and domineering Palmiro could be relaxed, even sentimental. Earlier in his career, Togliatti offered a series of lectures giving voice to his humanistic sensibility in the following terms:

> Fascism has divided, broken, annihilated, all the relationships between man and man since it began its organisation, because it has activated the sterilizing virus of blind obedience, which finds expression in the slogan *"credere, obbedire, combattere"* [believe, obey, fight]. We communists must resume the defence of human freedom, give back faith to Italians, urge them to unite, discuss, fight … We must provoke a wave of horror and reprobation against the perversion of human sentiment perpetrated by the fascists among the Italian people.[69]

In a lighter vein, journalist Vittorio Gorresio captured Togliatti's gentler side with the following words:

> His origins and dispositions were middle class, and even though he did not have friends, in the strict sense, he loved socializing with Giovanni Amendola and Eugenio Reale, two jovial communists who could talk both over dinner and while taking a stroll, about matters that were not necessarily connected with the life of the party. He did not shy away from gossip, he liked to indulge in mischievous behavior and in jests, and a joke or a well pulled off prank delighted him.[70]

Pietro Nenni

Of this study's three protagonists, Pietro Nenni was the most *simpatico*. Where De Gasperi was restrained and resolute, and Togliatti cool and rational, Nenni was excitable and spontaneous. Candid almost to a fault, he was much more approachable than his Communist or Christian Democratic counterparts. As the veteran Radical politician, Francesco Saverio Nitti quipped following the war: "In Italy there is only one revolutionary: Nenni. Fortunately we have Togliatti to restrain him."[71] For Pope Pius XII and his coterie of conservative Vatican integralists, Nenni was feared more than Togliatti as an unyielding and unrepentant anti-cleric, native as Nenni was of Romagna—a region which had for centuries been known as a hotbed of anti-Church sentiment.

Pietro Nenni was born in 1891, the son of an impoverished peasant couple. At age five Pietro was placed in a Catholic orphanage for poor children following the death of his father. The next decade of his life was marked by bitterness and humiliation. He chafed at the provincialism, insularity, and—most of all—the intellectual and cultural poverty of orphanage. At night and unbeknownst to the orphanage authorities, he read Hugo, Garibaldi, Leopardi, Zola, and (his favorite) Mazzini.[72] A proud autodidact, Nenni "looked down upon men who came across as strong, yet were less cultivated, and in fact weaker than him." As he would later tell Randolfo Pacciardi, he had not been able to attend "regular schools, had nevertheless read and studied much," confessing however that he feared (unjustifiably, in Pacciardi's view) that he "lacked a sufficiently solid base to separate the true from or the false." [73]

As he was later to reflect: "Those cloistered years marked me with a rebellious streak which has never left me."[74] Restless, imaginative, and inquisitive, the youthful Nenni was attracted in different ways to radicalism, anarchism,[75] and republicanism—embracing in this respect divergent ideological strands, which were to commingle, however uncomfortably, in early Italian socialism. Divided already before the First World War between reformist and revolutionary wings, the party found in anti-clericalism a much needed unifying creed.

His doctrinaire distrust of Catholicism stuck with Nenni through his interwar years. In 1926, he fled Italy for France, where he and his family found refuge for the next seventeen years. A pivotal hiatus for Nenni was the years he spent in Spain helping to defend the republic against Franco's nationalist, clericalist insurgency. He co-founded and led the Garibaldi Brigade, which fought valiantly in the unsuccessful defense of Madrid. While in Spain, Nenni first met Togliatti when the latter was visiting that country clandestinely in 1936 and again in 1937 as a representative of the Comintern. The two leaders knew of each other already, having sparred long distance in the pages of leftist newspapers. Previously sympathetic toward Europe's communists as his fellow Marxists, Nenni denounced Stalin's abrupt 1928 break with European socialists and other "bourgeois" parties—no matter how progressive—which the Soviet leader now lumped with dictatorships of the right as "social-Fascists." Forcefully rebutting Nenni's criticisms, Togliatti scorned his Socialist counterpart in the following terms:

> Signor Pietro Nenni proclaims himself to be a gentleman. He ignores the incompatibility between the morality of a political dilettante/adventurer and the way in which we understand political life… the democrats and social-democrats are no better than traitors.[76]

In his seminal biography of the Communist leader, Giorgio Bocca observed how Togliatti was "wont to describe his socialist counterpart as a mere 'journalist,' which is to say that Nenni dealt with problems by the seat of his pants (in Italian, 'by his nose'), day by day." Togliatti also "smiled condescendingly at Nenni's pretense to interpret the spirit and emotional impulses of the workers."[77]

After returning to France at the devastating end of the Spanish Civil War, Nenni and his family moved from location to location north of the Pyrenees. His nearly two-decade-long exile in France had taken him first to Paris and later to the southern countryside; henceforth, his sartorial trademark would remain a dark beret, testifying to an undiminished affection for French customs and culture.

Finally, in April 1943, the Socialist leader was allowed to return to his native land. He wound up quarantined for the next three months on the island of Ponza. Released early in August, he travelled to Rome. Shortly after his arrival in the Eternal City, a woman passerby excitedly hailed him as "the most famous politician in Italy." Nenni was pleasantly surprised to hear this; in fact, his Socialist Party at the time had the largest membership of any Italian anti-Fascist party.

The stage was now set for Nenni to meet De Gasperi. Unlike any of his political Catholic peers, De Gasperi was able, on occasion, to soften Nenni's deeply rooted anticlericalism. Between October 1943 and February 1944, St. John Lateran Seminary offered refuge, along with other prominent members of the anti-Fascist Resistance, from the revived Fascists (e.g., forces of Mussolini's Republic of Salò) and Nazi authorities occupying Rome. Huddled in this sanctuary, the Socialist and Christian Democratic leaders spent long hours reviewing the past two decades, seeking to determine whether the Socialist and Popular Parties might have found common ground during the early 1920s, thereby heading off the rise of Fascism. Memories of the earnest conversations, and sometimes debates, between the reserved Trentine and the exuberant Romagnuol would remain with them even after they become political enemies. In Giulio Andreotti's engaging 1956 memoir, De Gasperi's junior colleague has recounted that Alcide regularly attended mass with the seminary's Monsignor Ferrero di Cavallerleone. Nenni boycotted the religious services and would deliberately turn up the volume on his radio. At that point, the moderate Ivanoe Bonomi would go out to ask him to lower it.[78]

Togliatti's *Svolta di Salerno* drew a surprisingly moderate comment from Nenni. Amidst the uproar provoked by the Communists' dramatic shift, Nenni commented with uncharacteristic calm that "Behind Ercole is Stalin with the immense prestige of his victories, and with Stalin are the Anglo-Americans." The Socialist Party has no way to prevent the Allies from having their way. This tactical accommodation with Togliatti's party would repeat itself frequently in coming years. Socialist-Communist ties ran hot and cold during the interwar years, warming in Italy—underground and then above ground—during the Second World War, deepening with the two parties' formal political alliance during the *secondo dopoguerra*, and finally ending in divorce between the two Marxist parties in the mid-1950s.

Nenni and Togliatti each analyzed Italy's societal situation and revolutionary potential in broadly Marxist terms. Dedicated alike to the cause of the Italian proletariat, however, they diverged intellectually and temperamentally with regard to both tactics and strategy. The more orthodox of the two, Togliatti held fast to the dialectical materialist certainty that socialism would inevitably triumph over capitalism; a conviction that reinforced his tactical flexibility. Far less patient than Togliatti, Nenni connected intuitively and emotionally with Italy's commoners. Responsive to the immediate winds of change more than longer-term eventualities, he shifted course more impetuously than his Communist peer did. Yet his repeated and abrupt shifts of position were not a matter of capriciousness. Instead, they were prompted by a sudden recognition of new elements manifesting themselves on the political scene.

Throughout his political career, Nenni struggled to reconcile a deeply rooted faith in democratic liberty with an equally unshakable belief in revolutionary socialist change. Like many early twentieth-century converts to socialism, he never entirely transcended previous radical, anarchist, and republican convictions. Nenni formally joined the Republican Party in 1908 and remained a fiercely partisan Republican for a decade and a half before he embraced the Socialist standard in 1922.[79] Fundamental to each of these creeds was an unshakable faith in the dignity, common sense, and perspicacity of the people.

Indefatigable in parliament, in party conclaves, and on the stump in the piazza, Nenni was fated to experience a great number of disappointments and defeats. American historian Alexander De Grand has tarred Nenni as the least effective of all of Italy's major twentieth-century leaders.[80] Yet as author Orianna Fallaci underscored in her evocative interview with the Socialist statesman toward the end of his life, his personal decency and genial humanism offered a much-needed tonic to his countrymen during the "Years of Lead" (*anni di piombo*) of the late 1960s and 1970s.[81] His eloquence as a chronicler of his era arguably constitutes his greatest legacy. None of the republic's founding fathers could match his pungent wit, so often expressed in memorable *bon mots*.

Despite his reputation in some quarters as a "pure politician," biographer Giuseppe Tamburrano notes that the Socialist leader felt a strong need to marry action and theory. Although not a "Marxologist" (Tamburrano's term), Nenni was convinced that Marxist doctrine was necessary to realize the mission of the proletariat. On the other hand, Nenni asserted in two of his more memorable aphorisms "ideas walk on the legs of men" and "a fact, even the most modest one, counts more than a mountain of hypotheses."[82] He had little patience with "idealist philosophy" or with "abstract" invocations of "liberty," much preferring to concentrate on concrete political situations.[83] Yet in his almost romantic rhetorical exuberance, Nenni himself wrapped terms like "revolution" with a breadth of sentimental and historical connotations bordering on abstraction. In conversation with Nenni, journalist Indro Montanelli was struck by the way the Socialist leader savored pronouncing the word "proletariat" in all of its plasticity.[84]

Reflective of the polemical charge carried by these linguistic constructions were telling remarks made by De Gasperi in a Committee of National Liberation meeting in March 1944. "We Christian Democrats," he said,

> are not afraid of Revolution: but I tell you frankly that it is a word which annoys us after having heard the phrase "Fascist revolution" for so many years, and having heard all of fascism's misdeeds justified in the name of "revolution." We are not afraid of revolution: but what we want is not revolution—it is Liberty. Here there is a difference between us. We wish to preserve the method of democracy[85]; you speak of democracy but hold in reserve the option of *il colpo di mano* (literally "a blow of the hand," i.e., forceful action).[86]

Even as they crossed swords over their respective ideologies, the two men retained a measure of personal regard. Like De Gasperi, Nenni was a deeply devoted husband and father to four daughters. Like the Trentine statesman, too, Nenni struggled at times to square his political commitments with his familial duties. In any event, he found strength and solace in his role as *pater familias* even in the face of bitter political disappointment and repression. Still, as he confided to his diary in March 1943:

> Mine is the destiny of a man who has always found himself in a cross fire (*sparaglio*), passing from prison to war, from war to exile, from one struggle to another without ever yielding, yet unsparing in my judgments of myself, tormented by a realization of the suffering which I have imposed on my own. Perhaps the Church is justified in prohibiting its priests from marrying and starting a family. [87]

Nenni's deepest grief came from the arrest and then death of his youngest, and perhaps most gifted, daughter Victoria in the waning months of the Second World War—a loss which earned him the sympathy of a wide spectrum of his fellow politicians.

Opinions differ as to Nenni's ability to sustain close, lasting friendships. Biographer Maria Grazia D'Angelo Bigelli maintains that the Socialist leader's continual relocations, his exile, and his succession of political combats, taken together, impeded him from consolidating the kind of amicable relationships whose chief attribute was their own perpetuation[88]—in Aristotelian terms "friendships of virtue." More persuasive is the testimony of stouthearted Republican leader Randolfo Pacciardi, according to whom, beginning with the two men's close association during the Spanish Civil War, Nenni displayed a singular "fidelity to friendship." This trait of Nenni's struck Pacciardi as almost childlike in its simplicity. Formidable as he was on the stump, in private Nenni could open his heart in a disarmingly gentle, often self-critical manner.[89]

All three founding fathers were deeply committed to the vocation of politics. In one of his writings on Gramsci, Togliatti offered a grand apology for politics as the best expression of man, as an activity in which all the moral and ethical expressions/aspirations of man are sublimated/realized. De Gasperi and Nenni shared this respect for the autonomy and dignity of the political vocation. Among Nenni's favorite Gallicisms was the slogan *politique d'abord* ("at all times, politics first!"). In his letters to Montini and to the Pope himself, De Gasperi repeatedly asserted that he was a professional politician who legitimately operated in the contemporary, secular realm in favor of democracy, and for this work, he required a measure of autonomy of action.⁹⁰ The depth and endurance of this calling are perhaps expressed best in the following passage from a 1927 prison letter written by De Gasperi to his wife:

> There are many who enter politics as dilettantes, regarding it as a mere diversion, and others who see it, and for whom it is an accessory of secondary importance. But for me, ever since childhood, it has constituted my career and my vocation ... I will always be a *popolare*, the Degasperi of my youth and my maturity ... just as a surgeon remains always a surgeon ... and an engineer an engineer.⁹¹

As they traversed their lengthy public careers, each man displayed impressive resiliency and adaptability. Their greatest assets as leaders complemented each other. In Aristotelian terms, De Gasperi's greatest strength as a founding father lay in his *ethos* (his credibility as a person, rooted in his upstanding character), while Togliatti most embodied *logos* (his logical appeal to his audience), and Nenni *pathos* (his emotional appeal to his audience). Collectively, the three statesmen would have to draw deeply and persistently on each of these gifts as they faced Italy's tremendous societal challenges in the wake of dictatorship and war.

Notes

1 Miriam Mafai, "Quei due carissimi nemici nell'Italia che rinasceva," *La Repubblica*. August 19, 1984.
2 Literally, "friend-enemies." The mercurial evolution (then devolution) of the De Gasperi–Togliatti relationship between 1944 and 1954 is detailed in chapters 4–7 of this book.
3 Hughes, *The United States and Italy*, 141. Hughes' association of the two men's appearance here is unusual. More typical were cartoons of the day emphasizing De Gasperi's erect, rather gaunt figure compared with Togliatti's shorter, squat physique. Marzia Marsili, "De Gasperi and Togliatti," 254.
4 Hughes, *The United States and Italy*, 141.
5 What Ferdinand Tonnies and Max Weber term *Gesellschaft*, in contra-distinction to the earlier form of societal organization, *Gemeinschaft*. In *Gemeinschaft*, "personal relationships are defined and regulated on the basis of traditional social rules. People have simple and direct face-to-face relations with each other." *Gesellschaft* is "the creation of rational will and is typified by modern, cosmopolitan societies with their government bureaucracies and large industrial organizations." http://www.britannica.com/topic/Gemeinschaft-and-Gesellschaft, accessed October 17, 2018.

6 Writing late in the Roman imperial period, St. Augustine emphasized the communal nature of *civitas* (a foundational Latin term encompassing, among other meanings, civilization, the state, and a citizenry displaying civility, eloquence, urbanity, and cordiality) in public life. "What is a *civitas*": he asked in a letter to a friend, "except a multitude of men brought together in a sort of bond of *concordia?*" This resembles a second definition offered in his masterpiece *The City of God (De Civitate Dei)*: "nor can a *civitas* consist of one person, since it is nothing other than a multitude of men bound together by some bond of association." Donald Earl, *The Moral and Political Tradition of Rome* (London: Thames & Hudson, 1976), 123–124. See also anthropologist Sydel Silverman's penetrating discussion of *civiltà*, the Italian equivalent of *civitas*, in *Three Bells of Civilization: The Life of a Tuscan Hill Town* (New York: Columbia University Press, 1975).

7 See Hannah Arendt, *The Human Condition* (New York: Vintage Books, 1958) and *Men in Dark Times* (New York: Harcourt, Brace, Jovanovich, 1968), as well as William Rawlins' synthetic *The Compass of Friendship: Narrative, Identities, Dialogue* (Los Angeles: Sage, 2009).

8 Cicero, "Treatise on Friendship," in Marshell Carl Bradley and Philip Blosser, eds., *Of Friendship: Philosophical Selections on a Perennial Concern* (Wolfeboro, NH: Longwood, 1989), 89.

9 Appropriate for Togliatti during the final twenty years of his life (commencing with his return from his Muscovite exile), he had, however, gone along with many of Stalin's interwar purges of potential rivals within the Soviet Communist Party.

10 A. C. Grayling, *Friendship* (New Haven: Yale University Press, 2013), 32.

11 Aristotle, *Nichomachean Ethics*, trans. and ed. Martin Oswald (Indianapolis: Bobbs-Merrill, 1962), 1160a7–8.

12 Pakaluk, "Political Friendship," 203–205.

13 Cicero, *On the Commonwealth*, trans. and ed. G. H. Sabine and S. P. Smith (Columbus: Ohio State University Press, 1929), V, 3, 5; VI, 1. 16, 29.

14 Donald Earl, *The Moral and Political Tradition of Rome*, 16–17.

15 Neal Wood, *Cicero's Social and Political Thought* (Berkeley: University of California Press, 1988), 136.

16 John M. Reisman, *Anatomy of Friendship* (North Stratford, NH: Irvington, 1979), 36–40.

17 Ibid., 33–34.

18 Maria Romana Catti De Gasperi, *De Gasperi Uomo solo* (Milan: Mondadori, 1964), 168.

19 Gabriella Fanello-Marcucci, *Giuseppe Spataro: lineamenti per una biografia* (Rome: Cinque Lune, 1982), 60–61.

20 Giulio Andreotti, *De Gasperi visto da vicino* (Milan: Rizzoli, 1986), 19, 138.

21 Elisa Carrillo, *Alcide De Gasperi: The Long Apprenticeship* (Notre Dame: Notre Dame University Press, 1965), 63, 110.

22 Enrico Nassi, *Alcide De Gasperi: l'utopia del centro* (Florence: Camunia, 1997), 9–10; Carrillo, *Alcide De Gasperi*, 63.
23 Catti De Gasperi, *De Gasperi, uomo solo*, 81–82.
24 Ibid.
25 Elaborating on this kind of political friendship, William Rawlins observes that "Through collective activities, storytelling, respectful dialogue, and resolute debate about salient concerns, political friends work to perceive others within the contingencies and narratives of their own lives." Rawlins, *Compass of Friendship*, 191.
26 Massimo Franco, *Andreotti visto da vicino* (Milan: Mondadori, 1989), 79.
27 Carrillo, *Alcide De Gasperi*, 150.
28 Hannah Arendt, *Men in Dark Times*.
29 L. J. Disch, "On Friendship in 'Dark Times'," in B. Honig, ed., *Feminist Interpretations of Hannah Arendt* (University Park: Penn State University Press, 1995), 287–288.
30 Enrico Nassi, *Alcide De Gasperi: L'utopia*, 10–14.
31 Steven White, "Like Father, Like Sons? Alcide De Gasperi's Search for Christian Democratic Heirs." Paper delivered at the American Catholic Historical Association Semi-Annual Meeting, Princeton, NJ, March 2010.
32 Paolo Pombeni, *Il primo De Gasperi* (Bologna: Il Mulino, 2008), 73.
33 In point of fact, "intellectual" is not a term often applied to De Gasperi. Maurizio Cau makes an engaging case that a more apt characterization is "thinking politician." Maurizio Cau, "Alcide De Gasperi: A Political Thinker or a Thinking Politician?" *Modern Italy* 14:2 4 (November 2009), 433–436.
34 Pombeni, *Il primo De Gasperi*, 227
35 Alcide De Gasperi, *Lettere dalla Prigione, 1927–1928*, 2nd ed., (Rome: Cinque lune, 1987), 198. *ADG I*, 460-1. Throughout his life, De Gasperi's faith sustained him at times of isolation. His strength in solitude brings to mind the reassuring Catholic dictum *solitude pluralis*, a "solitude in communion with all of the faithful." Barbara Taylor, "Separations of Soul: Solitude, Biography, History," *American Historical Review* 114:3 (June 2009), 644.
36 Giulio Venneri's review essay, "Man of Faith and Political Commitment: Alcide De Gasperi in the History of Europe," *Journal of Modern Italian Studies* 13:1 (March 2008), 89–92.
37 Angelo Braschi, *Mussolini e De Gasperi: vite divergenti* (Bologna: Cappelli, 1983).
38 Speech delivered in Bologna, as reported in *Il Popolo*, March 19, 1948.
39 Craveri, *De Gasperi*, 101–122.
40 Carrillo, *Alcide De Gasperi*, 149.
41 Comment by Pope John Paul II, cited in Giovanni Battista Re, *Alcide De Gasperi, vol. I. Dal Trentino all'esilio in patria (1883–1943)* (Soveria Mannelli: Rubbettino, 2009), 12.

42 Silvio Lanaro, *Storia dell'Italia repubblicana: dalla fine della guerra agli anni novanta* (Venice: Marsilio, 1992), 94.
43 Guido Gonella, *Il Centro* 1:29, Archivio Guido Gonella (hereafter AGG), busta 149, serie 9.2, fascicolo 5.
44 Cardinal Domenico Tardini, *Memories of Pius XII* (Westminster: Stackpole Press, 1961), 119. De Gasperi is the only named perpetrator in a series of four linguistic or social gaffes, which Tardini relates at this point in his memoir.
45 Indro Montanelli, *Incontri italiani* (Milan: Rizzoli, 1982), 25.
46 Prior to transferring his own papers to the Istituto Luigi Sturzo, Francesco Bartelotta shared this citation with the author. Thus, there is no specific *serie* and *fondo* designation here. Apropos of De Gasperi and Lincoln, Doris Kearns Goodwin's magisterial *Team of Rivals* opens with the following epigram, taken from a *New York Herald* editorial of May 1860 printed at the time of Lincoln's nomination for president at the Republican National Convention: "The conduct of the republican party in this nomination is a remarkable indication of small intellect growing smaller... they pass over statesmen and able men, and they take up a fourth rate lecturer, who cannot speak good grammar."
47 Miriam Mafai, *Vie Nuove*. September 3, 1964, 3, colored insert, as cited in Marsili, "De Gasperi e Togliatti," 254.
48 Luigi Barzini, *I communisti non hanno vinto* (Milan: Mondadori, 1955), 36 and Paolo Spriano, *Le passioni di un decennio* (Milan: Garzanti, 1986), 50 as cited in Marsili, "De Gasperi and Togliatti," 260.
49 Eric Terzuolo, "The Uncongenial Realism of Palmiro Togliatti." Paper delivered at the Society for Italian Historical Studies Annual Meeting, Washington, DC, January 2018.
50 Agosti, *Palmiro Togliatti*, 6.
51 Giorgio Bocca, *Togliatti* (Milan: Feltrinelli, 2014), first published in Bari: Laterza (1972), 32.
52 Agosti, *Palmiro Togliatti*, 5.
53 Ibid.
54 On Gramsci's foundational concept of hegemony, see James Joll, *Antonio Gramsci* (New York: Penguin Books, 1977), 89–90, 139–140.
55 Ibid., 117–134.
56 Luca Salvi, "Togliatti and the Hotel Lux," review article of Gianni Corbi, *Togliatti in Moscow: Story of a Bond of Iron*, in *World Affairs* 154:3 (Winter 1992), 115.
57 Ibid., 116.
58 Ibid.
59 Ibid., 117.
60 Marco Innocenti, *L'Italia del 1948... quando De Gasperi battè Togliatti* (Milan: Mursia, 1997), 68.

61 Palmiro Togliatti, "L'elugio del cinico," in Ernesto Ragionieri, ed., *Opere*, I (Rome: Riuniti, 1967), 201–202 as cited in Sante Cruciani, "L'immagine di Palmiro Togliatti nel communismo italiano," *Memoria e Ricerca* 34 (May–August 2010), 201–202.
62 Andreotti, *Visti da vicino,* 79.
63 Tony Judt, *Postwar: A History of Europe since 1945* (New York: Penguin, 2005), 207.
64 Stalin made this remark while conversing with Marshall Tito, still his fair-haired boy at the time. *Yugoslav Record of Conversation of I. V. Stalin and the Yugoslav Delegation Headed by J. Broz Tito, 27–28 May 1946,* in Wilson Center Digital Archive, retrieved from http://digitalarchive.wilsoncenter.org/document/117099, accessed October 28, 2018.
65 Marsili, "De Gasperi and Togliatti," 259.
66 Party comrade Umberto Terracini's candid reflections on this side of Togliatti's character are detailed below in the section of chapter 3 dealing with the Salerno Turn.
67 Agosti, *Palmiro Togliatti,* 37.
68 On the political and personal relationship between Togliatti and Iotti, see Gianni Corbi, *Nilde* (Milan: Rizzoli, 1993).
69 Quoted in Agosti, *Palmiro Togliatti,* 110. Agosti finds in this passage the seeds of Togliatti's conception of "progressive democracy," discussed below in chapter 3.
70 Vittorio Gorresio, *I carissimi nemici* (Milan: Loganisi, 1977), 117, 127.
71 Giuseppe Tamburrano, *Pietro Nenni* (Bari: Laterza, 1986), 133.
72 Ibid., 15; Vittorio Emiliani, "Il talento del grande giornalista," in Giuseppe Tamburrano, ed., *Nenni dieci anni dopo* (Rome: Lucarini, 1990), 151.
73 Randolfo Pacciardi, "Il ricordo di un amico mazziniano," in Giuseppe Tamburrano, ed., *Nenni dieci anni dopo,* 23.
74 Maria Grazia D'Angelo Bigelli, *Pietro Nenni dalle barrecate a Palazzo Madama* (Milan: Giorgio Giannini, 1970), 28.
75 Among Nenni's favorite aphorisms, reflective of his early anarchism, was "the Italian State acts powerfully toward the weak, and weakly toward the powerful." http://www.imiglioriaforismi.com/2012/07/pietro-nenni-aforismi.html, accessed October 29, 2018.
76 Bocca, *Togliatti,* 195.
77 Ibid., 378.
78 Giulio Andreotti, *De Gasperi e il suo tempo: Trento-Vienna-Rome* (Milan: Rizzoli, 1956), 141. See also Ivanoe Bonomi, *Diario di un anno* (Milan: Garzanti, 1947), 131.
79 D'Angelo Bigelli, *Pietro Nenni,* 36–37.
80 Alexander De Grand, "To Learn Nothing and to Forget Nothing: Italian Socialism and the Experience of Exile Politics, 1935–1945," *Contemporary European History* 14, 539–558.
81 Oriana Fallaci, *Interview with History* (Boston: Houghton Mifflin, 1977).

82 https://www.aforism.it/pietro_nenni/23October2018, accessed October 29, 2018.
83 Pacciardi, "Amico mazziniano," 20.
84 Montanelli, *Gli incontri,* 99.
85 "Method of democracy" and "Method of liberty" were among De Gasperi's favorite rhetorical tropes—ones that he would return to again and again.
86 Francesco Malgeri, *Alcide De Gasperi*, vol. II, *Dal fascismo alla democrazia (1943-1947)* (Soveria Mannelli: Rubbettino, 2009), 26–27. For De Gasperi's full remarks on this occasion, see Alcide De Gasperi, *Scritti e discorsi*, III:I, ed. Paolo Pombeni and Giuliana Nobile Schiera, (Bologna: Il Mulino, 2008), 524–526.
87 D'Angelo Bigelli, *Pietro Nenni, 9.*
88 Ibid., 47.
89 Pacciardi, "Amico mazziniano," 20.
90 Paolo Spriano, "De Gasperi e Togliatti: protagonist e antagonisti," in Gaetano Arfè, ed., *De Gasperi e Togliatti: politiche a confronto* (Rimini: Maggioli, 1985), 28.
91 Paolo Pombeni, *Il primo De Gasperi: la formazione di un leader politico* (Bologna: Il Mulino, 2007), 13–14.

2

A Daunting Prospect

As the Second World War ended, Italy's prospects for a democratic future were far from auspicious. Two decades of Fascist opportunism followed by military humiliation and foreign occupation had left most Italians confused, frightened, isolated, and impoverished. Age-old social, economic, and political cleavages between north and south, and between center and periphery, had been aggravated during the halting two-year Anglo-American military advance up the peninsula against stubborn German and Italian neo-Fascist forces.[1]

The successful Allied invasion of Sicily in July 1943 precipitated Benito Mussolini's fall from power in Rome. The Anglo-Americans landed on July 10; encountering minimal resistance, they occupied the island in a matter of weeks. Palermo fell to American forces on July 22. On the evening of July 24, the Fascist Grand Council met and, at the end of a tense all-night session, voted nineteen to seven for the Fascist Party to the transfer of its powers to the State, and for the Duce to surrender his powers to the King.[2] On July 25, King Victor Emmanuel III secured Mussolini's resignation as prime minister, and then had him arrested. Over the next forty-five days (referred to henceforth as the Forty-Five Days), it appeared as though Italy had freed herself from Fascist authoritarianism. But this was not to be. The German rescue of Mussolini from captivity, coupled with disastrously prolonged negotiations between the Italians and the Allies over an eventual armistice, allowed the Nazis to occupy the entire boot, and subject Italians to even more brutal repression than that imposed during the Fascist *ventennio*.

Following the September 8, 1943, announcement of the armistice between the Allies and the Italian government, the King, his Prime Minister Marshall Pietro Badoglio, and their rump ministries fled from Rome to Brindisi. A weak, patchwork "cobelligerent" Italian government, known as "King's Italy," struggled to reassert a minimal measure of effective sovereignty in the portions of the Mezzogiorno nominally returned to Italian jurisdiction behind the advancing

Allied forces.³ "King's Italy" garnered uncertain respect—at best—from the Italian populace, yet the Anglo-American American authorities continued to recognize it, since the Italian monarchist regime remained legally bound to uphold the terms of the armistice agreement. The country's emergent anti-Fascist parties (described more fully in Chapter 3) were kept at arm's length early in the campaign, while the Vatican was, from the outset, a key interlocutor for Allied policymakers.

On June 4, 1944, the day before D-Day took place in Normandy, Rome was freed by advancing Allied troops. The nation's anti-Fascist parties were now invited to enter a new Italian co-belligerent government headed by the elderly, moderate Socialist Ivanoe Bonomi. It took nearly another year for Allied forces, assisted by anti-Fascist partisans, to complete the liberation of the peninsula. On May 2, 1945, the last German forces surrendered, ending the Italian campaign. Five days earlier, partisans had apprehended Mussolini, disguised as a German soldier, and his mistress Clara Petacci, as the two tried to escape into neutral Switzerland. The Duce was then shot and his and his mistress' mutilated bodies were hung upside down in Piazza Loreto in Milan. The twin ordeals of Fascist authoritarianism and foreign invasion were over. But at what cost?

Allied Occupation

The Anglo-American military campaign, and the occupation policies accompanying it, proved to be a profoundly mixed blessing for the Italian people. Early euphoria at the arrival of Anglo-American liberators gave way, time and again, to exasperation, disillusionment, and even despair among ordinary Italians. Focused first and foremost on military strategy and tactics, the Allies had to jump-start civil affairs policy,⁴ and to retool repeatedly during a campaign lasting far longer than any would have wished.

Allied Military Government (AMG)'s default policy was aptly encapsulated in the phrase "keep existing administration and temper de-fascistization with discretion."⁵

Further complicating their efforts were the dissimilar traditions and competencies which British and American officials brought to their responsibilities. In the initial stages of AMG, British and American officials alike were trained to discourage indigenous Italian initiative, the better to maintain law and order behind the lines. With regard to local populations, the officials were ordered to "avoid political implications of any kind"—an unrealistic stipulation in practice.⁶ British officials often reached out to local notables, inevitably tilting the conduct of affairs in a conservative direction. American officials were divided between reformists confident of their ability to promote democratic change and skeptics doubtful of the prospects for sweeping innovation in the midst of war.⁷

For the first five to six months of the Italian campaign, American policymakers deferred to their British counterparts in civil affairs matters, focusing instead on military strategy. The first Chief of Civil Affairs in Sicily was Lord Rennell of Rodd, a British aristocrat who had headed up military government in British-occupied areas of north and northeast Africa between 1941 and 1943. In Italy, Lord Rennell implemented a policy of "indirect control" of the indigenous population which had long served as a hallmark of overseas British colonial governance.⁸ The advantages of relying as much as possible on existing local officials such as prefects and mayors to carry out policies framed by the Anglo-Americans were twofold. This approach conserved Allied manpower while diffusing local resentment of stern Allied-mandated measures. In a memorandum written in early August 1943, Rennell reported:

> The decision to maintain the local administration in [Sicilian] towns has so far proved successful. In a number of places advisory municipal councils have been nominated... Local private people and businessmen have proved helpful and public spirited in trying to restore normal conditions especially in heavily damaged areas. Ecclesiastic personages have also been helpful.⁹

This memo reflects wider British skepticism (elaborated further below) as to the depth of grassroots Fascist indoctrination among local elites. Yet as American historian John Diggins has pointed out, "in a country where many of the most capable men had gone underground or fled, AMG had to work with unsavory elements."¹⁰ Notorious in this regard was the reemergence of the mafia in Sicily. Lord Rennell's defensively attributed the "regrettable resurfacing of the mafia"¹¹ to some of his fellow Allied officials' "exuberance to remove Fascist Podestas and Municipal officials in rural towns," adding that these officers "have in some cases, by ignorance of local personalities, appointed a number of 'Mafia' bosses or allowed such bosses to propose suitable malleable substitutes."¹²

Beginning with the liberation of Sicily, the Allies struggled to forge a consistent policy for screening and, if warranted, dismissing Italian officials tainted by Fascist connections.¹³ The process of investigating and removing such individuals from office was termed in Italian *epurazione*—a word whose connotations were less punitive than "purge" but sterner than the French derivative "epuration." As they sought to separate the Fascist wheat from the chaff, Allied Civil Affairs Officers relied heavily on a cumbersome vetting form which satisfied neither radical nor conservative Italian public opinion.

From the outset, Allied *epurazione* policy was subject to contradictory pressures. Prominent American civil affairs officers such as ex-New York Lieutenant Governor Charles Poletti took the process seriously throughout the campaign. On the other hand, Lord Rennell argued that the Allies needed to proceed cautiously, and retain as many competent Italian officials as possible. Rennell's Administrative Instruction Order No. 1 noted:

> The Fascist Party machine ... cannot be broken or Fascist influence be eliminated in a day. Since also nearly all Italian administrative officials are, at any rate nominally, members of the party, it will not be possible to remove or intern all members of the party. This would only cause a breakdown ... of the whole of the Italian administrative machine.[14]

As for the Italian populace as a whole, Allied planners envisioned that, to the degree possible, it should be treated with benevolence. Interestingly, Lord Rennell took a harder line, urging that the printed manual of guidelines drawn up for soldiers in preparation for the Sicily landings include the maxim that "You will be guided by the memory of years of war in which the Italians fought against your people and your Allies." This belligerent passage was excluded from the manual. On the subject of "benevolence," Rennell referenced his prior tenure in colonial northern and eastern Africa, where his "experience [was] not having to restrain the troops, at any rate the British troops, from being vindictive and brutal, but rather of having to prevent immediate fraternization and treatment of the local population as domestic pets."[15]

Nowhere was Allied occupation policy more problematic than in Naples between the fall of 1943 and the spring of 1945. The dire state of that city six months after its liberation was vividly evoked by Palmiro Togliatti in the following terms:

> A shower of fine ash was hovering over the gulf, covering the fields and the streets ... The appearance of the motherland, after eighteen years of [Togliatti's Russian] exile, was somehow apocalyptic, ... the city looked ill, with a fever mixed with exhaustion, anxiety for the present and the future, the anxious search for life's necessities to be obtained at any cost [...] There was the feeling that Italy, as an organized society, did not exist anymore, that it had to be rebuilt.[16]

Prior to the Allies' arrival in the city in October 1943, the Germans had blown up the great city aqueduct in seven places and the power station. In his initial report, Lord Rennell ruefully noted that the Germans "had removed all the food and goods they could lay their hands on. Naples had no water for three weeks. There was very little food in town."[17]

Sadly, the Allies' occupation and administration of that city, coveted strategically for its port, wound up compounding the socio-economic and even the moral suffering of Neapolitans. "Amlire," the AMG currency, flooded the city, with Franklin D. Roosevelt's Four Freedoms—freedom of speech, freedom of religion, freedom from want, and freedom from fear—printed (in English!) on the backside of the bills to uplift the local population. Ironically, the material impact of the circulation of so much issue was a drastic increase in inflation.[18] The heavy Allied bombardment of the zones surrounding the port had left 200,000 Neapolitans homeless. Through the fall of 1943, Naples had little water and the sewers did not function at all. In the chaos of evacuations and disrupted family life (often involving the death of one or both parents), hundreds of children ranging from age six to sixteen were reduced to the status of street urchins. Bewildered, hungry, and dressed in rags, many resorted to petty crime, pimping, or prostitution. Epidemics of venereal disease and typhus ravaged civilian and military populations alike.[19] John Horne Burns' scathing 1947 novel *The Gallery* (so named for Naples' spacious enclosed shopping arcade *Galleria Umberto I*) confirmed American GIs' callous—and indeed exploitative—treatment of the Neapolitans.[20]

A very different portrayal of American AMG impact on the ground emerges from John Hersey's upbeat novel *A Bell for Adano*. Based on a true story, the novel won a Pulitzer Prize in 1945 and formed the basis for a series of popular postwar movies. Hersey's book focuses on Major Joppolo, an AMG official who helps a group of Sicilian villagers to replace their church bell, which the Fascists had melted down for munitions. To accomplish this task, Joppolo must overcome the objections of Major Marvin, who disapproves of such feel-good favors to an undeserving native populace. In the end, however, the villagers' quest for a new bell emerges in the novel as a metaphor for the wider rebirth of Italian democracy.[21] Taken together, Hersey's and Burns' works gave new meaning to the turn-of-the-century Basilicatan proverb, "America accommodates some and ruins others."[22]

American and British civil affairs officers did not receive adequate advance training for the complicated situations awaiting them. In the United States, a School of Military Government had been created at the University of Virginia in Charlottesville in late May 1942. The school's operational capacities and instructional aims proved to be unequal to the task assigned to them. It had been widely assumed that the liberation of Italy would be accomplished expeditiously, and that this would largely limit civil affairs officers' responsibilities to the maintenance of calm and order. Rapid military success would hopefully preclude situations in which civil affairs officials might find themselves enmeshed in local social and political controversies. In any case, prompt, decisive intervention would have a better chance of prevailing over a stunned local populace than would slower action, where even more modest actions might well encounter stronger resistance. However sensible in theory, this principle proved irrelevant in the Italian theater, since the Allies themselves lacked any consensus as to what kind of "prompt, decisive intervention" needed to be undertaken.

Circumstances confronting civil affairs officers during the Second World War transcended the challenges involved in prior American experiences, including the occupations that had followed the war with Mexico, the US Civil War, the Spanish American War, and the occupation of the Rhineland after the First World War.[23] Now civil affairs required more specialization than ever, drawing upon the expertise of a range of officers; no longer "could a good soldier be a jack of all trades."[24] In an internal memo dated June 1942, the Commandant of the Charlottesville School of Military Government reflected on the fact that prior to the Second World War:

> [T]he only form of military government contemplated…arises upon the occupation of *enemy* territory. American forces may however, find themselves in the occupation of their territories of neutrals, quasi-neutrals, puppets or even allies. An entirely unexplored field of international law is in the prospect.[25]

Nuanced as the commandant's memo was, a simpler binary approach followed, whereby civil affairs officials were instructed to treat "enemy peoples" in one manner, liberated "friendly nations" in another. In the former instance, civil affairs officers were "immediately to extirpate totalitarian governments and economic systems." Administrative strategies appropriate for previously oppressed, friendly nations instead directed officials to move "as soon as possible to aid in restoring indigenous systems and authorities." In either instance, Allied civil officers "were to make an all-out effort to effect gradual transition toward the envisaged post-war national and international order."[26]

Italy did not fit either of these prescriptions. Though Mussolini prided himself for having promoted the term *totalitarianism*, Fascism fell short achieving "totalitarian" mastery of the Italian nation. In varying degrees, the Church, the Savoyard monarchy, and the Roman bureaucracy each preserved a measure of independence from Mussolini's wishes. Italy's aggressions against Balkan and African states prevented Great Britain in particular from fully embracing Italy as a political or military counterpart. Italy was designated in the armistice as a "co-belligerent" power.

As for Allied prescriptions for a postwar Italian or (broader international) order, these remained inchoate as the Italian campaign got underway. Already on the eve of the July 1943 Sicily landings, differences in the two Allied nations' perceptions of Fascism spelled trouble. While the UK's Foreign Office took seriously the threat of rivalry with an expansionist Italy in the Mediterranean and in Africa, Britons paid rather less attention to Fascism per se.[27] Their country lacked America's history of Italian immigration, and harbored fewer anti-Fascist exiles than either France or the United States. In 1941, British scholarship did produce a first-rate study: D. A. Binchy's *Church and State in Fascist Italy*. For all its factual scruples and attempt at objectivity, Binchy's study reinforced British dislike for Mussolini and measured sympathy for the Catholic Church. While the author did not ignore clerico-Fascism, fundamentally he portrayed the Church as the defender and the embodiment of Italy's "universalist and cosmopolitan genius" against the regime's nationalism and totalitarianism. Binchy criticized the anti-Fascist exiles on both sides of the Atlantic for their anti-clericalism and "extremism."[28]

The Schools

A complex, longer-term challenge arose in the field of education. This field, as much as any, revealed contradictions between Allied war-making and ground-level democratic reconstruction. Misplaced preconceptions, divergent agendas, and insufficient up-to-date information on Italian social realities each obstructed satisfactory evaluations of Fascism's educational legacy and stood in the way of crafting a consistent or effective reform strategy. Allied experience in the field of educational reconstruction foreshadowed broader policy cross currents and inconsistencies which would characterize the United States' impact on Italy's nascent republic throughout the *secondo dopoguerra*.[29]

British and American educators envisioned a two-stage process of reconstruction. First, ideologically committed Fascist teachers and administrators had to be purged, and explicitly Fascist doctrines expunged from textbooks and lesson plans. Second, instructional practices and materials needed to be redefined to foster democratic rather than authoritarian values. Here the revision of national primary and secondary school curricula would be especially significant.[30]

The Anglo-Americans' first educational leader (September 1943 to February 1944) was the English physical anthropologist George Robert Gayre.[31] Gayre had received recognition in the interwar period as a spirited critic of Nazi racial theory. Overall, he viewed Italian Fascism very much as he did National Socialism, except that the latter had "gone a little deeper and been a little more efficiently organized." Initially an educational advisor attached to the AMG central command, with the creation of the Allied Control Commission (ACC) in November, he became the director of its Educational Subcommission, which now encompassed the existing AMG staff and a small liaison group in Brindisi.[32]

Gayre's successors as education directors under ACC auspices both came from the United States, as did 80 percent of its officers. Thomas Vernor Smith, education director from February to September 1944, was a political philosopher at the University of Chicago and an ex-Congressman at large from the state of Illinois. Smith's successor, Carleton Washburne, was a disciple of John Dewey who had won national recognition for the reforms he had pioneered as superintendent of schools in Winnetka, Illinois.

The enthusiastic Washburne epitomized the activist approach noted above. He viewed the Education Subcommission's mission as two-fold:

> First, there is the emergency job of getting schools open on a non-fascist basis... Second, there is the assisting of the Italian Government in its attempt to organize its schools in a way which will foster healthy living, good citizenship, decent world attitude, while preserving the best cultural traditions.[33]

Smith on the other hand wrote in his "swan song" (as he characterized his final report as education director) that he "did not propose in a single season to try to straighten Italy's old Leaning Tower of Learning—but only to clear it of the poison ivy of fascism."[34]

Large numbers of schools were damaged or demolished in the course of the Italian campaign. Collateral damage was particularly extensive in the Mezzogiorno. The Sicilian campaign destroyed or severely damaged 25 percent of the island's schools; in Palermo, Catania, and Messina, destruction was even greater. Damage was also grave in Salerno and Naples. In areas adjoining the front lines and in strategic cities, schools were used as troop billets, hospitals, and shelters for homeless civilians. Troops were particularly prone to vandalize school property, often burning desks, chairs, blackboards, and even window and doorframes in order to keep warm during the winter months. Neither educational officers nor even the AMG leadership were authorized to remove such destructive occupants, however. Only local tactical army commanders could order school buildings cleared—a step they took strictly based on military or administrative convenience. In Palermo and Salerno, some schools were thus tied up for six to nine months; in Naples and in Apulia for as much as a year and a half. The consequent spectacle of hungry, ragged children living and working on the streets, in villages and towns as well as cities, alarmed AMG officials and visiting Anglo-American journalists as both immoral and unsafe, but remedies were slow in coming.[35]

On the average, formal instruction in any given locale resumed four months after the arrival of Allied forces. Pressures exerted by local gentry often enabled private and parochial schools to open several weeks before their state counterparts. Even after school buildings were physically repaired, it took much longer to restore heat, light, or adequate sanitation to classrooms. As winter set in, pupils' attentions centered more on the warmth provided by solitary classroom stoves than on their teachers' words.[36]

While the temporary closing of schools silenced Fascism's most extensive agency of political indoctrination, it also reversed much of the progress made in recent decades to extend a network of elementary schools throughout the Mezzogiorno's countryside. The war also wrought havoc on transportation and communication systems, making it hard for many children to reach schools even after they had reopened. In the south, the results were especially unfortunate, as much of the progress since the turn of the century in lowering illiteracy was temporarily undone.

At the same time, the material destruction of the war, followed by the uncontrolled influx of Allied military currency, especially via free spending GIs, into the Italian marketplace, was economically catastrophic. The ensuing inflation struck hardest at lower-level state employees, such as teachers.[37] The endemic southern specter of economic want now assumed menacing proportions: no wonder Allied educational officers so often found themselves distracted from their pedagogical mission by individual teachers seeking only a new *padrone*. Such disenchanted teachers were hardly prepared to serve as catalysts of a new democracy. Furthermore, twenty years of Fascist sloganeering, followed by an unpopular, misguided war, had left not a few school heads and teachers cynically deferential and conformist, incapable any longer of investing their faith in anything except their own advancement.

Such indigenous cynicism might seem to have confirmed some Allied invasion planners' doubts as to the extent of Fascist penetration of Italian popular schooling. A case in point was Henry Rowell, an American with extensive interwar exposure to Italian affairs, who asserted that elementary and secondary school materials would need "little revision based on his familiarity with what schools were using several years ago." Rowell had been tapped to head Allied reeducation efforts in Italy, but was transferred to another post just prior to the Sicily landings.[38] Also revealing is language appearing in the Political Warfare Executive's (PWE) *Italian Basic Handbook*, published in May 1943. That seminal British document reaffirmed Binchy's view that the predominantly ecclesiastical private schools made minimal concessions to the "Fascist atmosphere" around them. In general, the PWE handbook also emphasized how "indifferences and skepticism" on the part of the teachers and officials ultimately hindered the "the full application of Fascist theories" even in state institutions. Indeed, this report asserted:

> [T]here has been no Fascist revolution in the schools but rather a long war of attrition between a school which had its own life and developed according to its own needs and a political movement without any definite views on education.[39]

It did not take Gayre long to repudiate such judgments as "absolutely unfounded." Shortly after arriving in Sicily, Gayre paid an impromptu visit to a Palermo primary school. Alarmed by the ideological content presented to students even in the beginning grades, he proceeded to review a complete set of the *libri di stato*, the state-mandated series of textbooks. Gayre summarized his findings for Lord Rennell as follows:

> Starting with the second class (for children 7 years of age) we have such subjects as "The little sentry," "The little soldiers," an account of armoured weapons, and Italy's right to dominate the Mediterranean. All this is mixed up with "Tears of the Virgin" and "The sign of the Cross" in the best style of authoritarian propaganda. By the time we reach the third class (8 years) the indoctrination becomes even more intense, and more subtly interwoven with religious and moral themes. We have "Exercises of Tomorrow," the "March on Rome," "Italy on the March," "The War of the People," "The Servants of Mussolini," "The Duce," "The Ballila" and much more.[40]

Allied-approved textbooks, hastily scrubbed of Fascist content, did not become available until the spring of 1944. In the south, elementary students had to make do with make-shift textbooks in which offensive passages had been inked over or clipped out. In many cases, even these tattered materials were unavailable at first. That absence was serious indeed, in light of the reluctance of many elementary school teachers to depart from textual dictation as a method of teaching.[41]

The task of textbook and curricular revision at both the primary and secondary level fell mainly to Washburne. This affable American, with his unsoldierly bearing, got along readily with local schoolteachers, if not always with his military superiors. In many ways Washburne resembled "Major Joppolo," the protagonist of Hersey's novel *A Bell for Adano*. Like Joppolo, Washburne was imbued with the progressive American faith in grassroots activism. He believed that, for all their present flaws, Italy's public schools could be reformed "from below."

Struck by the inadequacies of popular education at the lower secondary and still more at the elementary levels, he collaborated with Gino Ferretti, a leftist anticleric from Palermo, to fashion a new primary school curriculum. A new subject entitled "moral and civic education" was introduced, aimed at refashioning "the minds and spirits of the new generations within a free society." In addition, the syllabus introduced a new form of religious instruction, emphasizing the Gospel rather than the catechism. The latter provision outraged Church authorities and was reversed.[42]

Educational reconstruction by outsiders, however well-intentioned, enlisted neither the approval nor the assistance of the most prominent Italian anti-Fascists who had found refuge in the United States. In comparison, anti-Nazi refugees at least contributed moderately to American proposals for educational reconstruction in their homeland. In the summer and fall of 1943, the New York journal *The New Leader* sponsored a series of symposia on the theme "What to do with Italy?", inviting the participation of a spectrum of anti-Fascist exiles, from the radical historian Gaetano Salvemini to the veteran Catholic leader Luigi Sturzo. In addition to sessions on such questions as the future of the Italian monarchy, one symposium confronted the possible re-education of Italian youth after the defeat of Fascism. Italian participants concurred that their countrymen would have to be "re-educated" to the virtues of democracy, but looked to indigenous anti-Fascist and pre-Fascist experiences for remediation.[43]

Several months after these anti-Fascist exiles gathered at the New York symposium, H. Stuart Hughes of the Office of Strategic Services (OSS) penned a revealing memorandum concerning educational reconstruction. "In view of the delicacy of issues touching on Italian cultural pride," Hughes wrote, Allied educators officials needed to tread proceed cautiously. For its part, the Catholic Church "had been too closely associated with the fallen regime" to be trusted to lead educational rehabilitation. Instead, Hughes asserted, "only a 'liberal' could be entrusted to lead Italians through the difficult emotional summersault of transforming education for a dictatorship into education for a democracy," urging that the next Italian minister of public instruction be a "man of universally recognized Liberalism, integrity and practical realism."[44] Hughes belonged to what diplomatic historian James Miller in his fine study *The United States and Italy, 1940–1950* has described as the New Deal progressive or "liberal" wing of the American policymaking establishment.[45] Like other State Department reformists, Hughes placed great stock in leaders such as Count Carlo Sforza of the Action Party.[46]

Between April and December 1944, the post of minister of public instruction was occupied by two of Sforza's fellow Action Party intellectuals, Adolfo Omodeo and then Guido De Ruggiero. Their counterpart as Allied Education Subcommission head at this time was T.V. Smith. Omodeo and Smith would seem to have been well matched: both were philosophically inclined, and both were deeply suspicious of the Church.[47]

But when the strong-minded Omodeo—determined to restore decorum and discipline to Italian schooling—resisted popular demands to enlarge Italy's university system, he rapidly became a lightning rod for attacks, especially from middle-class families, who looked to an easing of academic standards as a means of advancing from a disheartening present to a brighter future. To restore calm, Smith pressed the education minister to adopt a more conciliatory stance. Omodeo refused: "Such compromise methods might work in America," he said, "but in Italy one must be stern."[48] The Allied education director coolly conceded that his Italian counterpart was "too energetic for lethargic times." Omodeo was succeeded in June by the more patient and even-tempered De Ruggiero. By this time, however, Smith concluded:

> We do not hold ourselves responsible for the poverty, illiteracy, dense population of these tired people of a dazed land. Not without sympathy but with a touch of mature realism, we cannot but observe that for others too easily to save the foolish from the consequences of their own folly (even if they could), is one sure way to fill the world with fools."[49]

By the conclusion of his Italian sojourn in September 1944, Smith added:

> The minimum of our duty, internationally defined, was to uphold during the period of our interim sovereignty the maximum advantage wrested by the Church from Fascism. Moreover, it would have made no sense at all for us to [not] appreciate as fully as possible the influence of the greatest Agency for Order perhaps on earth, when the primary job of military government is to keep order among conquered peoples.[50]

How Smith's assessment of the Church had changed! This endorsement of the appropriateness of Church interests and actions foreshadowed steady Catholic ascendancy over Italian educational policy through the last year of the war and deep into the postwar period.

The Vatican had opposed American liberal reformers from the onset of the Italian campaign. The Church accused the advocates of radical "democratization" of harboring anti-clerical and even "anti-Italian" prejudices. The American Catholic hierarchy also feared the reformist potential of American policy in Italy. Hoping to curb liberal influence, the Knights of Columbus passed a resolution in August 1943 that American military government officials in liberated Italy be of the Catholic faith "in proportion to the Roman Catholic population of Italy."[51] Also allies of the Church were conservative officers within the traditionally Republican and isolationist State Department, such as the prominent Irish-American diplomat Robert Murphy.

A defining incident in this regard concerned Father Agostino Gemelli, the Franciscan friar and experimental psychologist who had founded the Sacred Heart University of Milan in 1921. One of interwar Italy's best-known and most influential Catholic educators, he was selected by Pius XI to head the Pontifical Academy of Sciences. Between 1937 and 1941, he gave a number of widely publicized speeches and articles that praised Fascism as Catholicism's partner in the international crusade against communism. What's more, Catholicism and Fascism shared the "lofty principles of hierarchy, order, discipline and sacrifice."[52]

Gemelli was among those singled out to be purged when Allied educational representative Arthur Vessolo arrived in the Lombard capital on May 15, 1945. For their part, the Americans had hardly endeared themselves to Gemelli when, late in the war, their bombers flattened the Father's psychological laboratory in Milan. Despite ample evidence of his pro-Fascist sympathies, Gemelli's influential connections within the Vatican prevented Vessolo from suspending the rector according to the usual criteria and procedures. Instead, Vessolo was compelled to place all vetting at the Catholic University in the hands of a special vetting committee, to be appointed from a list drawn up by the Vatican. In an August letter to Pius XII, Pro-Rector Monsignor Ogliati confided that Vessolo was apparently under the influence of "occult" (e.g., Masonic or Protestant) forces bent on the elimination of the long-suffering Gemelli. By the fall, the vetting committee had suspended eleven members of the Catholic University's faculty. But upon its recommendations, Gemelli remained rector, on the grounds that he had defended Jews and offered asylum to certain partisans.[53]

The final defascistization of Italian schooling fell to postwar Christian Democratic-led governments. Between July 1946 and July 1951, Guido Gonella served as Italy's Minister of Public Instruction. A close associate of De Gasperi's since the 1930s, Gonella also enjoyed the confidence of the Vatican hierarchy. Under Fascism he and his family had found shelter in a modest Vatican City apartment. Near the conclusion of his tenure as Minister of Public Instruction, he also assumed the post of DC Party Secretary (1950–1953).

The Church

The Church's educational involvement formed part of its overarching *magisterium*—the privileged role it claimed in safeguarding personal morality and all matters relating to marriage, family, and the socialization of the young. This centuries-old prerogative was confirmed in the 1929 Concordat between the Vatican and the State of Italy. The Concordat mandated instruction in the catechism in all Italian primary and secondary schools, public as well as private and parochial. Catholicism was honored as the established religion of the Italian state. In the Concordat, the Fascist regime accommodated Catholic Action, the sprawling organization of Catholic laity dedicated to advancing Church interests throughout Italian society,[54] granting this exception to its own claims to totalitarian societal control on the condition that Catholic Action focus solely on social as opposed to political matters.

Linked to the Concordat were the Lateran Accords, whereby the Holy See at last recognized the legitimacy of the Kingdom of Italy while establishing the sovereign nation of Vatican City. The advantages garnered by the Church by this resolution of the "Roman Question" came at a heavy cost. Pius XI's acclamation of Mussolini as "a man sent to Italy by Providence" would not be easily forgotten or forgiven. The Church supported an imperial war against Ethiopia whose cruelty prompted widespread international condemnation and severe economic sanctions by the League of Nations. Italy's intervention on the nationalist side in the Spanish Civil War of 1936–1939 was justified too as a crusade to rescue Spanish Catholicism from an anti-clerical Spanish republic. Also animating the Church's support for Franco's cause in Spain was its deeply rooted antipathy toward republicanism, seen as intimately linked with socialism and communism.

The Church's anti-republican hermeneutic of suspicion dated back to the French Revolution—a traumatic watershed whose anti-clerical excesses haunted Catholic officialdom as if they had happened yesterday. The Syllabus of Errors, promulgated in 1864, condemned democracy and liberalism in all of their political expressions—including republicanism and unfettered individualism.

Four years later, the Church proclaimed the doctrine of *Non-expedit*, barring Catholics from the political life of unified Italy.[55] This doctrine was abandoned in 1918, opening the way for the formation of Italy's first Catholic political party, the Popular Party. Yet fearful of the unpredictability of multi-party parliamentarism, and open to the possibility of an accommodation with Mussolini's regime, the Church disavowed the Popular Party in 1925. In lieu of parliamentary legislation recognizing Catholic rights and interests, Pius XI preferred to negotiate concordats with many Western governments in the interwar years, which would guarantee the Church's institutional privileges and prerogatives "from above"—an approach consonant with the Church's own hierarchical structure.[56]

The legacies of each of these prior Church actions were to embarrass Catholic anti-Fascists such as De Gasperi and foster anti-clericalism among their secular peers during and immediately following the Second World War. Also problematic was Pius XII's diplomacy of a neutrality between the Axis and Allied powers. Between 1938 and the early years of the Second World War, he refrained from criticizing either Nazism/Fascist authoritarianism or Western parliamentary democracy. The Pope's hesitancy reflected as well his exceptional solicitude for Rome herself. The descendant of an aristocratic Roman family, he was deeply committed to a Catholic brand of *romanità*.[57] He feared that public denunciation of Nazi racism might prompt retribution against Catholics, and possibly his own forced exile from Vatican City. He also feared the military violation of Rome, which had been largely spared from destruction until the summer of 1943. Acclaimed by Rome's vulnerable populace as *Salvator Urbis* (Savior of the City) and *Salvator Civitatis* (Savior of the civilization that Rome represented), he could not prevent the American bombing of Rome which, ironically, damaged the Church of San Lorenzo, thereby unearthing many of the Pacelli family graves interred there. The Pope soon visited the damaged church to offer pastoral solace—a gesture deeply appreciated by local Romans. By contrast, King Victor Emmanuel III's inspection of the site was met by insults and catcalls from the crowd.[58]

As Allied victory became more and more probable in the last two years of the war, Pius XII began to reconsider the Church's traditional hostility to democracy, conceding that, properly led, democracy might reveal itself "morally superior and philosophically preferable." In his celebrated Christmas Message of December 1944, the Pope explicitly linked freedom, democracy, and Christian values. At the same time, Pius XII warned that external agents promoting erroneous, morally corrupt ideas and ideologies endangered this auspicious trend. Specifically, he decried the usurpation of the discourse of democracy by "collectivist regimes" purporting to advance the will and needs of the "masses."[59]

In the immediate Italian context, however, he remained devoted to the House of Savoy. The Vatican steadfastly supported the monarchy as a fellow guarantor of law and order in the face of wartime chaos. As discussed further in chapter 4, the Vatican was to escalate its rhetorical support of the House of Savoy in the months leading up the June 1946 institutional referendum; in this campaign, the Pope redoubled his predecessors' loathing of atheistic socialism and communism, portraying republicanism as but a precursor to Marxist ascendancy—an evil and indeed existential threat to the Church's God-given mission.

The most controversial aspect of the Pope's wartime behavior was his response to the Holocaust. Pius XII's dualistic mindset, continually separating faithful insiders from fallen outsiders, bore tragically on his inability to extend his pastoral concern beyond Christian circles. Cognitively and emotionally, he found himself paralyzed when confronted by the calamity overtaking Europe's Jewry. Especially troubling was his failure to intervene when the Nazis rounded up the Jews of Rome's ghetto. The Vatican's chimerical attempt to remain above the fray of war and to remain detached from the reality of the Holocaust sowed confusion and remorse within the Church hierarchy as well as among the Roman Catholic faithful. Here and there, individual Church leaders faced up to the existential anti-Semitic threat and beseeched the Holy Father to intervene. More typical, however, was the hesitation of clerics, in Italy and elsewhere, to act without papal sanction.[60]

The Monarchy

In the eyes of many Italians, King Victor Emmanuel III's affiliation with Mussolini and his regime severely compromised the Crown's legitimacy following the Duce's fall. For two decades, the Fascist regime had largely eclipsed the Savoyard dynasty as the embodiment of national unity. Even after Mussolini's downfall, the reclusive and uncongenial Victor Emmanuel III was hard-pressed to reclaim the mantle of unifying national leadership. Indeed, the diminished stature of the monarchy exacerbated dissociative pressures already in evidence between North and South, and in peripheral regions such as Sicily, Trentino-Alto Adige, and Trieste.

Victor Emmanuel III's character weaknesses did not help matters. Obstinate, cynical, and cold even to his ministers, he took less interest in policy matters than in maintaining appearances as a worthy scion of the House of Savoy. A lonely sovereign (save for his comfortable marriage and relationship with the queen[61]), he lacked friends. Mussolini intimidated Victor Emmanuel throughout the *ventennio*. The King turned on the Duce only when *Fortuna* at last abandoned the latter. In sum, Victor Emmanuel was an opportunist; he fashioned himself a liberal monarch before the First World War, a flustered reactionary until 1922, and a Fascist enabler until 1943.

Victor Emmanuel's individual foibles aside, for a period the monarchy benefitted from external sympathy. Winston Churchill and other British policymakers wished Italy to remain a monarchy—a position seconded even by Stalin for the time being. FDR felt otherwise, as did his Kitchen Cabinet and a number of progressive officials in the US State Department. In the wake of his September 1943 flight to Brindisi, the American Office of War Information broadcast an analysis calling Victor Emmanuel a "moronic little king" and "the Fascist king."[62] The broadcast infuriated Churchill and caused an uproar among conservative American commentators. FDR wound up repudiating the broadcast.[63]

The King's decision to elevate his son Umberto II *Lungotenente* (Lieutenant General of the Realm) on June 5, 1944 (discussed further in Chapter 4), did not, in the end, rescue the monarchy from its fate. More congenial and handsomer than his father, Umberto was less intelligent and completely untutored politically. A soldier at heart, he floundered in trying to navigate the shoals of policymaking. Though sympathetic to the monarchy as an institution, Benedetto Croce dismissed the Lieutenant General's character as "entirely insignificant."[64]

Miseria

For ordinary Italians, the last two years of the Second World War, and indeed the two years immediately following the war, were a time of immense suffering. That suffering can be summed up by the word *miseria*. This term has no precise translation into English, as it embraces poverty, misfortune, misery, all-enveloping trouble, and, all too often, a sense of hopelessness. This mélange of pain, insecurity, and despondency greatly complicated the efforts of the country's political leadership to launch a stable new democratic polity. Hunger, disease, homelessness, economic devastation, and lawlessness were all factors contributing to an epidemic of *miseria* afflicting every corner of the peninsula. As we have seen, the Mezzogiorno was especially hard hit, as decades of the uneven but significant socio-economic, political, and cultural progress were set back.

There was great damage to buildings, shipping, heavy industry (especially iron and steel), and internal communication. On the eve of the war, there were 31 million rooms available to the population; by the end of the conflict, 6.7 million had been destroyed.[65] It was discovered that 48 percent of households had no kitchen, 73 percent no bathroom, and only 7.4 percent of homes were fitted with running water, electricity, and an indoor toilet. Much of the country's railway and harbors had been destroyed. The typical form of transportation in the countryside was still the mule and cart, and in the cities the tram and the bicycle. Italy's cheapest car, the FIAT 500 Topolino, cost about twice the annual income of industrial and white-collar workers in 1950, and was therefore unaffordable.[66] At the war's end, the typical factory worker spent 95 percent of his income on food. In 1945 real wages were half what they had been in 1938–1939. Inflation reached catastrophic proportions; between 1945 and 1946, the cost of goods doubled, while the cost of living increased twenty-fold. The problem worsened over the ensuing year: by 1947, the wholesale price index had risen to fifty-five times its prewar level.[67] Hunger was endemic; even in the capital, the last months of German occupation in the spring of 1944 saw lines of famished residents streaming north into Tuscany to beg for food.[68]

In the north, political authority shifted continuously between Nazi forces, Fascists, and partisans. Individuals were "faced with moral, political and, above all else, existential choices" on which their lives, and those of their loved ones, could depend.[69] South of Rome, as we have seen, *miseria* brought equally desperate choices to the populace. Peasants such as those immortalized by Carlo Levi in *Christ Stopped at Eboli* knew very little about the wider course of the war until their lives were turned upside by the encroaching conflict. The gentry portrayed in Levi's narrative were better informed, yet many, like Gagliano's mayor, continued to be seduced by Fascist idolatry until it evaporated, much like Baum's Wizard of Oz. In larger Italian towns and cities, the commercial and bureaucratic bourgeoisie's typical allegiance to Mussolini's regime rapidly eroded as their income proved less and less sufficient in the face of a skyrocketing cost of living. Such economic tribulations bred anxiety and rancor over their increasingly imperiled social status, accompanied not by political radicalization but by scornful indifference.[70]

In the transition from war to peace, as detailed below in chapter 3, the anti-Fascist political parties did provide a skeleton of sorts around which a healthier, more functional political culture could grow. Yet a large portion of the historical, sociological, and political studies of that period have documented:

> [A] fragmented country, beset by irreducible particularisms and by intense, vicious familial and clientelistic interactions which squandered resources, often [fed] corruption. All of this rendered inefficient, and fundamentally unjust, the State itself. Indeed, the nation became virtually ungovernable.[71]

Overwhelmed by malignant fortune, some Italians testified to losing the very sense of history. In September 1943, the collapse of the central government and fracturing of the Italian boot signaled what Rosario Forlenza and Bjorn Thommasen have characterized as a "psychic regression" of the their country back to its condition preceding its unification in 1861. Italians found themselves in the arms of foreign armies, as had happened so many times in the past.

In the words of one contemporary, "we lived outside our time, a parenthesis between two ages" and the approaching age "lacked any sense of reality"—a blank screen upon which one could project almost anything. As eminent author Cesare Pavese recalled in his autobiographically based novel *The House on the Hill*, "Nothing has happened. I've been at home for six months and the war still goes on. Another winter will pass, we will see snow again, we'll make a circle around the radio by the fire."[72]

In her novel *La Storia* (a title which means both "History" and "Story"), author Elsa Morante similarly distinguishes between the relentless, chronological march of History and the difficult quotidian experiences of her Roman protagonist, the elementary schoolteacher Ida Mancuso. Frightened and vulnerable as Ida is, she possesses a deep-seated human compassion, demonstrated in her steady witness to the disorientation and suffering of family members and acquaintances in the novel. Herself half-Jewish, Ida frequently visits residents of the Roman Ghetto, mostly peddlers and ragmen,[73] until they are torn away by German troops and sent north to Nazi concentration camps. Ida lives in fear of being "found out" as a result of Mussolini's anti-Semitic legislation of 1938. Her apprehension connects her to her Jewish neighbors.[74] Author Morante repeatedly associates Ida with oppressed others in the novel. In one early passage, Ida fretfully compares her subaltern status to that of blacks in America. Another passage reads "her black hair, barely streaked with gray, disheveled, down her back, [was] curly and full as an Ethiopian's."[75] Later in the novel, Ida and a group of others left homeless by an American bombardment, shelter an anti-Fascist partisan in their makeshift camp on the outskirts of Rome. Cumulatively, the reader recognizes in Ida a profound solidarity with fellow refugees from the inexorable oppression of history.[76]

Morante's novel affirms a central insight of Gaetano Salvemini's in his postwar essay "La guerra per bande," depicting the near biblical discouragement and disorientation afflicting the people of Italy—but also their redemptive capacity for mutual fellowship. In language worthy of Giuseppe Mazzini, he wrote:

> O Italian people, destitute of common sense, of political sense, of legal sense, of religious sense, of economic sense, of moral sense, of all possible senses ... but rich like no other people in one sense alone, the sense of humanity.
>
> —Gaetano Salvemini, Christmas 1949[77]

Notwithstanding the suffering and oppression which his countrymen had endured, Salvemini took heart in the "spontaneous participation of common people[78] in the Resistance between 1943 and 1945," for him "among the most luminous page's in Italy's history." It was Salvemini's fervent (if romantic) hope that the collective partisan experience would usher in a second—and this time genuine—*risorgimento* (resurgence) of the Italian nation.[79]

Notes

1. Paul Ginsborg offers an excellent account of the harsh wartime socio-economic conditions confronting Italians in his *History of Contemporary Italy*, 17–38.
2. Roy Domenico, *Remaking Italy in the Twentieth Century* (Lanham, MD: Rowan & Littlefield, 2002), 81.
3. Liberated Italian territory initially fell under the jurisdiction of a joint Allied Military Government (AMG) whose basic concern was to maintain law and order behind the lines. Once the armistice was signed, the Allies agreed that King's Italy would not fall under the control of AMG, but instead would coordinate its efforts with an Allied Control Commission (ACC). This body monitored Italian observance of the terms of the armistice, and, over time, mentored the performance of various Italian governmental ministries. Henry L. Coles and Albert K. Weinberg, *Civil Affairs: Solders Become Governors* (Washington, DC: Department of the Army, 1964), 217–222; 248–252. Charles R. S. Harris, *Allied Military Administration of Italy, 1943–1945* (London: Her Majesty's Stationary Office, 1957), 106–109, with an organization chart of AMG following page 32 and one for the ACC following page 126.
4. E.g. Allied occupation policy behind the advancing lines of combat.
5. Ginsborg, *History of Contemporary Italy*, 36.
6. John Diggins, *Mussolini and Fascism: The View from America* (Princeton: Princeton University Press, 1972), 424.

7   In the delicate area of education, Carleton Washburne epitomized the activist approach, while T. V. Smith was more skeptical about sweeping educational reform in the midst of war (see more detailed discussion of this theme below).
8   A number of British civil affairs officers in the Mezzogiorno had been recruited by Rennell from what he referred to as "the Colonial Services." Lord Rennell of Rodd, "Allied Military Government in Occupied Territory," *International Affairs* (*Royal Institute of International Affairs*) 20:3 July 1944.
9   Memorandum reproduced in Coles and Weinberg, *Civil Affairs*, 195–196.
10 Diggins, *Mussolini and Fascism*, 424.
11 Largely suppressed under Fascism, local mafia leaders re-emerged during the unsettled first months of Allied occupation. In addition, prominent Italian American bosses like Lucky Luciano took advantage of gullible AMGOT officials "as means of returning to their hunting grounds." Ginsborg, *History of Contemporary Italy*, 36.
12 Coles and Weinberg, *Civil Affairs*, 210.
13 On the Allies' overall approach to epuration, see Roy Domenico, *Italian Fascists on Trial* (Chapel Hill: University of North Carolina Press, 1991), 21–39.
14 See Rennell's discussion of his conservative approach in his preface to George Robert Gayre, *Italy in Transition: Extracts from the Private Journal of G. R. Gayre* (London: Faber and Faber, 1946), 12–13.
15 Ibid., 185.
16 Marcella and Maurizio Ferrara, *Conversando con Togliatti* (Rome: Riuniti, 1953), 312–313.
17 Rennell of Rodd, "Allied Military Government," 312.
18 Ginsborg, *History of Contemporary Italy*, 35.
19 Ibid., 35–36.
20 Burns based his novel on the year and a half he spent in military intelligence in Italy. The book documents "the tension between officers and enlisted men, the psychological effects of dislocation, economic and social inequality between Americans and those they defeated." Widely acclaimed (Burns was featured on the cover of *Time* magazine), the novel appealed to an American public that had grown tired of the saccharine, patriotic newsreels of the war years. Andrew J. Huebner, *Warrior Image: Soldiers in American Culture from the Second World War to the Vietnam Era* (Chapel Hill: University of North Carolina Press, 2008), 84ff.
21 Hersey spent three months with the Allied armies in southern Italy in preparation for his novel. Inspiring the work was Major Frank E. Toscani's successful effort to restore the bell of a 700-year-old church in the Sicilian port town of Licata. See also John Diggins' critical assessment of *A Bell for Adano* in his *Mussolini and Fascism*, 431.

22 Alex Korner, *America in Italy* (Princeton: *Princeton University Press*, 2017), 228. In its original sense, this proverb reflected the mixed experience of Italian immigrants to the United States in the late nineteenth and early twentieth centuries. Still, the vision of a shimmering America had persisted in the imaginations of many destitute southern Italians through the interwar years. In the late 1930s, when visiting the homes of his peasant neighbors while exiled to Basilicata, Carlo Levi was struck by the absence of any images of either the King or the Duce. Rather, along the walls, appeared the "sparkling eyes, behind gleaming glasses, and the hearty grin of President Roosevelt." Carlo Levi, *Christ Stopped at Eboli* (New York: Farrar, Straus & Giroux, 1947), 122.

23 Thomas R. Fisher, "Allied Military Government in Italy," *Annals of the American Academy of Political and Social Science* 267 (1950), 115.

24 Coles and Weinberg, *Civil Affairs*.

25 Ibid., 12.

26 Ibid., x.

27 Charles Loch Mowat, *Britain between the Wars: 1918–1940* (Boston: Beacon Press, 1955), 473–475, 480.

28 Daniel Binchy, *Church and State in Fascist Italy* (London: Oxford University Press, 1970), 434–438.

29 Steven White, "Soft on Catholicism: Secular-Clerical Rapprochement and American Policy in Italy, 1943–1948." Paper delivered at Society of Historians of American Foreign Policy Meeting, Charlotteville, June 19, 1993.

30 Carleton Washburne, "Education Under Allied Military Government in Italy," *Educational Record* XXVI, 4 (1945), 261–268.

31 Steven White, *Progressive Renaissance: America and the Reconstruction of Italian Education, 1943–1962* (New York: Garland, 1991), 47.

32 Gayre, *Italy in Transition*, 33, 112–113, 140.

33 Coles and Weinberg, *Civil Affairs*, 403.

34 Ibid., 404 and "Swan Song from the Ex-Director of the Education Subcommission, Allied Control Commission, Apologia for a Report That Is Personal and Philosophical," copy held in the archives of the University of California Library.

35 White, *Progressive Renaissance*, 60–61.

36 Ibid.

37 Ibid.

38 Ibid., 62, 74.

39 British Political Warfare Executive (PWE), *Italian Basic Handbook* (May 1943), 4, 45. NARA, Record Group 407, Box 2205.

40 White, *Progressive Renaissance*, 62–63.

41 Ibid., 73. Gayre asserted in a November 1943 report that "The Italian teacher virtually cannot teach without a textbook, so reliant has he become

42 Ibid., 65, 116.
43 John Diggins contextualizes this assessment within a broader arc of stateside perceptions of Italian education under Fascism in *Mussolini and Fascism,* 252–258.
44 Hughes may have had Croce in mind here. Steven White, "Liberal Antipodes: Omodeo, Smith and the Struggle over schooling, Naples and Salerno 1944," in *Italy and America 1943–1944. Italian, American and Italian American Experiences of the Liberation of the Italian Mezzogiorno* (Naples: Città del Sole, 1997 for the Istituto Italiano per gli Studi Filosofici), 488–489.
45 James E. Miller, *The United States and Italy, 1940–1950* (Chapel Hill: University of North Carolina Press, 1986), 40–49.
46 Hughes memorably characterized Sforza as "The tutelary genius of the Action Party ... the only important Italian exile of noble birth ... striking for his great enjoyment of both food and conversation [with his] air of a grand seigneur." Steven White, "'Gentleman Rebel': H. Stuart Hughes, the OSS and the Resistance," *Journal of Modern Italian Studies* 4:1 (Spring, 1999), 64–67. Hughes would go on after the war to become a leading intellectual historian, author of *The United States and Italy and Consciousness and Society: The Reorientation of European Social Thought, 1890–1930* (New York: Knopf, 1958).
47 On Omodeo's unorthodox take on early Christianity, and on Church-State relations during the Risorgimento, see Charles Delzell, "Adolfo Omodeo: Historian of the 'Religion of Freedom,'" in Hans A. Schmitt, ed., *Historians of Modern Europe* (Baton Rouge: Louisiana State University, 1971), 123–149. For his part, Smith wrote in 1941: "When diversity is valued less than commonality in religion," ... [that religion] "ceases to affirm divine creativeness through human hands [and becomes] sordid superstition exploited in the name of bogus control." White, "Liberal Antipodes," 484.
48 White, "Liberal Antipodes," 494.
49 Ibid., 498.
50 Ibid., 497.
51 See Arthur Vessolo, "Italy: Education under Allied Military Government," *The Educational Record* XXVI:19 (October 1945), 580.
52 Edward Tannenbaum, ed., *The Fascist Experience: Italian Society and Culture, 1922–1945* (New York: Basic Books, 1972).
53 Steven White, "The Politics of Psychology in Post-Fascist Italy." Paper delivered at American Historical Association Annual Meeting, New York, December 29, 1990.
54 Also protected by the Concordat was the Italian Catholic University Federation, from which would come any of Italy's postwar leaders. Domenico, *Remaking Italy,* 58.

55　This decree specifically forbade Catholics from voting in national parliamentary elections—a provision which was increasingly honored in the breach, and was formally rescinded in 1918. Spencer Di Scala, *Italy from Revolution to Republic, 1700 to the Present* (Boulder: Westview, 2004), 137, 226.

56　On this theme, see Paul E. Sigmund, "The Catholic Tradition and Modern Democracy," *The Review of Politics* 49:4 (Autumn, 1987), 530–548.

57　Logan, *"Pius XII: romanità, prophecy and charisma,"* 237–247.

58　Domenico, *Remaking Italy*, 81.

59　Pietro Scoppola, *La Nuova Cristianità perduta* (Rome: Studium, 2004), 17.

60　Renato Moro, *La Chiesa e lo sterminio degli ebrei* (Bologna: Il Mulino, 2002), 186–188.

61　Dennis Mack Smith, *Italy and Its Monarchy* (New Haven: Yale University Press, 1989), 149.

62　Charles Delzell, *Mussolini's Enemies: The Italian Anti-Fascist Resistance* (Princeton, NJ: Princeton University Press, 1961), 243.

63　Alexander De Conde. *Half Bitter, Half Sweet: An Excursion into Italian-American History* (New York: Scribners, 1971), 252.

64　Denis Mack Smith, *Italy and Its Monarchy*, 325.

65　Spencer Di Scala, *Italy from Revolution to Republic*, 3rd ed. (Boulder: Westview, 2004), 301.

66　Christopher Duggan, *The Force of Destiny: A History of Italy since 1796* (Boston: Houghton Mifflin, 2008), 554. https://www.lifeinitaly.com/history/italy-1945-to-1950, accessed October 30, 2018.

67　Dennis Mack Smith, *Italy: A Modern History*. Revised edition (Ann Arbor: University of Michigan Press, 1969), 493.

68　Iris Origo, *War in the Val D'Orcia: A War Diary, 1943–1944* (Boston: David Godine, 1947), 12.

69　Forlenza and Thomassen, *Italian Modernities: Competing Narratives of Nationhood* (New York: Macmillan, 2016), 154.

70　Andrea Riccardi, *Roma "Città Sacra"? Dalla Conciliazione all'operazione Sturzo* (Milan: Vita e Pensiero, 1979), 205–209.

71　Mauro Degl'Innocenti, "I socialisti," in *1945–1946: le origini della Repubblica*, vol. II. Edited by Giancarlo Monina (Soveria Mannelli: Rubbettino, 2007), 105.

72　Both sets of quotations are cited in Forlenza and Thomassen, *Italian Modernities*, 155.

73　According to Morante, the "only trades allowed to Jews in past centuries," 54.

74　Symbolically linking her to the ghetto as well is the proximity of her apartment to the ghetto.

75　Elsa Morante, *Storia* (Turin: Einaudi, 1971), 57, 81.

76　Sharon Wood, "Excursus as Narrative Technique in La Storia," in Stefania Lucamante, ed., *Elsa Morante's Politics of Writing: Rethinking Subjectivity, History and the Power of Art* (Lantham, MD: Rowan and Littlefield, 2015), 75–86.

Published in 1974, some three decades after the events depicted in the novel, Morante nevertheless draws on her own experiences, having fled Rome with her husband Alberto Moravia and living with the peasants of the southern Fondi region between September 1943 and June 1944. Gabrielle Elissa Popoff, "Once upon a Time There Was an S.S. Officer"; The Holocaust between History and Fiction in Elsa Morante's *La Storia. Journal of Modern Jewish Studies* 11:1 (March 2012), 2.

77 Gaetano Salvemini "La guerra per bande," reproduced in G. Agosti, ed., *Aspetti della Resistenza in Piemonte* (Turin: Books Store, 1977), 9.

78 Salvemini uses the term *contadini* (literally "peasants"), synonymous in this instance with "commoners" more broadly.

79 Roberto Rossellini's celebrated neo-realist film *Rome, Open City*, filmed in that city in 1944–1945, bears mention here too, masterfully evoking the themes of anti-Fascist idealism, hospitality, solidarity, and sacrifice. Peter Bondanella, *Italian Cinema from Neorealism to the Present* (New York: Ungar, 1983), 37–42.

3

From Resistance to Restoration

The nation's prostration, described in the previous chapter, was hardly unprecedented. Writing four centuries earlier, during the declining years of the Renaissance, Niccolò Machiavelli had chronicled analogous disarray befalling his beloved land.

> I ask myself whether the present hour is ripe to hail a new prince in Italy, if there is material here that a careful, able (*virtuoso*) leader could mold into a new form that might bring honor to him and benefit to all men: and I answer that all things now appear favorable to a new prince, so much so that I cannot think of any time more suitable... at the present time, if the power (*virtù*) of an Italian spirit is to be manifested, it was necessary that Italy be reduced to her present state; that she might be more enslaved than the Hebrews, more abject than the Persians, more widely dispersed than the Athenians; headless, orderless, beaten, stripped, scarred, overrun, and plagued by every sort of disaster.[1]

Nevertheless, Machiavelli perceived opportunity as well as calamity. In the Florentine savant's eyes, the chance of controlling events was offered to man only "in brief, fleeting moments. Therefore man must make use of a singular conjuncture in which there must be a meeting of circumstances and individuality."[2] For a brief period in war-torn Italy, circumstances and individuality seemed to meet auspiciously with the arrival of a collective "new prince"[3]: the anti-Fascist Resistance.

The suddenness of Mussolini's fall caught Italy's anti-Fascist forces by surprise. Emerging from underground at the beginning of the Forty Five Days, they found themselves acting as proxies for a scattered people—a people careening between early feelings of elation and, later, dread upon the king's flight from Rome and the ensuing Nazi occupation of the peninsula.[4] Piero Calamadrei recalled the joyful first days of post-Fascist freedom in the following terms:

> The sensation we felt in these days is best described as... having rediscovered our own country. Ah, what a breath! We could speak, could share our ideas clearly,

in the streets, on the trains, to the farmer laboring in the fields, to the worker bicycling by... beneath these shared words was an affection (*tenerezza*)... the mutual sympathy of the Italian people.[5]

Yet a month and a half later, in a letter dated September 17, Calamadrei's Action Party colleague Vittorio Foa soberly observed how "in the wake of the armistice and the double invasion, Italy no longer exists as an autonomous actor. It is today a simple object of military destiny."[6]

The Resistance and the Anti-Fascist Parties

Proceeding roughly from Right to Left on the political spectrum, the six anti-Fascist parties were the Liberal Party (Partito Liberale Italiano, PLI), Democracy of Labor, the Christian Democratic Party, the Action Party,[7] and the Marxist Socialist and Communist Parties. The day after Mussolini's fall, De Gasperi was freed from his "inner exile" as a librarian working under the protection of the Vatican. On August 6, Nenni returned to the capital from his exile in France. De Gasperi's and Nenni's views—different though they were—played key roles in defining the initial parameters of ideological discourse within the recently formed Committee of Anti-Fascist Currents. The Socialist and Catholic leaders extended their acquaintance as political refugees in the fall and winter, hiding out at St. John Lateran Seminary. Communist Chief Togliatti had to wait until late March 1944 to return from his Moscow exile to the liberated Mezzogiorno. Well before then, however, his writings and radio addresses from the USSR were also helping to shape anti-Fascist strategizing. The remaining months of the war saw De Gasperi, Nenni, Togliatti, and their fellow anti-Fascist leaders enter into an intense, often difficult process of political dialogue.

United in the struggle to free Italy from German and neo-Fascist oppression, Italy's anti-Fascists differed markedly as to the underlying nature of Fascism and as to the best way to transcend its legacy. Already in the latter 1920s, exiled anti-Fascist statesmen and intellectuals like Salvemini and former Popular Party leader Don Luigi Sturzo saw in the anti-Fascist Resistance a "second Risorgimento," which would bridge differences of class, region, and creed in an Italian rebirth of freedom. In fact, this metaphor obscured as much as it revealed. Enthusiasm for a sweeping re-foundation of the Italian State, grounded in the anti-Fascist Resistance experience, was far more widespread north of Rome than it was in the capital or in the *Mezzogiorno*. Partisan idealism and militance of any kind were suspect to broad segments of the southern Italian population, eager more than anything for a return to peace, healing, and stability.[8]

The Italian anti-Fascist Resistance unfolded in stages. Between the mid-1920s and 1943, underground anti-Fascist groups kept vigil, awaiting the day that Mussolini and his regime would be relegated to the ashbin of history. Assisting them from exile were Nenni, Togliatti, and De Gasperi,[9] along with other prominent opponents of the regime. Then, between the Allied Sicily landings and the end of the war, partisan guerilla fighters engaged in military actions against the Germans and Italian neo-Fascists. At their peak, the partisans numbered some 100,000 armed partisans; by the war's end, more than half of these had died, were wounded, or had been deported to Germany.[10] Joining partisan units were citizens from all walks of life, rising up to liberate their cities even before the arrival of Allied troops, first in Naples[11] and subsequently in Florence, Milan, and Turin. Overlapping with these military efforts was the political dimension of the Resistance, embodied in Committees of National Liberation in northern Italy (the *Comitato di Liberazione Nazionale di Alta Italia*, or CLNAI) and the central CLN in Rome.

Resistance participants, as well as scholars[12] of the period, differ sharply over the degree of continuity which existed between the ethos of the grassroots Resistance experience and the praxis of the anti-Fascist political parties. In Carlo Levi's[13] novel *The Watch*, the character Andrea (modeled on the Action Party leader Leo Valiani) recalls how, initially, party members and ordinary Italians spoke a common language, adding that:

> All understood one another... both in the city and in the country. You could knock at all doors and they'd open without the use of a password. We recognized each other then by a mere glance, by a sniff. We all agreed. Everyone was at his post and felt he belonged there, and was able to accomplish things he never imagined he could.[14]

In the novel, such silent solidarity contrasts with the bombast of the Duce. Levi's sentimental passage evokes the existential sympathy that bound anti-Fascists together as they confronted Mussolini's regime.[15] Valiani himself, in his immediate postwar work of historical reflection entitled *L'avvento di De Gasperi*, laments the erosion of this sense of transformational urgency as the anti-Fascist parties were drawn into protracted maneuvers for political preeminence.[16]

The single largest number of partisans belonged to the Communist-organized Garibaldi Brigades. Of all the anti-Fascist currents, the Communists' network of clandestine cells had enabled them to sustain the most extensive grassroots presence during the Fascist era. The Socialist rank and file had not fared so well, having been more extensively repressed by the Fascists while Nenni and other key leaders were forced into exile. Despite the disbanding of the Catholic Popular Party, Catholic Action provided a measure of cover for some Catholics to begin to develop their own critique of Fascism. In mid-December 1942, some 250 political Catholics from all over Lazio gathered to plan anti-regime political and military action as opportunities presented themselves. Remarkably, the meeting went unobserved by the ostensibly omniscient police.[17]

The most impatient of the anti-Fascist parties was one of the smaller ones: the Action Party. Led by their implacable commander "Maurizio" (Ferruccio Parri), Action Party members played a significant role in the Northern armed resistance. The Action Party was primarily, but not entirely, composed of northern intellectuals who drew inspiration from Giuseppe Mazzini's ideas and example.[18] Leading voices within the party, destined only to last from the late 1930s to 1946, were Sicilian journalist Ugo La Malfa, Florentine jurist Piero Calamandrei, and Turinese Carlo Levi,[19] the author of the novel cited above and editor of the party publication *Italia Libera* during the period 1945–1946. The Actionists advocated thoroughgoing decentralization in Italy, displacing the "dead hand" of the old Roman bureaucracy with the democratic ethos and experience of the anti-Fascist Resistance.

But, as had been the case a century earlier during the Risorgimento, fears over the centrifugal pressures pulling the peninsula apart would trump the need to engage ordinary Italians politically by granting them more grassroots autonomy. Related to its decentralist bent, the Action Party was vehemently republican, regarding the Savoyard Monarchy as the lynchpin of an antiquated and bankrupt political order. The Actionists also advocated a thoroughgoing purge of the country's political and socio-economic elites as a prerequisite for the foundation of a vibrant, genuinely democratic post-Fascist state and society.

Positioned at the right end of the CLN political spectrum was the Liberal Party, whose forefathers had led many of Italy's pre-Fascist governments. Never very disciplined, the Liberals fragmented during the 1920s and 1930s into electoral coteries surrounding privileged individuals. The most prestigious and influential of these individuals was Neapolitan philosopher Benedetto Croce. This monarchist intellectual and political leader regarded Fascism as a "parenthesis" in the history of modern Italy. In Croce's view, the pre-Fascist Liberal Monarchy had made important strides toward greater democracy before the savage, unexpected interruption of Fascism. Croce equated the Fascists with the Hyksos invaders who had ravaged ancient Egypt. At the head of the modern band of barbarian interlopers was the Duce, whom Croce depicted as a vacuous poseur.

Croce's detractors rejected this formulation, as it seemed to free the Italian people as a whole of any responsibility for their subjugation by the Fascists. Interestingly, the Neapolitan sage acknowledged that there was some merit in this charge, but he justified and reiterated his formulations as "necessary impostures," designed to try to buck up his countrymen as they shouldered the tasks of postwar economic recovery, political reconstruction, and moral rehabilitation.[20]

Like the Liberal Party, the Democracy of Labor Party was primarily a southern Italian political formation tilting in a monarchist direction. Enjoying only modest public support, however, the Democrats of Labor's influence depended heavily on the stature of its two main exponents, Ivanoe Bonomi and Meuccio Ruini.[21]

The Christian Democrats regarded Fascism and its legacy in a variety of ways. Some political Catholics believed the time had come to reenter the partisan political arena alongside non-Catholic anti-Fascist forces. Other Catholics, especially those active in the lay Catholic Action organization, engaged in mass mobilization outside of conventional party channels. Catholics were divided as well over the fate of the Savoyard Monarchy: conservative Catholic voices within and outside the Vatican valued it as a bulwark of law and order, while more progressive Catholics distrusted the monarchy due to its deep complicity with the fallen Fascist regime.

It was Alcide De Gasperi's achievement to finesse these differences and to establish himself from mid-1942 onward as the clear leader and spokesman for the Christian Democratic Party in its contacts with non-clerical political forces. De Gasperi regarded anti-Fascism as a moral as well as a political imperative. Essential to Mussolini's regime, in his eyes, had been its celebration and reliance upon violence. At the same time, De Gasperi distrusted what he saw as the intolerance and even fanaticism of the partisan movement. In a letter he wrote to Catholic interlocutor Sergio Paronetto on September 10, 1943, De Gasperi advocated an "anti-Fascism which is not a haphazard combination of reprisals, bands and denunciations, but which becomes the criterion by which to judge even anti-Fascists and non-Fascists." In De Gasperi's conception of anti-Fascism, there could be no room for "the anti-liberalism of any type of dictatorship, be it bourgeois-republican, militaristic-royalist or proletarian-communist."[22] There was nothing to be gained, he said, by "indulging in ideological debates about the ideal State or being caught up in myths of a revolutionary palingenesis."[23]

Already in the late 1930s, De Gasperi had begun to frame his critique of the Fascist cult of violence. Internationally, that violent impulse fostered arrogant and brutal forms of imperialism. Despite the temporary ascendancy of "Mussolini's Roman Empire" in the second half of the 1930s, the Second World War had exposed Fascist foreign and domestic policies as unsustainable. The regime's vainglory had engendered pervasive cynicism and corruption in the Italian people, and indeed the apparatus of the State. For De Gasperi, the State itself was perhaps Fascism's chief victim.[24]

For their part, the Communists and Socialists interpreted Mussolini's movement and regime in orthodox Marxist terms. From the outset, Fascism represented the violent and extreme bulwark of bourgeois privilege aimed at repressing the legitimate interests and aspirations of the peasants and workers. For both the Socialist and the Communist Parties, such doctrinaire class analysis hampered their ability to comprehend the novel interclass appeal of Mussolini's movement. Indeed, some historians have argued that Italian Marxists fell back on their own version of "Fascism as parenthesis," promising to revive an unsullied proletarian movement and shepherd its ascent to hegemony after the war.[25]

However orthodox in theory, Togliatti's Communists were tactically pragmatic and circumspect with regard to the conduct of the liberation struggle and postwar political reconstruction. This two-track approach echoed that of Stalin's USSR during the war. The most controversial example of this surprising moderation was the so-called Salerno Turn of March 29, 1944: the party's abandonment of its prior hostility to the monarchy, and its readiness instead to cooperate with Marshall Badoglio and the king in fashioning a new, broadly inclusive governing coalition.

By comparison, for much of the period 1943–1945, the Italian Socialists advocated positions to the left of their Marxist brothers. In Socialist eyes, the monarchy had compromised itself irremediably with Mussolini's regime, and needed to be replaced by a republic as soon as possible. Nor should the armed forces (fatefully merged with the black shirts) or the central bureaucracy—sullied by having executed baneful Fascist laws and policies—be allowed to continue to function without a serious purge. The societal influence of big industry, big landlords, and the Church also needed to be checked. In order to constrain all of these reactionary forces, a unity pact with the Communists needed to be preserved at all costs.

Systematic clandestine cooperation between the six anti-Fascist parties dated from December 1942. Emboldened by Allied military successes in North Africa and on the Eastern Front, representatives of the various anti-Fascist parties clandestinely formed a "Committee of Anti-Fascist Currents," and began meeting in private residences scattered about Rome. Particularly significant were gatherings at the legal study and apartment of Roman Christian Democratic lawyer and journalist Giuseppe Spataro on Via Cola di Rienzo, a broad street in the city's central Prati district. Spataro would distinguish himself militarily as well as politically: by mid-March 1944, he arranged for arms to be distributed not only to Christian Democratic partisans, but to members of other parties as well. Committee of Anti-Fascist Currents gatherings initially included Christian Democrats, Liberals, Democrats of Labor, and Socialists. By early January 1943, representatives of the Action and Communist parties also began to attend the clandestine meetings hosted by Spataro.

De Gasperi had opposed Communist involvement up until then, fearing that direct contact, even within a multiparty setting, might compromise the Christian Democrats' image, presumably in Vatican eyes. He may also have stalled, awaiting some specific guidance from the Vatican on the matter.[26] Spataro pressed De Gasperi to relent, arguing that Communist involvement was only appropriate in view of the Soviet Union's presence in the Allied Coalition. For his part, Socialist Giuseppe Romita threated to abandon the dialogue if the Socialists' fellow working-class party was not allowed to be present.[27]

The seventy-two-year-old Ivanoe Bonomi formally presided over these gatherings. For politicians of Bonomi's generation, the Cola di Rienzo gatherings revived the dialogue begun among democratic and anti-Fascist forces dating back to the 1920s and symbolized by the Aventine Secession.[28] A reformist Socialist in the pre-First World War era, Bonomi moved further to the right over the next several decades, neither serving nor actively opposing the Fascist regime. Still, the fall of Mussolini found Bonomi in a favorable position to lead the nascent anti-Fascist counter-regime due to his lengthy political career, moderation, and flexible, accommodating manner.

Though the affable Bonomi formally led the gatherings of the Committee of Anti-Fascist Currents' sessions, it was De Gasperi who came to dominate the meetings. De Gasperi had refined his self-assured, quietly charismatic manner in separate clandestine gatherings of Christian Democrats, dating from the late 1930s. A participant in one of those sessions recalled the Trentine statesman "perched on a stool, elegantly dressed in one of his cream-colored shirts, running his hands through his hair ... as he dispatched a fretful patrol of lieutenants."[29]

False Dawn

The sudden collapse from above of the Fascist dictatorship coupled with Marshall Badoglio's rapid appointment surprised the Committee of Anti-Fascist Currents. Though the Duce had been removed and the Fascist Party outlawed, the Italian state remained an authoritarian one. Badoglio was an old-fashioned military man, deeply committed to king and country but not an ideological Fascist. A commander already in the First World War, he had opposed the March on Rome. Yet his career flourished under Mussolini. Badoglio became a national hero as conqueror of Ethiopia in 1936. His entry in Addis Ababa astride a white horse reinforced the Duce's claim to have created a New Roman Empire across the Mediterranean and Red Seas.

On July 25, the Committee of Anti-Fascist Currents met and debated whether to collaborate with—or indeed join—Badoglio's new government. Could the anti-Fascists in good conscience participate in a government led by a figure like Badoglio? At the meeting on July 25, De Gasperi cautioned against such participation in the short run. Here he distinguished between two objectives. One was the defeat of Mussolini and Fascism. The other was negotiating an armistice with the Allies. The first objective appeared to have been essentially accomplished. As for the second objective, it would be better for the anti-Fascists to hold back, so as not to compromise themselves in what was likely to be a messy, controversial process.[30]

De Gasperi's caution was confirmed when, much to the dismay of the anti-Fascist leadership, Badoglio announced that *la guerra continua*[31] ("the war continues") and that Italy would continue to fight at Germany's side. Though the Fascist Party was dissolved and many Fascist laws repealed, his government was slow to arrest prominent *gerarchi* (leading Fascists). Huge protest demonstrations broke out against the remaining legacies of Mussolini's regime. Badoglio firmly suppressed these demonstrations for fear that they might develop into a republican-led or even a communist revolution.[32]

For his part, Nenni was taken aback by the streamers he saw flying from windows in Terracina proclaiming "Viva Badoglio." These streamers represented the face of Italy—"one that applauds every victor"—which the Socialist leader despised. The education of the masses provided by socialism would be needed to tame the "fickle fantasies of the *popolo mezzano* ('middling population')." Fascist miseducation, Nenni lamented, "has reduced us to *spagnolismo settecentisco* (the servile 'Spanishism' of the 1600s). Here too, we would need to start from scratch."[33] Three days after the events of July 25, Nenni confided to his journal that "Italy needs to be led away from the euphoria surrounding the gift of freedom, towards the hard tests ahead."[34]

Even as De Gasperi and his anti-Fascist peers kept their distance from Badoglio, conservative integralist Luigi Gedda, head of Catholic Action's youth branch (*Gioventú Italiana di Azione Cattolica,* or GIAC), wrote a letter to the General on August 11 offering the new head of government the backing of Catholic Action's 2,500,000 members. As Gedda put it: "this morally sound, patriotic force, untouched by political partiality" (*scevro di passionalità politica*) could be placed at the disposition of the new executive the better to "strike back at communist proselytism."[35] His readiness to speak on behalf of Catholic Action as a whole, and not just GIAC, reflected the trust which Pope Pius XII had come to place in him. While Badoglio did not respond to Gedda's overture, the contrast between De Gasperi's reserve and Gedda's impetuousness would resurface in years to come.

Underground Once More

After six and a half weeks of difficult negotiations, the Allies finally concluded an armistice with the Badoglio government. When Marshall Badoglio broadcast word of the September Armistice, he directed Italy's armed forces to stop fighting the Allies. He did not tell them to fight the Germans. Nor did he provide any further instructions, except "to react to eventual attacks from whatever quarter."[36] This cryptic instruction confused Italian soldiers; as recalled by Nuno Revelli, a resident of the northern city of Cuneo, there were "those who don't understand, those who half understand. Soldiers embracing, caps flying. The soldiers were in high spirits as if the war were really over." Tens of thousands soldiers flung away their weapons and uniforms and headed for their homes, however distant.[37]

Already the war had turned disastrously against Italy: of the nearly 4 million soldiers who served in the Royal Italian Armed Forces during the Second World War, roughly half were captured, first by Allies and then, after the signing of the Armistice, by the Germans.[38] Casualties had numbered nearly 160,000 in combat with Allied troops; subsequently some 70,000 would die at the hands of German forces. Nearly an additional 80,000 perished first in Allied and then in Nazi prison camps.[39]

Dismayed at the ensuing flight of the king and much of the Badoglio cabinet south to Brindisi on September 9, the Roman anti-Fascist organization, now adopting the title of Committee of National Liberation (CLN), issued a stirring appeal to the people of Italy to join in resisting the Germans who had begun to flood into the peninsula. Headed by the moderate Bonomi, the CLN was formally composed of three representatives from each party. The full membership of the CLN was as follows: De Gasperi, Spataro, and Gronchi (DC); Nenni, Pertini, Romita (PSI); La Malfa, Bauer, Fenoaltea (Actionists); Scoccimarro, Amendola, Roveda (PCI); Ruini, Cevolotto, Bassano (Democracy of Labor); and Casati, Brosio, Cattani (Liberals).[40] Soon however, logistical challenges, and the dangers of capture, encouraged the creation of a more restricted leadership committee composed of Bonomi (remaining as head), De Gasperi (DC), Nenni (PSI), Scoccimarro (PCI), Casati (Liberals), Ruini (Democrats of Labor), and La Malfa (Action Party).[41]

This leadership group comprised a colorful and diverse set of personalities, deftly evoked by Nenni in his diary. Personally honest and conscientious, the elderly Bonomi was often indecisive and overly compromising as head of the CLN. He seemed too wed to "the contingencies of immediate situations." By contrast, the youthful Action Party representative Ugo La Malfa focused too little on such realities, tending rather to abstraction and moral judgmentalism. Such behavior seems to have gotten under De Gasperi's skin. In conversation with Spataro, the Christian Democratic leader expressed frustration with certain CLN colleagues (doubtless including La Malfa) who would resort to demagogy when speaking of topics about which they actually knew little. "They want to discover America" was the Christian Democratic leader's wry remark.[42] For his part, Nenni found De Gasperi "as prudent and diffident as the Church which stands behind him." Of Meuccio Ruini, Nenni remarked that Democrats of Labor Party leader "tended to promise more than he could deliver, given the fragile base of his party." The highly cultured and refined Liberal Casati was "a typical Lombard conservative" who was chronically slow "to advance new ideas or courses of action." A seasoned Communist party member, Scoccimarro possessed a genial, frank manner, which reassured his non-Communist peers.[43]

The Nazi occupation of Rome in September once again drove anti-Fascist leaders underground. Between early December 1943 and early February 1944, De Gasperi found refuge within the walls of St. John Lateran Church and Seminary. He was soon joined by other anti-Fascist leaders, including nearly the entire CLN.[44] Top leaders assumed the names of the seminarians of the rooms they occupied. Saragat's room came first down the hallway, followed by those of Ruini, De Gasperi, Casati, Bonomi, and Nenni. Sunday masses were generally said by Monsignor Ferrero di Cavallerleone, with De Gasperi assisting. Nenni did not attend these masses; instead, he often turned up the volume on his radio, at which point Bonomi would go out to ask him to turn it back down.[45]

While they were sheltered at St. John Lateran, De Gasperi and Nenni engaged in lengthy conversations; the two leaders were determined to prevent the kinds of misunderstandings and mutual intolerance between the Popular Party and the Socialists, which had opened the door to Fascism after the First World War. The colloquies between the reserved Trentine and the exuberant Romagnuol "became quite lively at times... even later, when De Gasperi and Nenni became political foes, there remained the memory of the friendly debates in the Lateran Seminary, held in what seemed an oasis of security amid the military terror which then gripped Rome."[46] As their discussions continued, De Gasperi became convinced that the Socialists—and perhaps the Communists were no longer as eager to take power as earlier appeared to be the case.[47]

Though appreciative of the refuge offered by the seminary, De Gasperi chafed at the regimen imposed by the meddlesome Seminary Rector Monsignior Roberto Ronca.[48] In a letter addressed to the latter, De Gasperi acknowledged that his stay at the seminary had afforded him the opportunity to confer with a number of friends, but that those conversations had served their purpose. Feeling "cut off" from events, the Christian Democratic leader stated that it was urgent that he now leave to carry on other work within the anti-Fascist movement.[49] From his exile in Moscow, due to end in late March when he would return to the liberated Mezzogiorno, Togliatti expressed similar impatience.

From time to time individuals would slip out of the seminary in order to confer with such anti-Fascist figures as the Communist Scoccimarro and the Christian Democrat Spataro who were hiding out elsewhere in the city. As the winter wore on, conditions in Nazi-occupied Rome became more and more dire. On February 8, 1944, German and Fascist agents stormed St. Paul Outside the Walls, violating its neutrality as Vatican territory. Apprehensive that a similar action might be in the offing against St. John Lateran, Nenni took shelter in various comrades' homes, returning to the Lateran Seminary for a period in April. De Gasperi moved to the palace of *Propaganda Fidae,* where Cardinal Celso Costantini offered him shelter until the beginning of June.[50] When Communist activist Giorgio Amendola secretly met De Gasperi there to discuss resistance strategy, the Communist underground had just staged a successful military action. In his memoirs Amendola recorded that, in the wake of that event, De Gasperi had commented, with a certain tone of admiration, "that you think of an action once and carry it out a thousand times" (in Italian, *voi una ne pensate e mille ne fate*).[51]

The Salerno Turn

As noted in Chapter 2, Togliatti reached Naples on March 27, ending his eighteen-year exile. The CLN found itself deeply divided over the institutional question, with the leftist parties insisting on the abolition of the monarchy, and the Christian Democrats and rightist parties resisting such a move. In a February posting from Moscow, Togliatti had forcefully affirmed the leftist position, stating that:

> [T]he Communists call on the king to abdicate, since he was an accomplice in the formation of the Fascist Regime and in all of Mussolini's crimes. At present, he is also the central, unifying figure for all the reactionary, semi-fascist and fascist forces who oppose the democratization of the nation.... The communists refuse to participate in the current government and denounce the present government's policies as an obstacle to the genuine participation of the Italian government in the war against Germany.

As for Marshall Badoglio, Togliatti asserted that he deserved to be "abandoned to his fate."[52]

Then in speeches delivered to Italian party colleagues on March 30–31 and again on April 11, Togliatti dramatically reversed course. The Communist leadership now asserted that resolution of the institutional question needed to be deferred until the war's conclusion. Togliatti urged all of the other anti-Fascist parties to follow suit. With typical terseness, Togliatti characterized the existing stalemate in Italy between and Badoglio and the King on the one hand and the CLN on the other as futile—opposing a "government with power but no authority" and "a popular movement with authority but no power."[53]

To break this pernicious stalemate, Italians needed to unite to defeat the German and Fascist Republican enemy, Togliatti argued. In furtherance of national unity and cooperation against a common foe, he also promised that the PCI would renew itself as a patriotic force—a "new party"—prepared to compromise and come to power within a democratic context. The goal of "proletarian revolution" needed to give way to the pursuit of "progressive democracy."[54] Togliatti's shift of position soon came to be known as the "Salerno Turn" (*Svolta di Salerno*).

What accounts for this remarkable *volte face*? The answer begins with Joseph Stalin, who had concluded earlier in March that, fortified by British support, the Savoyard Monarchy was strong enough to withstand short-term pressures and that it needed to be accommodated. Consequently, the

Soviet Union recognized the Badoglio government, and Togliatti was directed in a forty-five-minute nighttime face-to-face meeting with Stalin to toe the new line. In point of fact, a conciliatory half step toward the Salerno Turn (albeit directed to the Church rather than the monarchy) had already been taken by the party during the Forty-Five Days. When *Osservatore Romano* editor Count Della Torre approached Communist activist Giorgio Amendola about whether the PCI would honor the 1929 Lateran Treaty and Concordat, Amendola replied that the Party accepted the inter-state terms of the Lateran Accords, but opposed the domestic prerogatives granted to the Church in the Concordat.[55]

Nenni termed Togliatti's drastic reversal the "Ercoli Bomb." "Ercole" had been the moniker leftist Italians had given Togliatti during his years of exile. The Socialists and Actionists were outraged at this sudden undermining of the CLN consensus on the institutional question which they had painfully hammered out the previous October. Much of the Communist rank and file also opposed the new party line. In his journal, Nenni compared Togliatti to an "elephant in a china shop, moving as cavalierly as if traversing the desert, heedless of what he might be smashing to smithereens."[56] Nenni went so far as to compare the disorientation produced by the Salerno Turn to that which resulted from the Molotov-Ribbentropp Non-Aggression Pact of 1939. Bitter though he was, Nenni would not repudiate the unity of action agreement, which his party had with the Communists.

Though with mixed emotions, in late April the anti-Fascist parties entered a reshuffled Badoglio government. Custom dictated that they be sworn in by Victor Emmanuel III, the same sovereign who had conferred power to Mussolini twenty-three years before. Togliatti described the following "pathetic spectacle:"

> The king had to read his declaration but he fumbled in a trouser pocket before finding the crumpled piece of paper, and then reading it he stumbled and changed the text, so that different versions circulated. He looked grotesque.... He couldn't put two words together that made sense, not even words of welcome.[57]

Hoping to blunt continuing public resentment and suspicion toward his own figure, King Victor Emmanuel III transferred functional governing powers to his son Umberto II on June 5, the day after the liberation of Rome. Umberto II received the title of Lieutenant General of the Realm, but his father chose not to relinquish the formal title of King.[58] This odd arrangement frustrated and confused many Italians, including monarchists who would have preferred a complete transfer of power and office to Umberto.

Four days after the liberation of the capital, the leaders of the CLN met in Rome's Grand Hotel, intent upon forming a new government to be led by Ivanoe Bonomi, and embodying a more explicitly anti-Fascist orientation. Representatives of each of the six CLN parties, including Togliatti, De Gasperi, and Nenn, huddled in a small room in the hotel. Their initiative irritated Allied authorities, as it raised questions about continuing Italian accountability for the armistice agreement, which Badoglio had signed the previous September. Churchill charged that the new Italian government was illegitimate, while FDR adopted a more accommodating stance toward the Italian move.[59] Badoglio himself balked at stepping aside. It was Togliatti who finally prevailed upon him, praising him for making this final sacrifice for the well-being of the nation.[60]

While expressing a broader spectrum of Italian political opinion, the new government possessed a decidedly provisional quality, given the incomplete liberation of the peninsula. Anglo-American military, diplomatic, and economic priorities all constrained the neophyte Italian government's freedom of action. The Allies' decision to hold off on a major military push against the Gothic Line until the spring of 1945 contributed to a more cautious political equation in Rome, and left the partisans of the North vulnerable to German and Fascist counter-attacks.

Concerned to reassure the Allies of his countrymen's gratitude and goodwill, future foreign minister (he would assume that post in the Parri government of June–December 1945) De Gasperi gave a major speech at Brancaccio Theater on July 23. Warmly acknowledging his countrymen's debt to the Anglo-Americans, De Gasperi asked that Italians be allowed to fight at the Allies' side to advance "their moral and civil reconstruction" and to save their "dignity, honor and strength." Elected unanimously as party secretary at the fourth Christian Democratic Party congress in November, De Gasperi extended his Brancaccio remarks, invoking "the renewal of moral conscience among all of Italy's social classes as the indispensable premise for the nation's material reconstruction."[61]

At the Bonomi government's first cabinet meeting on June 26, Nenni recommended the abolition of the title "excellency" for ministers. De Gasperi, as foreign minister, voiced concerns about the implications for diplomatic ceremonies. Though Nenni's motion passed, it would remain a dead letter. Years later, when Nenni himself occupied the post of foreign minister, he had a sign posted outside his office which read "You will recall that the title of Excellency has been abolished." Yet every bureaucrat who entered his office addressed him as "Excellency," without fail.[62]

In November 1944, the first Bonomi government fell, weakened by continuing discord over the institutional question and other issues. Bonomi's decision to submit his resignation to Umberto II, rather than the CLN, outraged the Action and Socialist parties. Disregarding an impassioned plea by Togliatti that they remain, the Actionists and Socialists refused to enter a second Bonomi coalition government which took shape later that month.

Having remained outside the new Bonomi government, Nenni penned a stinging December 4, 1944, editorial in the pages of *Avanti!* He castigated Bonomi as expressing "the Italy of the prefects and the Fascist generals as over against the Italy of the Committees of Liberation, of the Italy that finds shelter under the wings of the troops of occupation as over against that of the people, of the Italy in the rear as over against democratic Italy."[63]

Problems with the Purge

With the re-establishment of the Italian government in the capital in the summer of 1944, thousands of Roman bureaucrats had returned to their previous ministerial posts, resuming "business as usual." Some of these civil servants had been sincere supporters of the Duce, while others had merely paid lip service to Fascist doctrine or practice.[64] Nevertheless in the eyes of many partisans, all too many Roman bureaucrats retained deeply rooted presumptions of class and caste privilege vis-à-vis ordinary Italians citizens—thereby constituting an insidious threat to grassroots, democratic renewal. In an impassioned series of editorials in the Socialist newspaper *Avanti!* (which then enjoyed the largest circulation in Rome), Nenni evoked a radical "Wind from the North" which could disperse the "gloomy clouds" that he saw settling over the capital. Yet for all of its promise, this northern wind, generated out of the Resistance struggle, was to exhaust itself in Rome where, in the words of journalist Antonio Gambino, it proved itself to be, at best, a "gentle breeze."[65]

Ever since the Forty-Five Days, the three parties of the Left had gone out of their way to stress the necessity of purging from the central governmental apparatus officials compromised by Fascist leanings. From the start, however, Italian attempts to carry out this process confronted many of the same problems which had bedeviled AMG. Little of lasting value in the area of *epurazione* was accomplished until Rome had been liberated and the first Bonomi government formed. Responsibility for the purge was then assigned to Count Carlo Sforza. A hardnosed anti-Fascist, Sforza nevertheless saw himself more as a coordinator than as a crusader for the purge.[66]

On July 27, Royal Legislative Decree (RDL) Number 159 created the High Commission for Sanctions against Fascism. Though disinterested in the technicalities of *epurazione*, Sforza articulated the overarching policy objective of "striking firmly at the top, and letting the small fry go." He leaned heavily on four lieutenants, each of assumed responsibility for a different type of sanction and each of whom came from a different political party. The first office, focusing on Fascist criminal actions, was headed by Sardinian Actionist Mario Berlinguer. Labor Democrat F.S. Stangone took charge of the second office, concerned with sequestered Fascist property. The third office, dealing with illegal profits, was headed by Christian Democrat Mario Cingolani. Communist Mauro Scoccimarro held the brief for the fourth—and most sensitive—office, charged with which purging the central governmental bureaucracy.[67]

Scoccimarro devised his own vetting document as he began the screening of bureaucrats. A harsh verdict could mean suspension or dismissal, often on reduced pay (with one-twelfth normal pay). Loss of political rights often accompanied these judgments. Even so, most punishments meted out by the *Alto Commissariato* (High Commission) for epuration would be *sanzioni minori*, nothing more than letters placed in the person's files.

In January 1945, upon the formation of his second government, Bonomi weakened the High Commission, among other steps lifting the temporary ban from office for suspected Fascists that had been implemented in July 1944.[68] For their part, the British and the Americans continued, as they had since the signing of the armistice,[69] to resist the purge of the monarchist government or the bureaucracy, the better to maintain stability. Admiral Stone and prominent figures from the American economic sector such as Amadeo Giannini were also determined to shield top Italian business figures, despite records of Fascist collaboration.[70]

A dejected Nenni felt that such reversals "had all the characteristics of a first-class funeral." Still, the Socialist leader had a chance to re-strengthen *epurazione* in August 1945, when he assumed the leadership of the High Commission. He labored valiantly to draft a more equitable, efficient vetting instrument, seeking to re-instate Sforza's policy of focusing on high-ranking offenders. Nenni counted among those who defined "top" in a very broad manner, including strategic elements of the Fascist dictatorship, the bureaucracy—the more "permanent" element of the Italian government—and even private business.

In November, a new draft law (DDL 702), popularly dubbed "the Nenni Law," proposed that state employees with a civil service grade of 8 or lower be exempted from the purging process unless individuals were particularly active collaborationists. On the other hand, all administrators above grade 8 were subject to scrutiny, including those in government, in publicly controlled businesses and in private entities with government contracts. Persons tied to Mussolini's Republic of Salò, either as officials of that government or as members of the Republican Fascist Party, were to be dismissed.

To Nenni's dismay, insufficient time remained to implement this broadening of the purge. With the fall of the Parri government, consummated in early December 1945, the High Commission ceased to be an effective instrument of de-Fascistization. Nenni now realized that purging could only have been effective six months earlier at the conclusion of the liberation struggle. He had only taken the position of high commissioner out of a sense of duty, wanting to demonstrate that the Socialists were willing to do their part in bringing Fascists to justice. Yet from the beginning of the Parri government, he dedicated himself more enthusiastically and steadily to his duties as minister for the Constituent Assembly than as high commissioner for the purge.[71]

The final chapter in the history of the purge was to be written by Togliatti, who served as minister of justice from June 1945 to July 1946. On June 22, 1946, he issued a decree granting amnesty for most former Fascist political prisoners. Togliatti justified this controversial step by invoking the need to inaugurate the neophyte Republic "from its first steps as a regime of peace and reconciliation." Entering too into this action was the calculation that his party had to compete with the Christian Democrats for the support of broad sectors of the Italian populace (especially within the middle class) who had been unsettled about the purge from the start.[72]

Uomo Qualunque

Indicative of the broad public backlash unleashed by *epurazione* was the rise of the reactionary *Uomo Qualunque* (The Common Man Front). Responding to the "cry of pain" produced by the purge across the nation, this disruptive movement was founded by Guglielmo Gianinni, an overweight and extroverted Neapolitan playwright. Founded in 1944, his movement was to steadily gain strength over the ensuing two years.[73]

Giannini's newspaper, also called *L'Uomo Qualunque,* ridiculed the Wind from the North, dubbing it instead the "Belch from the North" *(Il Rutto del Nord).* By mid-1945, the paper's circulation had soared to 800,000—a very large number for the time—with most copies selling in the Mezzogiorno. In its solicitude for potential victims of the purge, Giannini's movement appealed especially to conservative elites and to government employees and other resentful and frightened members of the middle classes. Giannini himself had been denounced by the High Commission for the Purge in early April 1945, though without consequence.

Uomo Qualunque capitalized on persisting monarchist sentiment in the Mezzogiorno. There the Resistance Movement was broadly disliked as an alien and untrustworthy import from the north. By contrast, the Savoy dynasty represented an honorable superiority untouched by political intrigue, gamesmanship, and impotence.[74] Rhetorically, Gianinni scorned formal ideology and the professionalization of politics. Disgusted by the "sordid and corrupt" jockeying for position characteristic of coalition politics, he advocated "technicians" as officeholders who, like "good bookkeepers enter government service on January 1 and leave on December 31, strictly ineligible for re-election for whatever reason."[75] *Abbasano tutti!* ("Down with Everyone!") was among the movement's most popular slogans.

Beneath *Uomo Qualunque*'s iconoclasm lay considerable nostalgia for Fascism. Much of the movement's funding came from ex-Fascist southern bosses who, scorned even by the right-wing Liberals, turned to Giannini for a political outlet. The movement lent its name to a new epithet in Italian politics: *qualunquista*: "a digger of one's own garden, a cynic, a potential Fascist."[76]

The prolonged partisan negotiations required to put together new anti-Fascist, multi-party governments in June and again in December 1945 (outlined just below and in chapter 4) frustrated and bewildered a populace buffeted by lingering fears of epuration on the one hand and by economic hardship on the other. Speaking at a national Christian Democratic gathering in August 1945, De Gasperi fretted at a widespread proclivity among his countrymen to keep the anti-Fascist political parties at arm's-length, and to lapse into an *atarassia dilagante* (roughly "widening stupor").

From Parri to De Gasperi

The full liberation of Italy in late May 1945 heralded the formation of a new Italian government, one possessing fuller legitimacy and authority than the preceding Bonomi governments, which had been forced to function under overarching Allied tutelage. Nenni's was the first name put forward for the prime ministership.[77] Inexperienced in the subtleties of closeted political diplomacy, he counted on the negotiating savvy and clear vision (*chiaroveggenza*) of Togliatti, who however held back.[78] A seemingly less probable supporter of Nenni's candidacy was the conservative but anti-clerical Benedetto Croce. Despite initial support from across the spectrum of anti-Fascist parties, Nenni's impetuosity compromised his candidacy. Though appreciative of the Socialist leader's goodwill, the prominent Action Party leader Leo Valiani stated that Nenni "didn't know any other way to reach his goal than to broadcast high-sounding slogans, preferably in large rallies." Nenni acknowledged in a note made in June 1945 his fear that he would not be able to "adjust to being a man of government; for I am a journalist, a journalist I must remain, a journalist I will die."[79] Personally affable and engaging, nevertheless he employed a rousing, even provocative, rhetoric which unsettled his counterparts. Among Nenni's favorite aphorisms, well suited to the excitement of the piazza, was the following: "Politics is not made on the basis of sentiments... we count instead on resentments."[80]

On June 1, representatives of the Socialist and Christian Democratic delegations met. Speaking for the latter party, Mario Scelba acknowledged that, in view of the rapport existing between De Gasperi and Nenni, the Socialist leader was viewed more favorably by Christian Democrats than any other member of his party. However, he added, as a matter of principle a Socialist prime ministership would shift the political equilibrium to the Left, and the resulting Socialist-Communist linkage would bring unacceptably grave internal and international risks.

After Nenni's name was dropped from consideration, De Gasperi's was put forward. In Valiani's words,

> [T]his man from the North possessed a sober, bourgeois manner reminiscent of an earlier age. Conceding the value of *epurazione*, workers' rights and agrarian reform, De Gasperi emphasized the necessity of a government which would stand above political factions.

Such a government would address the pressing need to restore "the prestige and authority of the State, respect for the Law, and its efficacy."[81] A disciplined, direct speaker, De Gasperi focused on the essential.

As a meeting of CLN leaders at the time drew to a close, a leader of the Action Party present remarked that "this man will govern us for five years."[82] But De Gasperi's time had not yet arrived; beginning in December 1945, he would lead Italy for better than eight years, setting a record for continuous service as prime minister destined to last until the coming of Silvio Berlusconi at the century's end. For now, intransigent leftist opposition, both among politicians and on the streets, blocked De Gasperi's candidacy. In a journal entry dated June 5–6, Nenni noted that posters and banners had appeared all over Rome proclaiming "Nenni and Togliatti at the head of the government." At the same time the Christian Democratic leader told Nenni that his own residence had been defaced with graffiti stating "De Gasperi to the sacristy, power to Nenni."[83]

After Nenni's and De Gasperi's candidacies each faltered, Action Party leader Ferruccio Parri formed a new coalition government in early June 1945. Parri represented a compromise choice. He was widely admired for the Resistance military leadership he had shown under the pseudonym of "Maurizio." Like Giuseppe Mazzini at the time of the Risorgimento, his was a puritanical creed of personal hardship and self-denial in service to a higher cause. An upstanding figure, he brought little administrative experience and even less political savvy to his new position. In American journalist Max Ascoli's description, "the hardworking, fanatically honest, unsmiling Parri was the atonement for twenty-four years of clownishness."[84] He slept on a simple cot in his Viminal office. He approached the day's work stoically, methodically, and scrupulously, without however distinguishing between major and minor tasks. Parri allowed himself to be overwhelmed day and night by administrative minutiae and by ceaseless delegations of partisans and others. Fearless and decisive as a partisan leader, he proved tentative as head of a supposedly innovatory government.[85]

De Gasperi was far more effective in his role of foreign minister in the Parri government. He and his fellow Christian Democrats differed with Parri over the purge, the institutional question, and other issues. As the months passed, De Gasperi grew more and more disillusioned with the manner in which Parri governed. The Action leader failed to hammer out a consensus on the agrarian crisis, or subsequently industrial or monetary policy. The prime minister's political naivetè riled the Christian Democratic leader as well. In De Gasperi's eyes, Parri was simply out of his league by virtue of "his temperament, his mentality and the blinkered outlook of his chancellery."[86]

Togliatti and Nenni also harbored reservations about Parri's leadership. Like De Gasperi, they felt Parri was losing touch with the common people's pulse. Nenni regretted the prime minister's "poor oratory"—the fact that he "read from notes, and read poorly, without emphasis or liveliness."[87] In a cautious mid-June letter to party colleague Luigi Longo, Togliatti stated:

> It seems to me, following the dealings we had, that with him [Parri] we can definitely move towards the constituent assembly and towards a republic. He won't be so determined in the [political] battle against what is left of fascism.

He is, in the end, completely insensitive to the social problems and above all basically hostile to the socialist developments.[88]

Partisans like Parri had confronted a Machiavellian reality, forced to pit their *virtù* against the *fortuna* of war. But the end of the war and the restoration of more conventional politics eclipsed the arena in which classical, heroic virtue could express itself. The epic arena of the Resistance now gave way to old-fashioned practices of horse-trading (the equivalent Italian term is *mercato delle vacche,* cow market[89]) and intrigue over the distribution of ministerial posts.[90]

The transition from Resistance idealism to parliamentary pragmatism proved to be far more problematic than expected. However well-intentioned, Parri was unable to negotiate that passage. In his defense, however, it should be added that Parri was not the only member of his party to stumble. Other Action Party leaders confidently confronted the challenge of moving from the ethical and emotional certainties of partisan militance to the shifting exigences of conventional politics, only to regret the outcome. As Vittorio Foa recalled in his memoirs:

> Many of us fell in love with the techniques of politics. We got revenge on defeated Fascism by avidly rediscovering all the instruments that it had taken from us. We used them to the full: parties, free press, congresses, meetings, contacts conversations, tactics that were so refined as to exasperate us. We deluded ourselves into thinking we could defeat the restoration with its own arms.[91]

On November 24, representatives of the foreign and Italian press were invited to attend the CLN meeting that convened at the Viminal. Here the usually modest and soft-spoken Parri launched a vitriolic tirade, charging that a "coup d'etat" engineered by the Christian Democrats and Liberals was underway.[92] At this point De Gasperi leapt to his feet, beseeching the representatives of the press not to report Parri's outburst for the sake of Italy's international reputation. Speaking both as head of the Christian Democratic Party and as foreign minister, he vowed that neither his party nor the governing coalition had the remotest intention of carrying out a coup, a step which would only "expose the nation to a Fascist or reactionary turn, undermining its progress toward a government of liberty and order."[93]

In a celebrated passage from *The Watch,* Carlo Levi describes De Gasperi's behavior in this way:

> They all deplored this uncalled for reply, so strange and almost insane coming from an old and prudent politician, renowned for his moderation, capacity, weight and sense of responsibility. And yet, from his own point of view this

weathered old serpent was right. More than all the others had demonstrated, perhaps quite unconsciously, he knew what he was doing. He knew how to defend his own solid but limited position. Driven by holy indignation, he had been poetic in his own way. He found himself in this time of no parliaments, almost without realizing it, impelled by an innate parliamentary sense to make a speech for the opposition, that obligatory speech that asserts the privilege of the successor. Also, without realizing it, he had restored the old state.[94]

The restoration of the pre-Fascist state structure was a more incremental process than Levi's testimony might seem to imply. Leo Valiani attributed what he termed "the first victory of the continuity of the State over the revolution of the State" to De Gasperi's step-by-step actions, beginning with the ministerial crisis of mid-1945 and extending into 1946 under De Gasperi's first prime ministership. The Christian Democrat insisted repeatedly that legislation was the prerogative of the government, not Resistance organs like the CLN.[95] For British historian Elizabeth Wiskemann, the process of "more or less restor[ing] the old-fashioned structure of the liberal state which Mussolini had done his best to destroy"[96] continued throughout De Gasperi's eight years as prime minister.

We will be in a better position to calibrate this "Degasperian restoration" in the chapters to come. The Christian Democratic statesman brought a layered appreciation to the term *Stato* (State) as he prepared to assume the reins of leadership. At the most basic level, respect for the State meant recognition and respect for law. To uphold such a recognition, it was necessary to replace ad hoc CLN-appointed local officials with seasoned civil servants ostensibly habituated to perform their responsibilities without partisan bias. Yet as we will see in Chapter 4, De Gasperi could not rehabilitate the State at this level without sheltering, perhaps inadvertently, a host of bureaucrats, many of whom least desirable inclinations had been reinforced during the Fascist *ventennio*. Less problematic was De Gasperi's commitment to parliamentary values and methods as the surest scaffolding for implementing to a sound democracy. He reaffirmed this commitment beginning with his tenure as foreign minister in the Parri government and continuing through the difficult postwar negotiations surrounding the signing of a peace treaty with the Allies. To secure the least draconian terms in such a treaty, it was imperative that the Americans and British in particular believe in the reliability and solidity of the State with which they were dealing.[97]

Politically, Valiani disapproved of the restoration ushered in by De Gasperi. Still, the Action Party leader respected the high-minded manner with which the Christian Democrat proceeded. In Valiani's view, De Gasperi was conscientiously devoted to the dignity of the State as he conceived of it, "acting from a sense of personal responsibility, and not to further the interests of his party and still less the interests of the economic categories which stood to benefit from its restoration." While De Gasperi certainly consulted with the hierarchy of the Church, he was not, in the end, "the Vatican's man." De Gasperi was, above all, a man of the State.[98]

Notes

1. Machiavelli, *The Prince*, 69–70.
2. Felix Gilbert, "Fortune, Necessity, Virtù," in *The Prince*, Norton Critical Edition. (New York: Norton, 1992), 152.
3. Writing from his prison cell (he was imprisoned by the Fascist regime from 1926 until his death in 1937), Antonio Gramsci, the Italian Communist Party's foundational political thinker, called on his party to become a "Modern Prince." Antonio Gramsci, *The Modern Prince and Other Writings*, trans. Lewis Marks (New York: International Publishers, 1957), 135–188.
4. As radical democrats, the members of the Action Party were not positioned as far Left on the political spectrum as were the Socialists or Communists. In tactical terms, however, the Actionists were often more intemperate than their Marxist counterparts. Of the six parties noted here, only the Christian Democratic Party (heir to the post-First World War Popular Party), Socialist Party and Communist Party were proven political formations which had already attracted mass support prior to the establishment of the Fascist dictatorship.
5. Cited in Norberto Bobbio, *Dal fascismo alla democrazia. I regimi, le ideologie, le figure e le culture politiche* (Milan: Baldini & Castoldi, 1997), 134. Anti-Fascist author Natalia Ginzburg evokes a similar sentiment when she writes, "During fascism, poets found themselves expressing only an arid, cryptic dream world. Now [at the moment of liberation], once more, many words were in circulation and reality appeared to be at everyone's fingertips. So those who had been starved dedicated themselves to harvesting the words with delight. And the harvest was ubiquitous because everyone wanted to take part in it. The result was a confused mixing up of the languages of poetry and politics." Cited in Deborah Eisenberg, "The Driest Eye" (a review of three of Natalia Ginzburg's works), *New York Review of Books* LXVI: 13 (July 18, 2019), 14.
6. Vittorio Foa, *Il cavallo e la torre: riflessioni su una vita* (Turin: Einaudi, 1991), 137.
7. While lacking the Marxist ideological base of the Socialist and Communist parties, the Action Party adopted more radical and impatient positions than the Communists especially.

8   Claudio Pavone, *A Civil War: A History of the Italian Resistance* (London: Verso, 2013), 39–41.
9   As noted in chapter 1, De Gasperi's was an "inner exile" under the aegis of the Vatican.
10 Ginsborg, *History of Contemporary Italy*, 70.
11 Evocative of the Neapolitan revolt is Renato Luigi Sansone's testimony, highlighting the role of women, in Stanislao Pugliese, ed., *Fascism, Anti-Fascism and the Resistance in Italy* (Lanham, MD: Rowan & Littlefield, 2004), 251–252.
12 Guido Quazza has underscored the gap, which opened between the Resistance and the CLN on the one hand, and the anti-Fascist parties on the other, as noted in Pietro Scoppola, "Tessuto etico, forze politiche, istituzioni," in Agostino Giovagnoli, ed., *Interpretazioni della Repubblica*, 23 (Bologna: Il Mulino, 1998), 21. In his biography of Togliatti, Aldo Agosti suggests greater continuity between Resistance and party. Agosti, *Palmiro Togliatti*, 154–155.
13 Levi himself was a member of the Resistance in Turin before his arrest and exile to Basilicata during the Ethiopian war.
14 Carlo Levi, *The Watch*. Translated from the Italian (New York: Farrar, Straus & Young, 1951), 20.
15 Pietro Scoppola also credits in this regard the "innumerable forms of [partisan] civil resistance" which occurred "above and beyond the armed struggle." "Tessuto etico," 23.
16 Leo Valiani, *L'avvento di De Gasperi* (Turin: De Silva, 1949), 19–39.
17 Carlo Trabucco, *La prigionia di Roma. Diario dei 268 giorni dell'occupazione tedesca* (Rome: S.E.L.I., 1947), 131.
18 Gabriela Fanello-Marcucci, *Alle origini della Democrazia Cristiana, 1929-1944: dal carteggio Spataro-De Gasperi* (Brescia: Morcelliana, 1982), 31–32.
19 A physician, journalist (editor of the Action Party newspaper *Italia Libera*) and painter as well as the author of *Christ Stopped at Eboli* (1944–1945) and *The Watch*, among other works.
20 Pier Giorgio Zunino, *La Repubblica e il suo passato* (Bologna: Il Mulino, 2003), 285–289.
21 Fanello-Marcucci, *Alle origini della Democrazia Cristiana*, 31–32.
22 Maria Romana De Gasperi, ed., *De Gasperi scrive* I (Brescia: Morcelliana, 1974), 341.
23 Guido Formigoni, prefatory essay, *Alcide De Gasperi, Scritti e Discorsi Politici* (SDP hereafter) III, I (Bologna: Il Mulino, 2008), 13.
24 Giovagnoli, *La cultura democristiana*, 152.
25 Zunino, *La Repubblica e il suo passato*, ch. 7.
26 Piero Craveri, *De Gasperi*, 147.
27 Fanello-Marcucci, *Alle origini della Democrazia Cristiana*, 39–40.
28 Duggan, *Force of Destiny*, 445–448.

29 Catti De Gasperi, *De Gasperi, uomo solo*, 180. See also Emilio Bonomelli, "Il senso della sua autonomia politica," article published in *Concretezza,* August 16, 1964, reproduced in Di Capua, ed., *Processo a De Gasperi*, 192–199.
30 Formigoni, prefatory essay to De Gasperi, SDP, vol. III: I, 35.
31 Observing from the island of Ponza, where he remained quarantined, Nenni decried Badoglio's sibylline instruction as "absurd." Nenni, *Tempo di Guerra Fredda*, 22.
32 Domenico, *Italian Fascists on Trial*, 47.
33 The phrase *popolo mezzano* was one Nenni borrowed from beloved nineteenth-century poet Giuseppe Carducci. *Tempo di Guerra Fredda,* 28.
34 Ibid., 26.
35 Luigi Gedda, *18 aprile 1948: memorie inedite del sconfitto del Fronte Popolare* (Milan: Mondadori, 1998), 84–85.
36 Ginsborg, *History of Contemporary Italy,* 13.
37 Forlenza and Thomassen, *Italian Modernities*, 150–151.
38 http://www.lifeinItaly/com/historyitaly-1945-to-1950, accessed October 30, 2018.
39 http://en.wikipedia.org/wiki/Royal_Italian_Army during_World_War_II, accessed November 2, 2018.
40 Vera Capperucci, introduction to De Gasperi, *SDP* III, I (Bologna: Il Mulino, 2008), 156.
41 Ivanoe Bonomi. *Diario di un anno,* 97.
42 Spataro, "Le giornate della clandestinità," in Giovanni Di Capua, ed., *Processo a De Gasperi 211 testimonianze* (Roma: EBE, 1976), 875–877.
43 Nenni, *Tempo di Guerra Fredda,* 42. Entry of September 11, 1943.
44 Catti De Gasperi, *De Gasperi, uomo solo,* 182.
45 Carrillo, *Alcide De Gasperi, 123;* Bonomi, *Diario di un anno,* 139–141.
46 Carrillo, *Alcide De Gasperi,* 123.
47 Ibid.
48 Malgeri, *Alcide De Gasperi,* vol. II: *Dal Fascismo alla democrazia,* 19. De Gasperi and Ronca would remain in sympathetic contact with one another in the coming years, despite their differences as the 1952 Sturzo Operation drew closer.
49 Fanello-Marcucci, *Alle origini della Democrazia Cristiana*, 232.
50 Catti De Gasperi, *De Gasperi, uomo solo*, 184.
51 Giorgio Amendola, *Lettere a Milano* (Rome: Riuniti, 1974), 292.
52 Antonello Capurso, ed. *I discorsi che hanno cambiato l'Italia* (Milan: Mondadori, 2007), 143–144. Despite this harsh comment, Togliatti and Badoglio got along well privately after the communist leader returned to Italy.
53 Agosti, *Palmiro Togliatti*, 151.
54 Di Scala, *Italy from Revolution to Republic*, 296.

55 Amendola, *Lettere a Milano*, 124. For the specific provisions of both halves of the 1929 pact, see Mack Smith, *Italy: A Modern History*, 441–442.
56 Nenni, *Tempo di Guerra Fredda*, 62.
57 Marcella and Maurizio Ferrara, *Conversando con Togliatti*, 331.
58 Domenico, *Remaking Italy*, 89.
59 Malgeri, *Alcide De Gasperi*, vol. II, 33.
60 Both Togliatti and Badoglio came from the Piedmont and shared the practicality and pragmatism often associated with that region.
61 Malgeri, *Alcide De Gasperi*, vol. II, 36.
62 Nenni, *Tempo di guerra fredda*, 126.
63 Malgeri, *Alcide De Gasperi*, vol. II, 58–59.
64 Claudio Pavone, "La continuità dello Stato. Istituzioni e uomini," in Giancarlo Monina, ed., *Italia 1945–48. Le origini della Repubblica* (Soveria Mannelli: Rubbettino, 2007), 137–289.
65 Antonio Gambino, *Storia del dopoguerra. Dalla liberazione al potere DC* (Bari: Laterza, 1988), 4.
66 Domenico, *Italian Fascists on Trial*, 79.
67 Ibid.
68 Ibid., 122.
69 Miller, *United States and Italy*, 50.
70 Valiani, *Avvento di De Gasperi*, 33.
71 Enzo Santarelli, *Pietro Nenni* (Turin: UTET, 1988), 276.
72 Domenico, *Italian Fascists on Trial*, 207–210.
73 Gambino, *Storia del dopoguerra*, 92.
74 Matteo Truffelli, "L'antipolitica," in G. Monina, ed., *1945–1946: le origini della Repubblica*, vol. II (Soveria Mannelli: Rubbettino, 2007), 355.
75 Ibid., 345.
76 Ginsborg, *History of Contemporary Italy*, 99–100.
77 Tamburrano, *Pietro Nenni*, 159.
78 Valiani, *Avvento di De Gasperi*, 18.
79 Santarelli, *Pietro Nenni*, 265.
80 In Nenni's more pungent Italian, *La politica non si fa con i sentimenti…figuriamoci con i risentimenti*. http://www.miglioriafarismi.com/2012/pietro-nenni-aforsimi.html, accessed November 15, 2018.
81 Valiani, *Avvento di De Gasperi*, 24.
82 Ibid., 23–24.
83 Nenni, *Tempo di Guerra Fredda*, 121.
84 Max Ascoli, "Political Reconstruction in Italy," *The Journal of Politics* 8, 3 (August 1946), 324.
85 Valiani, *Avvento di De Gasperi*, 25, 30.

86 Even the Socialists and Communists had the workers behind them, De Gasperi acknowledged, but behind the Action Party, "there is nothing." Gabriella Fanello-Marcucci, *Il primo governo De Gasperi (dicembre 1945-giuigno 1946). Sei mesi decisivi per la democrazia in Italia* (Soveria Mannelli: Rubbettino, 2004), 19.
87 Nenni, *Tempo di Guerra Fredda*, 149.
88 Cited in Agosti, *Palmiro Togliatti*, 164. Togliatti's reticence was already evident in the summer of 1944. Upon Rome's liberation, Parri and other partisan leaders arrived in the city to meet their CLN counterparts. But Togliatti held back at first. To Parri, it seemed that the Communist leader "did not find it opportune to appear in the light as a man of the Resistance." Bocca, *Togliatti*, 331. In a 1964 article published shortly after Togliatti's passing, Parri judged the late Communist leader's overriding "prudence" (understandable though he found it in light of Togliatti's "cautious" character and the PCI's difficult history) unfortunate, compromising as it did much-needed institutional restructuring immediately following Italy's liberation. Ferruccio Parri, "In memoria di Palmiro Togliatti," *Il Movimento di Liberazione in Italia* 76 (1964), 87–89.
89 Valiani, *Avvento di De Gasperi*, 23.
90 Max Weber masterfully predicted this transition in his essay "The Vocation and Profession of Politics," decrying the displacement of "living for politics" to "living by politics." Max Weber, *Political Writings*, ed. Peter Lassman and Ronald Spiers (Cambridge: Cambridge University Press, 1994), 309–369.
91 Foa, *Il cavallo e la torre*, 171–172. In *The Watch*, Levi colorfully portrays Foa (thinly disguised as the character Fede) and some dozen other leading figures in the Action Party. See in this regard Ward, *Antifascisms*, 174–175.
92 Subsequently Parri apologized for his outburst, admitting that he had gone too far in the heat of the moment. See Ferruccio Parri, "La caduta del governo Parri," *L'Astrolabio*, January 1972, as reproduced in F. Parri, *Scritti 1915-1975* (Milan: Feltrinelli, 1976), 575.
93 Malgeri, *Alcide De Gasperi*, vol. II, 99; Gambino, *Storia del dopoguerra*, 99.
94 Levi, *Watch*, 206.
95 Valiani, *Avvento di De Gasperi*, 25.
96 Elizabeth Wiskemann, *Italy since 1945*, published posthumously (London: Macmillan, 1971), 23.
97 For a quantitative and diagrammatic treatment of De Gasperi's use of terminology such as *Stato*, and his political discourse more broadly, see the digitized platform ALCIDE at http://alcidedigitale.fbk.eu, accessed October 17, 2018.
98 Valiani, *Avvento di De Gasperi*, 37–38.

4

Monarchy or Republic?

De Gasperi's first year as prime minister confirmed his stature as Italy's preeminent statesman. His diplomacy, tenacity, realism, and self-confidence proved to be invaluable as postwar Italy took its first halting steps toward a functioning democracy. Three watershed developments in 1946 were the enfranchisement of women, the staging of the first free local elections since the early 1920s, and the dual vote of June 2 (consisting of a referendum on the monarchy and the election of members to a Constituent Assembly (*Constituente*) charged with crafting a constitution for the new state).

Togliatti and Nenni made important contributions to each of these achievements. All three leaders backed women's suffrage. But De Gasperi refrained from endorsing either a republican or a monarchist resolution of the institutional question, finessing deep divisions within his party and its electorate on the matter. Resolved to honor the ensuing republican victory in the referendum, he overcame challenges from Umberto II and his backers and, after ten days of escalating tensions, publicly cut the Gordian knot on June 12 on behalf of the newborn republic.

De Gasperi's First Government

Parri's dramatic exit from power in late November 1945 had left no obvious choice for a successor. On the 25th, the six CLN parties commenced an exceptionally arduous series of negotiations to form a new coalition government. Veteran 85-year-old politician Orlando's name surfaced first, but was vetoed by the Actionists, Communists, and Socialists. In Nenni's words, an Orlando government would signal an unacceptable shift to the right. "We don't want a Petain or Hindenburg style cabinet," asserted the Socialist leader.[1] In substance, an Orlando-led government would give Italy "a Hindenburg who would attempt to save the Monarchy."[2] Carlo Sforza's name surfaced next as a potential prime minister, only to meet stiff Liberal Party opposition. Ruini and De Gasperi also harbored reservations, lest Sforza's resolute republicanism give the Allies pause. Ruini then launched a short-lived bid on his own behalf as protagonist of the "smaller parties" in the CLN against the "Big Three" (i.e., the DC, PSI, and PCI).[3] After several more days of deliberations, Nenni broached the possibility of a De Gasperi-led government—a proposition that garnered unanimous CLN support. The Christian Democratic leader reacted with characteristic circumspection: if need be, he said, he would "accept the sacrifice" for the good of the nation.[4] On December 1, the lieutenant general empowered the Christian Democratic leader to put together a new coalition government.

A De Gasperi-led government recommended itself on several grounds. Politically, the Christian Democratic leader provided a bridge between the small Democracy of Labor and Liberal Parties to his right and the larger Socialist and Communist Parties to his left. Palmiro Togliatti backed De Gasperi as a way of sustaining a stable Popular-Front-style coalition into Italy's postwar period. A De Gasperi prime ministership would enhance the government's standing in the eyes of the Allies. For their part, De Gasperi's colleagues trusted him in his promise to conduct negotiations over cabinet positions in a balanced manner.

Still, clashes over cabinet positions between December 1 and December 10 severely tested De Gasperi's political tenacity and finesse. Having previously precipitated Parri's fall, the Liberals proved the most recalcitrant party in the ensuing horse-trading. The thorniest issue was the allocation of the ministry of interior. Always a position of great power, the post was especially important because it would fall to this individual to oversee the replacement of CLN-appointed prefects with career civil servants, and to supervise Italy's first democratic elections. The Socialists and the Liberals both claimed a right to the post, while suspecting the other of bad faith. In order to break the deadlock, De Gasperi floated the option of retaining that post himself. In fact, however, the Christian Democratic leader was prepared to relinquish the interior ministry for that of foreign affairs, thereby extending the sound relationship that he had already established with the Allied Powers under the Parri government. In the end, Socialist Giuseppe Romita secured the ministry of the interior.

Unable to secure that portfolio for themselves, the Liberals torpedoed an all-but-certain agreement on December 4 by insisting at the last minute on ten conservative programmatic conditions. Togliatti reacted vehemently, at one point equating the Liberals' decalogue to the program of the right-wing *Uomo Qualunque*. Outraged at Togliatti's analogy and disillusioned at their general lack of success within the negotiations, the Liberals abruptly withdrew from negotiations. Over the next several days, it appeared that a five-party coalition—minus the Liberals—might take shape. But the Crown insisted that the Liberals be included. De Gasperi himself strongly preferred the maintenance of a six-party government coalition, arguing that the full spectrum of anti-Fascist opinion—from the Socialists and Communists on the left to the Democrats of Labor and Liberals on the right—share responsibility for the difficult decisions a new government would face in coming months. Obstreperous though they were, the Liberals also represented a crucial ideological counterweight to the potent left-wing of the prospective governing coalition.

Even so, De Gasperi found it especially trying to deal with Liberal leaders and their Savoyard allies. After a particularly charged telephone conversation on the evening of December 6 with Minister of the Realm Lucifero, the usually composed De Gasperi exclaimed to Nenni "now our woes begin!"[5] An emotionally exhausted De Gasperi then resumed deliberations with Lucifero and with Ruini, only to suffer a brief fainting spell. Citing personal illness, the Christian Democratic leader then asked that the late evening CLN gathering be suspended until the morrow.

But how indisposed was De Gasperi? After the suspension of the gathering of anti-Fascist leaders, he immediately, and surreptitiously, went to see Prince Umberto in hopes of salvaging an inclusive (six-party) agreement—an outcome which, in the end, De Gasperi would obtain. The Christian Democrat's unusual late-night maneuver remains the source of both political contention and scholarly conjecture. The Christian Democratic statesman may indeed have been suffering from the after-effects of a bout with severe bronchitis.[6] Admiral Franco Garofalo, a top aide to the lieutenant general present at the time, recalled that, upon entering the antechamber of the Palazzo Chigi, the Christian Democratic leader indeed "looked like someone who was not well."[7] On the left, however, leaders like Socialist Sandro Pertini suspected that De Gasperi had resorted to an extraordinary and uncharacteristic subterfuge.[8]

Finally, on December 10, the new government was announced, with De Gasperi as prime minister and foreign minister, Togliatti as minister of justice, Nenni as vice premier and minister for the Constituent Assembly, and Nenni's Socialist colleague Giuseppe Romita as minister of the interior. Another key ministry was that of agriculture and forestries, held by Communist Fausto Gullo. Excluded from more important posts, the Liberals obtained the ministries of war (Manlio Brosi) and public works (Leone Cattani). Sole representative of a weakening Action Party was Ugo La Malfa, who became minister of reconstruction. Democracy of Labor statesman Enrico Molè became minister of public instruction. Though he would be largely ineffective in that position, Molè nevertheless represented a last ditch bulwark against undue Catholic influence in the Italy's war-ravaged school system.[9]

Though the cabinet crisis had finally been overcome, the De Gasperi government faced pressing problems at every turn. Banditry and politically motivated violence had become commonplace. Much of this took the form of retaliatory murders of former Fascists. Between May 1945 and August 1946, the police recorded 893 such "acts of violence" in Modena province—and that excluding the city itself.[10] Furthermore, unemployment was growing across the country, hunger was widespread—and that, in turn had driven even state employees to go on strike. In his diary, Nenni confessed, "I fear for tomorrow—I who have never feared anything."[11]

The ensuing months were contentious, with cabinet disagreements deepening over a host of issues. Especially divisive was the question of postwar economic recovery. As prices soared but jobs remained scarce, Treasury Minister Epicarmo Corbino, chief architect of the government's austere monetarist economic policies, became the target of mounting vituperation from the Left. The Communists took credit for his ultimate resignation in October, but his successors continued to carry out his orthodox Liberal line.

The purge continued to vex the government. By the beginning of 1946, support for *epurazione* had ebbed among each of the major anti-Fascist parties. Prime Minister De Gasperi recalled that the Fascists had required all government officials swear allegiance to their regime, whether by conviction or expediency, and therefore a coherent purge was simply not practicable. Two months later Justice Minister Togliatti announced the broad amnesty noted in Chapter 3 and shut down the High Commission on the Purge.

Another volatile issue within the cabinet centered on the pending Constituent Assembly. In January 1944, the CLN Bari Congress had pledged that such a body be elected as soon as possible following full liberation, to enjoy "full powers" to dispose of the institutional question. The Bonomi government in late June 1944 reaffirmed this authorization. Provocatively, Nenni was on record as having urged "all power to the Constituent Assembly."[12] From the opposite side of the political spectrum, Liberal supporters of the monarchy were beginning to advocate a popular referendum as an alternative mechanism for resolving the institutional question. Even De Gasperi warmed to the referendum alternative.

Debate over the question persisted through 1945 and came to a head during the first months of 1946. De Gasperi now pushed more forcefully for the referendum, arguing that resolution of the institutional question by means of a referendum would possess greater "moral weight" than a decision made by a Constituent Assembly. Political calculation also figured in the Christian Democratic leader's position, as referral of the institutional question to the Constituent Assembly threatened to deepen simmering divisions on the matter within his party, which in turn would damage party morale and influence. American policymakers have earlier endorsed referral of this decision to the Constituent Assembly. Now, concerned at the radical potential of that body, Secretary of State Cordell Hull and US Ambassador to Italy Alexander Kirk, joined by their British counterparts, sided with De Gasperi.[13]

Nenni countered by denouncing the referendum option as a reactionary cabal. For his part, Togliatti invoked the inter-party CLN pact, dating from the 1944 Bari conference, which authorized the Constituent Assembly, once elected, to decide the fate of the monarchy. The Communist leader feared the polarizing potential of a lengthy, volatile run-up to a referendum vote. A close outcome, he feared, might even prompt a civil war, as had broken out in Greece.

Finally, the Socialist and Communist leaders relented, agreeing to refer the institutional question to a referendum. Togliatti and Nenni feared that further delay would weaken their standing among an increasingly impatient public. Though a longstanding advocate of a strong Constituent Assembly, Nenni declared that he would accept a referendum on the monarchy if that vote were to be held contemporaneously with elections for the Constituent Assembly. This compromise proposal was accepted by the governing coalition despite vehement Action Party opposition.

The Administrative Elections of Spring 1946

The major political task carried out by the first De Gasperi government was the holding of spring local (or "administrative," in the Italian parlance) elections, to be followed by a second round of elections in the fall. These administrative elections offered an initial test of strength for the six CLN parties. For the first time in two decades, Italians could invest their political hopes and wishes in free, fair elections. Even more importantly, for the first time in Italian history, women had qualified for the suffrage. Slightly over two-thirds of the nation's *comuni* (communities) held administrative elections in the spring, with the remainder voting in the fall. Because they did not encompass the entire nation, yet broke historic ground, the spring elections were widely seen as a kind of democratic apprenticeship.

Ultimately, the decision of when and how the elections would take place fell to the ministry of interior, as it had prior to the Fascist *ventennio*. Electoral procedures and supervisory local boards were revived on the basis of that precedent. Given a free hand by the prime minister to select which communities would go to the polls in the spring as opposed to the fall, Interior Minister Romita chose a cross-section of communities across the peninsula which, he hoped, promised to favor the Left. Initial spring returns dramatically rewarded candidates of parties and groups favoring the republic in comparison with those favoring the monarchy. Upon receiving the results, Romita confidently claimed, "I have the republic in my desk drawer."[14]

The nature and timing of Italy's first post-Fascist free elections had occasioned considerable friction right from the middle of 1945. A variety of important factors merited consideration in scheduling these elections. It would take time until roads and railroads in war-ravaged areas could provide transportation to all polling places. Important provisions needed to be made with respect to suffrage rights, voting procedures, and electoral districting (e.g., proportional representation, majority rule in single member constituencies, or a combination thereof). The ministry of the interior itself had to be mobilized to adequately supervise the entire process, including the preparation of electoral rolls, casting of ballots and tabulation of results. In the months leading up to the elections, Interior Minister Giuseppe Romita focused special attention to addressing and the eliminating the banditry and political violence which had plagued immediate postwar Italy.[15]

Initially the Allied authorities had stipulated that nationwide ("political") elections should be held as soon as feasible following the conclusion of hostilities. Eager to capitalize on the energy and idealism of the left-leaning Resistance movement, the Socialists, Communists, and many members of the Action Party were also keen to hold an early vote, even as they recognized the presence of short-term logistical impediments. However, the Christian Democrats and the Liberals preferred to wait on the all-important national political vote, fearing the short-term potency of the Wind from the North. Instead, they argued that staggered administrative elections distributed across the Italian boot should come first. American officials had come to endorse this approach, viewing it as a "test" of Italian political maturity—a characterization to which many, especially on the Left, took exception.[16] In American eyes, it was only reasonable that Italians should demonstrate their democratic convictions through the ballot box at some level before the peace treaty with Italy would be concluded.[17]

All told, a total of 5,722 communities held elections spread over five successive weeks in March and April. The great majority of these communities had fewer than 30,000 residents. Only Milan, among Italy's large (500,000 plus) cities, held spring elections. Interestingly enough, the pre-Fascist practice of majoritarian voting was retained for communities under 30,000 in population. Individual candidates did not have to indicate formal party affiliation but were required to present a "declaration of political continuity" (here, "continuity" may be read as synonymous with "history"). This provision suggests a transition—in some locales more than others—away from a notable based patronage basis and toward a more ideological and partisan basis. In provincial capitals (66) and in communities of over 30,000 residents (49), the anti-Fascist parties confirmed their fundamental democratic role through the provision for proportional representation.[18]

In five rounds of voting between March 10 and April 7, 82.3 percent of eligible voters went to the polls—a striking figure in view of pre-election predictions of a turnout of perhaps below 50 percent.[19] Fears circulated among Italy's political and intellectual elites that a populace, unaccustomed after two decades to the ballot box, would widely ignore the vote—an inaccurate judgment reflecting nothing so much as their own elitist pessimism. Almost equal percentages of men and women voted (83 percent of eligible men and 81.7 percent of eligible women). Regional variation in turn out was relatively modest, with 85 percent of eligible northerners participating, 78 percent of southerners, and 71 percent of Sicilians and Sardinians.[20]

What accounts for the very high turnouts in the spring 1946 elections? In many ways, the 1946 elections constituted something completely novel for the Italian people. Voters were mesmerized by the frank and open political debate in the air. For a defeated, war-torn, impoverished, geographically disjointed country, the stakes could hardly be more dramatic. Compared with the major pre-Fascist parties, the post-Fascist parties made unprecedented, highly effective use of political slogans and images. In Milan, Togliatti and Nenni attracted large, enthusiastic crowds to their *comizi* (popular assemblies). In the words one participant, Togliatti "underscored his points not with his voice but with rapid yet measured gestures, which constituted the most dramatic 'words' of his address." Nenni, by contrast, "sought more to move (*commuovere*) his audience rather than convince them."[21]

Such events elaborated upon older forms of community engagement. Public squares and theaters were favored venues for election rallies: participants at these *comizi* were immersed in a multi-sensory environment, combining formal speeches by party leaders, music, slogans broadcasted by loudspeakers, flags, and political placards. For some participants, the *comizi* recalled village festivals, or *sagri*. At these settings, political arguments were kept simple and straightforward, the better to reach and motivate a heterogeneous audience.[22]

For newly enfranchised women voters, the spring local elections represented a historic watershed. Although the Fascist government had granted them the nominal right to vote in local elections in 1925, the imposition of a one-party state rendered that concession hollow. The chauvinist thrust of Mussolinian ideology steadily degraded Italian women to second-class civil status.[23] Upon entering the co-belligerent Italian government in 1944, the Resistance parties had lost little time in pushing for women's suffrage. In a decree dated February 1, 1945, Lieutenant of the Realm Umberto II extended to Italian women the right to vote at all levels. Strangely, however, what was then called "passive suffrage" (the right to stand for election by women as well as men) was not incorporated in the February decree. This omission was only corrected subsequently, as women would run to serve in the Constituent Assembly.[24]

Each of the mass parties favored women's suffrage, though they justified it in different ways. De Gasperi and his fellow Christian Democratic leaders overcame traditional fears, still evident in some Catholic quarters, as to the political maturity of women and the potential weakening of family coherence. In a December 1944 article, appearing several months before Italian women obtained the suffrage, De Gasperi greeted newly recruited female members of his party, describing *Democrazia Cristiana* (DC) as "a great family," within which women could participate "as mothers, spouses and sisters."[25] The Christian Democratic leader backed women's suffrage both as a matter of democratic principle and as a pragmatic asset, since most female voters leaned toward his party. In part to assuage reticence about that step in conservative party circles, De Gasperi praised newly enfranchised women on the grounds that they could be counted on as voters who would defend such traditional values as public propriety, the sanctity of marriage, and the centrality of the family.

In 1944, De Gasperi had turned to Angela Guidi Cingolani to organize the Christian Democratic Women's Movement. The daughter of one of the founders of the Popular Party, at a young age she had already organized a party propaganda course for the Union for the Catholic Women of Italy. Now this poised, well-educated Roman woman set out as a feminist pilgrim of sorts, explaining, cajoling, and recruiting members for the new party organization. By 1945, she had emerged as a well-known advocate of women assuming a more prominent role in politics. Dressed stylishly in dark hues, with her smiling visage framed by her carefully arranged hair, and speaking forcefully into a microphone, Cingolani established a well-known public image. Even so, she encountered widespread hesitance among women about joining the party or its affiliated organizations. Fathers and husbands could be more hostile.[26]

For their part, the Marxists set aside earlier fears that the conservative ballot box counsel of their parish priests would unduly influence women. On the Left, a significant inducement to broaden the suffrage was the many-sided contribution of women to the Resistance between 1943 and 1945.[27] Leftist leaders, including Togliatti, advocated women's suffrage because it epitomized the rejection of Fascism: female participation in the political arena confirmed the demise of Mussolini and of his sexist agenda. Cognizant of the short-term ideological challenge which women's suffrage posed for his party, Togliatti embraced the reform as part of a larger commitment to women's emancipation. In the words of fellow Communist Emilio Sereni: "If Fascism had blocked women from politics, anti-Fascist democracy calls on women to become involved."[28] In particular, the new democracy needed their "commitment to concord and to peace," "their sense of responsibility," and their "immediate sense of the necessities of daily life." Pietro Nenni embraced women's suffrage as well. In her definitive study of the 1946 campaign for women's suffrage, Patrizia Gabrielli stresses how crucial the authoritative backing of De Gasperi, Togliatti, and Nenni alike was in overcoming widespread rank and file reservations about this unprecedented reform.[29]

Another controversy surrounded the option of making voting obligatory. Advocated as an antidote to Fascist-induced passivity, especially among presumably timid women voters, this step was championed by the Right and by some Christian Democrats, but was firmly repudiated by the Left. Instead, the names of registered voters abstaining from the ballot box were posted at local polling stations—a form of social embarrassment which may have contributed, if only marginally, to the high turnout for the spring 1946 elections.

Clearly, the vote possessed a potent symbolic valence to ordinary Italians. By casting their votes in an open election, the population affirmed a measure of mutual reconciliation following the twin nightmares of Fascist oppression and renewed world war. As David Kertzer has argued, the participation in such rituals plays an important role in forging and sustaining social solidarity—something Italy desperately needed during the early postwar years. Indeed, ritual action may have been more important in this election than pre-existing political belief.[30] All of this sheds light on the short-term potency of what some scholars have termed republican Italy's "political religion."[31]

In the end, the March and April administrative contests awarded the parties of the center (Christian Democrats plus the small Republican and Liberal Parties and the Democratic Party of Labor), 45 percent of the candidates running for local office. The Left (Communists, Socialists, the Action Party, and other left-wing formations) won 41.5 percent of the candidates, and the Right (*Uomo Qualunque* Front, the Italian Democratic Party, and other right-wing formations), 11.8 percent. Milan went to the Socialists, and the Left did well, as expected in the northwest and center. These successes were offset by sweeping centrist victories in the northeast, the south, and the islands.[32]

The heady excitement surrounding the spring round dissipated by the time the final round was held in the fall. Absenteeism increased. There was an uptick of public disenchantment with the major parties which increased in comparison with the spring elections. Gaining confidence from the downturn in support for existing parties, Giannini's movement reorganized as a party of sorts in order to elect representatives to the pending Constituent Assembly. *Uomo Qualunque* captured 5.3 percent of the vote for that body (discussed in chapter 5), electing thirty representatives. Yet with the defeat of the monarchy in the June 2 referendum, and King Umberto's subsequent exile, the Common Man Front began to decline.[33]

June 2: The Republic Is Born

On June 2 Italian voters cast two ballots, one passing judgment via referendum on the institutional question and the other electing representatives to a Constituent Assembly. Once the fate of the monarchy had been resolved, Prime Minister De Gasperi called for a jurisdictional "division of the tables," whereby the *Costituente* would devote its energies strictly to fashioning a new constitution (discussed in chapter 5 below), while his sitting Italian coalition government (formed in December of the previous year) would continue to legislate on all other matters. This pragmatic arrangement was adopted.

As the June 2 election date drew nearer, the Church become more and more outspoken in its support for the monarchy. As summed up by political scientist Norman Kogan:

> The issue was shifted from Monarchy vs. Republic to Monarchy vs. Communism to Christianity vs. Communism. On June 1, 1946, the day before the referendum, Pope Pius XII himself addressed the Italian people. Without mentioning republic or monarchy, he called on voters to choose between materialism and Christianity,

between the supporters and the enemies of Christian civilization. Given the context of the campaign, it would be difficult to misunderstand the plea. (For the English translation of the text, see the *New York Times,* June 2, 1946.)[34]

As long as the military campaign in the Italian theater continued to be waged, Allied officials preferred that Italy's monarchy remain in place, as it was the king who had signed the armistice and begun negotiating a peace treaty. Reinforcing the Church's pro-monarchist stance were highly placed conservative voices within the ACC. In an early January 1946 meeting with Count Enrico Galeazzi, Admiral Ellery Stone, then chief commissioner of the Allied Commission, voiced a strong preference for a monarchy. He feared that even Umberto II's

> regency would not be able to preserve the Monarchy as an institution. After a Regency would come a Republic, and thanks to the swing of the pendulum, Italy would have an extremist Republic, probably a Bolshevik one.[35]

The admiral questioned the robustness of the Christian Democratic Party's grassroots mobilizational capacity on the eve of the June votes. Given its position of strength coming out of the previous year, he found it reprehensible that it had not enrolled a far larger number of new party members. Therefore, the Church needed to step up its own mobilizing efforts on behalf of the party. Should the clergy hesitate, outside help would have to be brought in. The anti-extremist, pro-monarchist message needed to be reiterated continuously, something the Communists understood all too well. Concluding in American commercial terms, he insisted that "a product has to be pushed again and again in order to sell."[36]

Among rank and file Christian Democrats, sentiment about the Savoyard dynasty broke along generational lines. At a heated gathering of the DC Roman sectional leadership prior to the vote, Domenico Ravaioli argued vociferously in favor of the republic. Given pause by Ravaioli's combative rhetoric, De Gasperi invited new party commissioner Umberto Tupini to play down the issue. Consequently Tupini suggested that the institutional question was "just a matter of hats"—the Savoyard crown versus the republican Phrygian cap.[37] As witnessed by Leopoldo Elia, the youthful audience disagreed "tumultuously."[38]

Nenni's diary entries detail the Socialist leader's mounting impatience with the prime minister's agnosticism during the lead-up to the June 2 vote. In March, Nenni pressed De Gasperi to "finally move beyond a position of *ni* (a whimsical hybrid between *no* and *sì*)."[39] De Gasperi demurred. On another occasion, it was De Gasperi's turn to tease his counterpart: "Why are you so obsessed with this republic business? This issue will divide the Italian people. Why don't we drop it and put together a nice agrarian reform instead?"[40]

Many of De Gasperi's critics, within the party and outside of it, were frustrated at what they regarded as his abstract and ahistorical view of the monarchy. In comparison with other contemporary politicians, the Christian Democratic leader's thinking focused more on the choice between monarchy and republic as formal constitutional orders, than on the merits of the Savoy dynasty, with all of the historical baggage it carried. He ruminated over the relative merits of monarchies and republics over the centuries, distinguishing between "despotic" monarchies, in which the ruler is irresponsible, and others—such as Great Britain's—which are sanctioned constitutionally. Had there not been liberal monarchies? One has the impression that he wanted the answer to be yes—while regretfully acknowledging that it had often been not.[41]

De Gasperi fretted about what he called "the myth of the Republic," especially as it was forged during the French Revolution. Here he rejected the claims of doctrinaire republicans such as Nenni, without however embracing monarchism either. De Gasperi continued to fear the "leap in the dark" implied in a republican referendum outcome. He worried about the possible breakdown of the State, which in turn would open the door to a "revolutionary Convention" intent upon unpredictable and uncontainable radical action. Nenni's sometimes fiery calls for just such a Jacobin-like body alarmed him. It is worth recalling here a May 1945 remark of the Christian Democratic leader regarding his Socialist counterpart, "a man who has written articles, shouldered responsibilities, etc. But could this man maintain discipline within the Nation?" Alarmed at the continuing, surreptitious possession of arms by radical ex-partisans, De Gasperi also insisted that the State had to possess "the force and will" to uncover those weapons, adding threateningly "either one vouchsafes democracy" through such resolve or "one would confront reaction."[42]

On the other hand, was the preservation of the monarchy necessary to guarantee the continuity of the State? De Gasperi had his doubts.[43] Which of these contrasting concerns carried the greater weight in the Christian Democratic leader's mind, inclining him either in a pro-republican or pro-monarchist direction? The answer to this question remains unclear. Be that as it may, De Gasperi welcomed a pair of articles published in *Il Popolo* by party colleague Guido Gonella which emphasized the fact that the eventual convening of the Constituent Assembly to draft a republican constitution would not mean "starting from zero." Given the Trentine statesman's central European roots, it is not surprising that he paid attention to the role of referenda in the political evolution of the Weimar Republic, Austria, and Czechoslovakia, as well as Ireland, Spain, and Greece.[44]

To this day, opinion remains sharply divided as to how the Trentine statesman finally cast his ballot. Minister of the Royal House Falcone Lucifero and Allied Control Commission President Admiral Stone were of the opinion that the prime minister preferred a monarchy. Interestingly enough, several of the prime minister's outspokenly pro-republic party colleagues concurred in this assessment. De Gasperi's obfuscation on the issue prompted the resignation of Giuseppe Dossetti, the Christian Democrats' unabashedly republican vice president. Dossetti accused De Gasperi of "having done everything he could to swing the party's political weight behind the monarchy."[45]

Other contemporary testimony from the period suggests that, in the end, De Gasperi voted for the republic after all. This is the view espoused by eldest daughter Maria Romana, De Gasperi's sometime *dauphin* Giulio Andreotti, Socialist leaders Pietro Nenni and Giuseppe Romita, and ironically Umberto II. The king felt that, however diffident, De Gasperi's heart was with the republican cause. Historian Giovanni Sale has argued, quite plausibly, that De Gasperi's eventual, if hesitant, *scelta repubblicana* reflected his "political realism." Here, Sale continues, "We can see De Gasperi's greatness as a political leader: setting aside his personal preferences, knowing how to implement changes which were in the interest of his Nation, first and foremost, and also of his party."[46]

On the eve of the referendum, Pietro Nenni asked once again whether his Christian Democratic counterpart would divulge his intentions. De Gasperi replied, maliciously, the vote is secret, but then added, "I am willing to bet you that my 'black' Trentino will give more votes to the republic than your 'red' Romagna." Nenni interpreted this as a "republican nod" by De Gasperi.[47] For his part, fellow Christian Democrat Amintore Fanfani wrote years later of a conversation in which De Gasperi related having voted for the republic, but having done so with such *riservatezza* that his wife mistook her husband's intentions as monarchist, and had voted accordingly herself."[48] Maria Romana recalled the family's experience of the referendum somewhat differently, stating that her mother refused to divulge to anyone how she had voted, but that De Gasperi's sister had voted monarchist, leaving her and her father with the illusion (impression) of carrying a majority within the family.[49]

On the balance, the referendum's endorsement of a republic seems to have relieved De Gasperi. Along with top Allied officials, he had feared that a monarchist victory would provoke a left-wing coup attempt. During the lead-up to the vote, Nenni and Togliatti had each threatened that a monarchist outcome would be unacceptable.[50]

Italy's pro-monarchist forces were hardly reconciled to the outcome. The ensuing nine days brought convoluted, increasingly contentious negotiations between the council of ministers and King Umberto II and his entourage. An indefatigable De Gasperi played a critical intermediary role in the high-stakes stand-off. On the one hand, he led the council of ministers in agreeing on successive negotiating positions during tense, almost daily gatherings during the crisis. On the other hand, he carried on delicate face-to-face meetings with the king or with his Minister of the Royal House Falcone Lucifero.

The immediate aftermath of the referendum seemed unremarkable enough. Late on the evening of June 2, the prime minister conveyed the results of the vote to Lucifero, suggesting that he immediately inform Umberto. The next morning the prime minister visited the Quirinal. The cordial tenor of this meeting reflected the personal regard in which the young king continued to feel for his guest. While acknowledging that the "probable hypothesis of a republican outcome" had to be confirmed by the Court of Cassation, De Gasperi recommended that the royal family begin to make preparations for departure. By the evening of June 4, plans seemed to be in place for the entire royal family of eighteen persons to go into exile and take up residence in Lisbon. De Gasperi even offered to accompany the nervous Umberto II if it should prove necessary.[51]

On June 5, Minister of the Interior Giuseppe Romita released a detailed summary of the referendum vote, including total counts of 12,182,000 for the republic and 10,362,000 for the monarchy. A province-by-province breakdown of the vote revealed a dramatic split between the republican northern and central parts of the nation on the one hand and monarchist Mezzogiorno. In Ravenna, 88 percent of the voters embraced a republic; in Lecce, 85 percent cast their vote for monarchy.[52] In order to preempt pernicious rumors which might inflame public opinion (by implication, particularly in the South), De Gasperi was intent on addressing the public on the outcome of the vote, even though the Court of Cassation had not completed its work. That evening, De Gasperi went on the radio to address the nation. He urged the Italian people to remain "firm and united...to defend the nation against the intrigues and selfishness (*cupidigie*) of those who want to deprive Italy of the possibility of cooperating, according to the genius of its civilization, in the renewal of international life."[53]

As the electoral review process dragged on at the Court of Cassation, patience grew short, especially within monarchist circles, among the king's sympathizers at the Vatican, and—out of a concern for stability—within the Allied Commission. Over dinner on the evening of June 5, one American official sought to encourage the disconsolate Umberto II by suggesting, remarkably, that the king might think of becoming the president of the new republic.[54] Other backers of Umberto II took a firmer line. Speaking for himself, British Ambassador Sir Noel Charles indicated that a second referendum should be held, on the grounds that a constitutional monarchy "best suited Italy."[55]

Leading Liberals also began to insist on a second referendum. They argued that the total republican vote represented only a relative plurality over monarchist votes, and not an absolute majority of all votes cast. Blank ballots, invalid ballots, and contestable (unclear) ballots all needed to be tallied in the total vote column. In a country only just returning to the practice of free elections, it was not surprising that the number of such irregular ballots was high. Yet inexperienced local electoral officials had not processed or preserved such ballots in a consistent manner. In addition, rumors of outright fraud circulated widely, especially in the South. As the days passed and the Court of Cassation balked at declaring a definitive republican victory, monarchist opposition stiffened against accepting the vote. Interior Minister Romita and Prime Minister De Gasperi were accused of acting illegitimately when they made public the initial referendum results. A note published in the Liberal Party newspaper *Risorgimento Liberale* cast further doubt on the June 2 election, claiming that—suspiciously—more than a million votes were cast for the Constituent Assembly than valid votes were cast in the referendum.[56]

At the June 8 cabinet meeting, the issues surrounding the referendum vote provoked a fierce argument between the intransigently monarchist Liberal Cattani and the resolutely republican Socialist Nenni. De Gasperi cut the dispute short, observing that the important thing was to recognize and to remember that the Court of Cassation would have the final say on the matter. Togliatti also urged calm. "We have won a battle," the Communist chief said, "and we have to bring around the other side which balks at accepting the outcome of the referendum."[57]

But in many respects, the time for temporizing had passed. The cabinet turned to substantive issues such as the registration of legislative proclamations, the design of the seal and emblem of the state, the designation of a festival for the republic, and the handing out of sentences and granting of amnesties. The cabinet prevailed upon an initially reluctant De Gasperi to announce that he would become "provisional head of a republican state" upon the Court of Cassation's certification of the republican victory, scheduled in two more days (June 10).

This last step outraged the monarchists, who now accused the government of staging a virtual *coup d'etat*. Addressing the press the next morning, De

Gasperi dismissed such charges as completely unfounded. Speaking with uncharacteristic bluntness, he said, "It is crazy (*pazzesco*) that one could accuse a democratic government of engaging in a *coup d'etat*."[58] Rumors circulating at the time suggested rather that it was a group of the king's intemperate advisors who were beginning to push for a military putsch. Speaking on June 11, Togliatti declared that a *coup d'etat* seemed unlikely, "on the condition that the government proclaim with absolute firmness that it would defend itself."[59]

Privately, the Vatican applied its own pressure upon the prime minister. Various intermediaries between the Pope and the prime minister cautioned the latter against acting "unconstitutionally"—an unmistakable reference to the latter's assumption of the position of acting Head of State. This shot across the bow may have recalled to the proud De Gasperi the snub he had received from Sardinian bishops a month earlier. Suspicious of his attitude toward the embattled monarchy, the bishops had effectively boycotted the prime minister's public appearances on an official trip to the island.[60]

Finally, at 6:00 p.m. on June 10, in the Chamber of Deputies' *Sala del Lupo* (Hall of the Wolf), the nineteen members of the Court of Cassation rendered their judgment. In his *Dairies,* Nenni described the atmosphere as "grey and yet lacking in true solemnity."[61] In a cold, undemonstrative tone, Court President Pagano announced that the republic had amassed 12,672,767 votes and the monarchy 10,688,905. But to the government's dismay, Pagano went on to say that the definitive tally would have to wait for a subsequent session, after the Court had evaluated contested votes and associated protests, and after it had incorporated votes from districts which still had not reported. Even more troubling, and ambiguous, was the statement that the total number of persons casting votes, including those whose ballots were void, would need to be calculated before the outcome of the referendum could be officially proclaimed. Pagano's unexpected provisos lifted monarchist hopes that the referendum's outcome might be reversed.[62]

De Gasperi now exercised the role of interlocutor brilliantly, moderating the more intemperate voices within the cabinet on the one hand, while first coaxing and then insisting that the king accept the result of the referendum. In summarizing for his governmental colleagues the tenor of his conversations with Umberto II, De Gasperi repeatedly underplayed the unrealistic defiance of the sovereign. In this way, he extended as long as possible the opportunity for the monarch to see the light of reason.[63]

Mario Bracci's recollection of De Gasperi's behavior in this difficult meeting with Lucifero and the king bears quoting:

De Gasperi took on his most dignified manner (*anima sua di galantuomo*).... He did not wish for conflict, but was convinced of the justice of the government's position, knowing that the people—in the majority—wished for a republic. He felt that it was his duty to represent them honestly, and that he felt the moral weight of this duty even more than its political weight. It was indeed moving to see this soft-spoken (*mite*) man, whose political roots were not republican, who perhaps had expressed many times his sympathy for the sovereign and yet now, as a gentlemen, confront the crown calmly but decisively on behalf of the people: I am certain he will not turn back.[64]

Togliatti's cool-headedness also served the government well in weathering this period of crisis. As minister of justice, he held jurisdiction over the magistrates involved in validating the vote. True, he reacted with atypical vehemence when Court of Cassation President Pagano announced the referendum outcome on such an inconclusive note. Within a matter of twenty-four hours, Saverio Brigante, another member of the Court of Cassation, conveyed to Togliatti word that Pagano had ad-libbed in his announcement "in order to discredit the outcome of the referendum" and "to delay the definitive certification of the results." Brigante denounced Pagano's extraordinary improvisation to the other members of the Court, and then confronted the president of the Court directly. At this point, Pagano broke into tears, acknowledging his wrongdoing. At the June 12 meeting of the council of ministers, De Gasperi reported that the members of the Court had been polled, and that a follow-up announcement confirming a republican victory from the Court would be forthcoming. De Gasperi, Togliatti, and Nenni then agreed to discretely turn the page on Pagano's actions so as not to add further fuel to an atmosphere already replete with accusations of conspiracy and fraud.[65]

For his part, Umberto II kept all of the participants in the post-referendum drama on tenterhooks for three days, before finally departing the country for Portuguese exile on September 13. During the interim, members of his entourage begged, unsuccessfully, for some form of Allied intervention on the king's behalf. Others revived the idea of armed rebellion, and some southerners even suggested establishing a separatist monarchical regime in Naples and Sicily.[66] The strain of waiting for word, finally, of the king's leave-taking took its toll even on the unflappable De Gasperi. In an interview granted years later with journalist Antonio Gambino, Guido Gonella recalled his shock when he came upon the prime minister "stretched out on the armchair behind his desk, smoking"—something which he believed De Gasperi to have given up since his youth.[67]

At Rome's Ciampino airport, Umberto tempestuously denounced the government. In historian Denis Mack Smith's words, the king

> issued a defiant proclamation against what he called a *coup d'etat* by ministers who were acting illegally and as revolutionaries. He therefore refused to recognize the legality of the republic and in so doing ensured that the change of regime took place in the worst possible way with bitterness and recriminations on both sides.[68]

De Gasperi then issued a counterstatement decrying the "unworthy page of history," which now ended the monarchy:

> We must strive to understand the tragedy of someone who, after inheriting a military defeat and a disastrous complicity with dictatorship, tried hard in recent months to work with patience and good will towards a better future. Now this final act of the thousand-year House of Savoy must be seen as part of our national catastrophe; it is an expiation, an expiation forced upon all of us, even those who have not shared directly in the guilt of the dynasty.[69]

In the end, the prime minister's determination, prudence, and calm—in contrast to Umberto II's volatility and recriminatory leave-taking—had guided the ship of state through to safe harbor. The royal family had agreed to go into exile, however ungracefully, without unleashing a much feared civil war. Most importantly, De Gasperi's actions, along with those of Romita, Togliatti, and other ministers, had confirmed the sovereignty of the infant republic.

Little known at the time by the general public, the prime minister's patience and restraint during the nerve wracking two weeks following the referendum vote were much admired by his peers. As Pietro Nenni observed with relief in a journal entry dated June 14, calm now followed the storm. De Gasperi's radio address to the nation had been

> conciliatory but firm. It is fortunate that [De Gasperi] is the head of government at this moment. He did not help us much to promote the Republic, but he is helping greatly to see it through its first difficulties.[70]

For Nenni himself, the pro-republican referendum was the source of enormous satisfaction: in a career filled with political frustration, he regarded the creation of the republic as his "greatest victory," for "no one wanted it with a commitment" equal to his.[71]

Notes

1. Malgeri, *Alcide De Gasperi,* vol. II, 101–102.
2. Ibid. Archivo Storico Istituto Luigi Sturzo (hereafter ASILS), Diario Bartolotta, vol. VI, 378–380.
3. Gambino, *Storia del dopoguerra,* 113.
4. Craveri, *De Gasperi,* 207–208.
5. Malgeri, *Alcide De Gasperi,* vol. II, 11–13.
6. Ibid.
7. Franco Garofalo, *Un anno al Quirinale* (Milan: Garzanti, 1977), 104.
8. Gambino, *Storia del dopoguerra,* 117.
9. For a complete rundown of the new cabinet, see Fanello-Marcucci, *Primo governo De Gasperi,* 60–62.
10. Danilo Braschi. "Le forme di anti-communismo alle origini della repubblica," in Monino, *1945–1946,* 304.
11. Tamburrano, *Pietro Nenni,* 202.
12. Pietro Nenni, *Vento del Nord: giugno 1944-giugno, 1945* (Turin: Einaudi, 1978), 196–198.
13. Craveri, *De Gasperi,* 186–216; Fanello-Marcucci, *Primo governo De Gasperi,* 96.
14. Spencer Di Scala, *Reviving Italian Socialism: Nenni to Craxi* (Oxford: Oxford University Press, 1988), 31.
15. Ibid.
16. Gambino, *Storia del dopoguerra*, 62–66.
17. Ibid., 70, 108–109; *FRUS,* 1945, 4:982, Byrnes to Kirk, August 22, 1954.
18. Rosario Forlenza, *Le elezioni amministrative della prima repubblica: Politica e propaganda locale nell'Italia del secondo dopoguerra* (Rome: Donizelli, 2008), 11.
19. Ibid., 12.
20. Ibid., 12, 20.
21. A. Benedetti, "Ecco la settimana elettoriale dei milanesi. *Risorgimento Liberale,* April 5, 1946.
22. Patrizia Gabrielli, *Il 1946, le donne, la Repubblica* (Rome: Donizelli, 2009), 129.
23. Victoria De Grazia, *How Fascism Ruled Women: Italy, 1922–1945* (Berkeley: University of California Press, 1992).
24. Gabrielli, *1946,* 78–79.
25. Ibid.
26. Ibid., Gabrielli, *1946,* 50–51.
27. Jane Slaughter, *Women in the Italian Resistance, 1943–1945* (Denver: Arden Press, 1997). For a compelling memoir by a leftist Catholic member of the resistance struggle, see Tina Anselmi, *Storia di una passione politica* (Milan: Sperling & Kopfer, 2006).

28 Forlenza, *Elezioni amministrative*, 15.
29 Gabrielli, *1946*, 67.
30 David Kertzer, *Ritual, Politics and Power* (New Haven: Yale University Press, 1988), 61–69.
31 In the long run, Michele Battini has amply documented the fragility of this "political religion." Battini, "Una debole religione politica civica: il patriottismo costituzionale," in Monina, ed., *1945–1946*. 229–238.
32 For a comprehensive analysis of the results of both spring and fall rounds of 1946, see Forlenza, *Elezioni amministrative*, 37–59.
33 Norman Kogan, *A Political History of Post-War Italy* (New York: Praeger, 1966), 52, 60.
34 Ibid., 37.
35 Giovanni Sale, *Dalla monarchia alla repubblica, 1943–1946. Santa Sede, cattolici italiani e referendum* (Milan: Jaca Book, 2003).
36 Ibid.
37 References to the respective symbols appearing on the referendum ballots.
38 Leopoldo, Elia "De Gasperi e la questione istituzionale," in Monina, ed., *1945–1946*, vol. II, 20.
39 Nenni, *Tempo di Guerra Fredda*, 196.
40 Eugenio Scalfari, *Interviste ai potenti* (Milan: Mondadori, 1979), 24.
41 European University Institute Historical Archives, archivio Alcide De Gasperi (hereafter EUIHA, AADG), Serie Referendum Istituzionale.
42 Roberto Gualtieri, "La nascita della repubblica. Dibattito politico e transizione istituzionale," in *Monina 1945–1946*, vol. II, 9.
43 Ibid., Much depended on the spirit and scope of the coming *Costituente* in the event that the referendum backed a republic. Gambino, *Storia del dopoguerra*, 150–151.
44 Elia, "De Gasperi e la questione istituzionale," 23–24.
45 Sale, *Dalla monarchia alla repubblica*, 49; Malgeri, *Alcide De Gasperi*, vol. II, 145–146; Guido Formigoni, prefatory essay, *Alcide De Gasperi. Scritti e Discorsi Politici* III, I (Bologna: Il Mulino, 2008), 87; Craveri, *De Gasperi*, 230–240.
46 Sale, *Dalla monarchia alla repubblica*, 49.
47 Nenni, *Tempo di Guerra Fredda*, 224.
48 Craveri, *De Gasperi*, 260.
49 Nassi, *Alcide De Gasperi*, 243.
50 Miller, *United States and Italy*, 189–190; ACS, Togliatti comments at council of ministers' meeting, May 10, 1946, Verbali del Consiglio dei Ministri, b. 7, f. 29.
51 (Malgeri, *Alcide de Gasperi*, 148, 148n; Sale, *Dalla monarchia alla repubblica*, 159–160.
52 Ibid., 149.
53 Diario Bartelotta, cit., 1208–1209, 1218.
54 The American official in question is not identified here. Letter, Borgognoni Duca to Montini, June 6, 1946, Sale in his *Dalla monarchia alla repubblica*, 164.

55 Ibid., 169.
56 Malgeri, *Alcide de Gasperi,* vol. II, 151.
57 Ibid., 152.
58 De Gasperi, SDP, III, I, 933–934.
59 Mario Bracci, "Storia di una settimana (7–12 giugno 1946)," *Il Ponte* II, 7–8 (July–August 1946), 607, as cited in Malgeri, *Alcide De Gasperi,* 158.
60 Sale, *Dalla monarchia alla repubblica,* 46.
61 Nenni, *Tempo di Guerra Fredda,* 228.
62 Catti De Gasperi, *De Gasperi uomo solo,* 215–216; Aldo Mola, *Declino e crollo della monarchia in Italia: I Savoia dall'Unità al referendum del 2 giugno 1946* (Milan: Mondadori, 2006), 128.
63 Craveri, *Alcide De Gasperi,* 236.
64 Bracci, "Storia di una settimana," 158.
65 Gualtieri, "La nascita della *repubblica,* Monina, ed., *1945–1946,* vol. II, 101–103.
66 Mack Smith, *Italy and Its Monarchy,* 339.
67 Gambino, *Storia del dopoguerra,* 245.
68 Mack Smith, *Italy and Its Monarchy,* 340.
69 Ibid.
70 Nenni, *Tempo di Guerra Fredda,* 230.
71 Fallaci, *Interview with History,* 253.

Figure 1 Alcide De Gasperi (April 3, 1881 – August 19, 1954): Italian politician, photo dated January 31, 1950. Credit: Photo 12/Universal Images Group/Getty Images.

Figure 2 Portrait of Palmiro Togliatti (March 26, 1893 – August 21, 1964), Italian Communist Party leader. Photo dated December 1, 1944. Credit: Margaret Bourke-White/The LIFE Picture Collection/Getty Images.

Figure 3 Portrait of Pietro Nenni (February 9, 1891 - January 1, 1980), Italian Socialist Party leader. Photo dated December 1, 1944. Credit: Margaret Bourke-White The LIFE Picture Collection/Getty Images.

Figure 4 Victor Emmanuel III (November 11, 1869–December 28, 1947) King of Italy. Credit: INTERFOTO/Alamy Stock Photo.

Figure 5 The Italian President of the Council Alcide De Gasperi countersigning the Constitution observed by President of the Italian Republic Enrico De Nicola, Rome, December 27, 1947. Credit: Mondadori Portfolio/Getty Images.

Figure 6 Pietro Nenni giving a speech. Credit: The History Collection/Alamy Stock Photo.

Figure 7 The President of the Republic Luigi Einaudi talks with Minister of the Interior Mario Scelba and the secretary of the Italian Communist Party Palmiro Togliatti, during a reception at the Quirinal; standing on the left, the senator Umberto Terracini, Rome, June 2, 1952. Credit: Mondadori/Getty Images.

Figure 8 Italian Communist politician Palmiro Togliatti casting vote in the ballot box during elections, Rome, June 7, 1953. Credit: Keystone/Hulton Archive/Getty Images.

Figure 9 Alcide De Gasperi in his office in Rome, Italy, August 1, 1948. Credit: Keystone-France/Getty Images.

Figure 10 Façade of Montecitorio Palace, seat of Italian Chamber of Deputies, Rome (UNESCO World Heritage List). Lazio, Italy, seventeenth century. Credit: DeAgostini/Getty Images.

5

The Constitution and the Peace Treaty

Between mid-1946 and the beginning of 1948, Italy's leaders accomplished two crucial tasks: drafting a constitution for the republic and negotiating a peace treaty with the victorious Allies. In law as well as in fact, the republic renounced it Fascist past. Democracy officially replaced dictatorship and a peaceable foreign policy supplanted chauvinism and militarism. Even as Cold War animosities deepened at home and abroad, De Gasperi, Nenni, and Togliatti managed to bracket reciprocal distrust in realizing these milestones. Neither accomplishment came easily. American sympathy at the Paris Peace Conference and American economic aid thereafter—elicited largely by De Gasperi—proved vital in overcoming public anger at the peace treaty's harsh terms. The constitution was greeted with relief as it went into effect; its weaknesses would only be revealed in years to come.[1]

The Constitutional Compromise

The June 2 election of delegates to the *Costituente* (Constitutional Assembly) brought to a close the transitional governance of the country by the CLN, dating from 1944. This election ended the awkward parity of representation which had prevailed among the six anti-Fascist parties. The time had come to assess the real, grassroots strength of all of the country's parties. Some 25 million Italians cast their ballots—a figure representing 89.1 percent of eligible voters.

The outcome marked a clear victory for the Christian Democrats, who garnered 35.2 percent of the votes and 207 seats. The Socialists came in second with 20.7 percent of the vote and 115 seats. To their great disappointment, the Communists came in third with 18.9 percent and 104 seats. Among the minor parties, the Liberals and the Labor Democrats ran together (as the National Democratic Union) and received 6.9 percent and 41 seats. *Uomo Qualunque* received 5.3 percent and thirty deputies. The Republicans re-entered the fray with 4.4 percent of the vote and twenty-four seats. Several monarchist groups banded together (as the National Bloc of Freedom) while the once-promising Action Party collapsed, earning only 1.5 percent of the vote and only seven seats.[2]

At De Gasperi's behest, the Christian Democrats' strategy of avoiding an official position on the institutional question clearly paid off. In addition to party members both supporting and opposing the republic, it drew the votes of many monarchists drawn to it as a hedge against the Left. For the Socialists, the election was both encouraging and worrisome: in Nenni's colorful image, it rewarded the party with a rose—though one with thorns. The Socialists had garnered the mantle of the country's leading Marxist party. Yet the Christian Democrats had amassed over a third of the votes, almost twice the combined strength of the Socialists and Communists.[3]

On the basis of *Costituente* election outcome, De Gasperi set about forming a new governing coalition, embracing the DC, the PSI, the PCI, and the Republicans.[4] Still smarting from the defeat of the monarchy, the Liberal Party refused to enter a coalition alongside the two Marxist parties, save for the appointment of fiscal conservative Epicarmo Corbino as minister of the treasury.[5] In view of their tiny share of the election, the Action Party and the Democrats of Labor were also left out. Nenni entered the government as minister without portfolio, with the understanding that he would become foreign minister. De Gasperi reached out to Togliatti too, but the Communist leader chose not to enter the coalition, the better to concentrate on Communist Party matters.[6]

Meanwhile, the newly convened Constituent Assembly tabbed Socialist Giuseppe Saragat to serve as its first president. The choice of this energetic and well-spoken figure reflected the Socialist Party's second place showing in the June 2 balloting. Mindful of the need for equilibrium and calm as the assembly commenced its work, it was De Gasperi who recommended that a Socialist be selected, thus counterbalancing Christian Democratic pre-eminence. Saragat served as president for nine months. His successor was Communist Umberto Terracini, who guided Constituent Assembly until the completion of its work at the end of January 1948.

After picking its president, the Constituent Assembly's next order of business was to select a temporary head of state,[7] to serve in that office until the new constitution had been completed and gone into effect. Togliatti displayed characteristic prescience and realism in advancing the candidacy of the respected Liberal Neapolitan jurist Enrico De Nicola. De Nicola had already served, when still a young parliamentarian, as president of the Chamber of Deputies prior to the Fascist *ventennio*.[8] De Gasperi and Nenni soon rallied to De Nicola's banner, after having briefly backed other candidates. De Nicola was widely respected for his personal probity, seriousness, and sense of State. More importantly, the election of such a prominent monarchist promised to help rally to the new state the sizeable number of Italians who had shared his institutional preference. In De Gasperi's eyes, it was also important to select a southern Italian, given the fact that northerners already held the positions of prime minister (the Trentine De Gasperi) and president of the Constituent Assembly (the Piedmontese Saragat).[9]

Notwithstanding the backing of the country's major political leaders, the modest Neapolitan jurist waivered as to whether he would accept this nomination.[10] On behalf of his senior colleagues, Giulio Andreotti finally begged him, "Your Excellency, please, decide to decide if you can accept to accept." At last, De Nicola agreed to allow his name to be put in the ring. In a striking show of solidarity, 80 percent of the Constituent Assembly's members voted for him.[11]

In a florid June 25 inaugural address to the *Costituente*, De Nicola leaned heavily on tropes dating back to the Risorgimento. He vowed:

> [T]o the Italian people, through the Constituent Assembly—its direct and legitimate representative—that I will carry out my brief but intense mission as provisional head of state, guided by a single ideal: to faithfully and loyally serve my Nation ... We must focus on the only power at our disposal: our unbreakable unity. United, we will be able to surmount the enormous difficulties confronting us; lacking that, we will fall into an abyss from which we will not recover.
>
> The parties—necessary preconditions of parliamentary governments—must reconcile and direct their battles toward the realization of the common good ... to fight as one .... If it is true that the Italian people participated in a war which—as the Allies repeatedly acknowledged even in the most acute and bitterest period of hostilities—was imposed upon them contrary to their sentiments, their aspirations and their interests, it is no less true that they contributed ably to the final victory.[12]

De Nicola's rationalization of Italy's wartime behavior, however convoluted, resonated widely at the time in Italy. How different De Gasperi's humble, direct address would be to the assembled Allies at the Paris Peace Conference.

Following De Nicola's opening remarks, De Gasperi delivered a brief address of his own in the capacity of prime minister. He concisely conveyed his good wishes and high hopes for the assembly as it began its work, acknowledging the "elevated psychological temperature" of the day. He congratulated his countrymen for carrying through "modern Italy's greatest transition (*rivolgimento*) legally and peacefully," culminating in the democratic selection of Enrico De Nicola as provisional head of state.

De Gasperi stressed the importance of preserving the continuity of the State—the two-decade hiatus of Fascism notwithstanding. Counterbalancing this comment was a forward-looking invocation of the three great post-liberal and anti-Fascist ideologies of the day:

> With fervor, tenacity and disciplined effort, we have thrown a bridge across the abyss between two epochs, and have completed the lengthy work without loss of men or materials. Three great national forces contributed to this remarkable accomplishment: the universal tendencies of Christianity, the humanitarian tendencies of Mazzini, and the solidarity and organized strength of labor."[13]

Missing from De Gasperi's trio of national forces, interestingly enough, was the Risorgimento liberalism of Camillo De Cavour.[14]

In concluding his remarks, De Gasperi reached out to a foreign audience, urging the Allied Powers then gathered in Paris to finalize peace terms for Italy not to humiliate or to undercut Italy's nascent, many-faceted democracy, which would be tantamount to "asphyxiating a newborn." Invoking Enlightenment rights language, he beseeched the Allies to permit Italy to

> fulfill the international mission which history and nature had vouchsafed for it... rather than risk extinguishing Italy's light, both new and old, at a time when the world already threatens to slide back into the darkness of the past.[15]

Given the occasion, the prime minister's address was quite brief, requiring only five minutes to deliver. Nenni was disappointed in the entire opening day, including De Gasperi's remarks, which he felt launched the *Costituente* on a distressingly perfunctory note.[16] In his diary entry for the day, Nenni judged the prime minister's speech severely, describing it as "two words which rapidly disappeared into a void."[17] Why didn't the prime minister choose to address the Constituent Assembly at greater length? One possibility, implicit in Nenni's comment, is that De Gasperi's brevity symbolically betrayed his continuing reticence over the *Costituente*'s powers.[18] Very different was Togliatti's address, linking

> the Republic and the Constitution to... a grand tradition, to a profound hope of all of the Italian people: the hope of finally having gathered an Assembly which can—in accordance with the needs and aspirations expressed by the entire population—set about a profound renewal of the nation's political, economic and social life.[19]

Nor was the Socialist leader impressed by the much longer remarks which De Gasperi delivered on July 15. On that occasion, De Gasperi presented the principles and policies which would characterize his newly formed quadripartite government. He reassured his audience that this government had preserved its predecessor's ideological balance, even though the rightist Liberal and leftist Action parties had refrained from joining it. By way of illustration, he offered a blunt equation. If, on the one hand, the Lateran Accords were to be retained in the republican constitution and if, for the first time, a Christian Democrat (Guido Gonella) had now assumed the post of minister of public instruction, this was balanced by a Communist remaining in charge of the ministry of justice.

Already in that address, tensions separating the Left from the Center-Right began to spill over. Pressed on the subject of a *premio* (an economic aid package directed especially at impoverished Italians), De Gasperi responded that its effect on the budget would have to be considered before a decision could be reached. At this point, a voice from the Left burst out "Corbino will decide!" The prime minister curtly observed that "the mania of continual *ad hominem* attacks" would "render impossible cordial and active collaboration within the government."[20] Exchanges of this kind were to be expected since the Communists and their Socialist partners had been expelled from the government seven weeks earlier. Yet the "separation of tables" held. As Communist Giorgio Amendola observed:

> At the time that the May 1947 crisis[21] occurred, the work of the *Costituente*'s had as of yet achieved but limited progress. Collaboration between the Communists, Socialists and Christian Democrats had functioned positively, particularly in the commissions.[22]

Amendola added that once his party was

> forced into an oppositional role, it had no choice but to make that opposition bitter. Yet it had to constrain that opposition within limits so that the constitution could be completed, because a crisis within the *Costituente* would have tremendously grave consequences, running the risk of destroying the accomplishments of the Resistance.[23]

An important early focus of deliberation concerned the form and competence of parliament under the republic. De Gasperi, Nenni, and Togliatti all envisioned a strong legislative branch vis-à-vis the executive. Initially, but unsuccessfully, the Communist promoted a monocameral chamber in lieu of a more traditional bicameral body consisting of a Chamber of Deputies and a Senate. A single legislative chamber would, they claimed, guarantee maximum expression of the will of the electorate, though at the cost of increased governmental instability.

In his 1943 *Idee ricostruttive della Democrazia Cristiana*, De Gasperi had identified parliament as preeminent among the branches of the state, in virtue of its status as supreme embodiment of the national community.[24] In September 1946, the prime minister gathered Catholics from within and outside the party at St. Paul Cathedral to deliberate various constitutional options still in the air. According to the testimony of Giuseppe Dossetti, De Gasperi firmly opposed the option of creating a presidential model of government, defying Vatican pressure in favor of the latter.[25]

On the floor of the Constituent Assembly, De Gasperi intervened to dissuade several party colleagues from following the West German precedent and creating a stronger, chancellor-like prime ministership. This attitude seems to have derived in part from De Gasperi's fears that the Socialist-Communist opposition might benefit from a more powerful prime ministership, should they win the first national parliamentary elections. For their part, the Socialists and Communists also opposed a stronger prime ministership, for fears of their present foes.[26]

The main body of the new constitution's text was divided into an opening section entitled "Fundamental Principles," followed by two parts: part I addressed "Rights and Duties of Citizens," while part II dealt with the "Organization of the Republic." The opening section and first part conveyed the progressive aspirations especially of the country's left-leaning, anti-Fascist parties. In the words of Florentine Action Party lawyer Piero Calamandrei, these early sections embraced "the spirit of the Resistance given juridical expression."[27] Part I's opening three articles strikingly recall the language of France's 1791 "Declaration of the Rights of Man and Citizen." An important symbolic victory for the Left was the affirmation that the republic was "founded on labor." Article 2 invoked Mazzini's renowned pairing of "inviolable rights" with "binding duties" as these pertain to the individual on the one hand, and to "social formations" on the other.

As constitutional scholar Nicola Occhiocupo has elaborated, it is through social formations that:

> [S]ociety itself takes form, and where individuals 'shape' their personalities. Typical social formations include (but are not limited to) the family, the school, churches, political parties, unions, workers' groups as a whole, business enterprises, cooperatives, etc.[28]

Article 49 affirmed the indispensable role of pivotal role of political parties in the functioning of democracy, stating that "All citizens have the right to freely associate in political parties, through which they compete democratically to shape the nation's policies." Speaking to the Constituent Assembly on July 24, 1946, Palmiro Togliatti anticipated the language of that article in asserting that "the parties embody democracy in the process of organizing itself, conquering definite positions that will never be lost again."[29] "We come from far away and we are moving far ahead," Togliatti asserted, "Without a doubt! Our goal is the creation in our Country of a society of free and equal persons, a society liberated from the exploitation by some men over other men."[30]

In a brief retrospective article about the Communist leader, Ferruccio Parri praised his contribution to the first portion of the Constitution, while also expressing disappointment that Togliatti and other Communist participants had not focused more on matters of institutional structure,[31] for example:

> Those essential factors (the imposing bureaucratic apparatus of the State, the concrete organization of the ministries, the efficiency of public administration) without which an effective operation of government can be exercised.[32]

By September 1946, Togliatti and Terracini themselves realized that their party comrades needed to pay more attention to juridical questions.[33]

Part II of the Constitution focused on foundational—if at times mundane—aspects of administration structure and procedure. Many of its provisions reflect the typical conventions of modern European parliamentarism. Two noteworthy breaks from the pre-Fascist State, as it had been defined by the Piedmontese *Statuto* (constitution) of 1848, were the establishment of a supreme Constitutional Court,[34] and the creation of regions to facilitate a measure of decentralization.[35] Yet lacking implementing legislation, these innovations were not realized until 1955 and 1970, respectively. A major reason for these delays, as we will see in Chapter 6, was the deepening of the Cold War and the concomitant determination of the ruling Christian Democrats to hold off implementing constitutional provisions which might benefit the leftist opposition.

While the constitution was still being drafted, the *Costituente* remained largely free from partisan maneuvers. It was Togliatti and Nenni—more than De Gasperi—who contributed most substantially to the drafting process. Of fundamental importance were the Communist leader's remarks concerning the place of political parties, as noted above. In contrast to Nitti, who remained nostalgic for the traditional, pre-Fascist "parties of notables," he championed the new, popularly based parties in the following terms: "the parties are necessary for democracy when—let us be frank—they transcend a little, oligarchic circle of several hundred thousand voters... instead bringing into the political arena 25,000,000 men and women."[36]

Togliatti also contributed in a major way to the defining of "the rights and duties of citizens." In the work of several assembly sub-commissions, he entered into productive deliberations with both the Socialists and with leftist Christian Democrats. He prepared a broad-ranging report on the subject of "social rights" which contributed in a major way to article 3 of the final text.[37] Already at the PCI's fifth party congress in December 1945, Togliatti looked forward to the convening of the *Costituente* with the following words:

> We require a Constitution, which permanently buries a past of social conservatism and reactionary tyranny, vowing to keep it from ever rising again. This means a Constitution whose originality will consist in being, in a certain sense, a blueprint for the future.[38]

Pietro Nenni's substantive engagement in the drafting of the republican constitution dated from mid-1945, when he assumed the role of minister for the *Costituente*.[39] His service in that role, frustrating as it often was, ended in mid-June 1946, when he submitted his resignation from that post. Indicative of deepening differences between De Gasperi and Nenni was the "laconic and bureaucratic" acknowledgment of the resignation which the Christian Democratic leader then sent to his Socialist counterpart.[40] Campaigning for delegates to the Constituent Assembly, the Socialist Party set forth a broad, if rather generic, vision of a new constitution, which would vouchsafe political, social, and economic equality "appropriate to a modern State." Nenni characteristically distilled that platform into a four-point pledge to promote "unity, democracy, secularism and sociability."[41]

De Gasperi was not particularly interested in matters of jurisprudence or constitutional engineering. He was more concerned about the overarching ethos of a government than in its specific institutional form. This bent of the prime minister has left him open to accusations—perhaps with some justification—of undervaluing the legitimizing force of the constitution as a formal document, as compared with the importance of the government's obtaining the consent and trust of the citizenry. In the proceedings of the *Costituente,* it fell to Christian Democratic colleagues like Guido Gonella to enunciate in detail how the party's fundamental political values should best be translated into constitutional language. Between the assembly's opening session on June 25, 1946, and its final meeting on January 18, 1948, De Gasperi's addresses to the *Costituente* referred fulsomely to domestic and international issues of the day rather than to specific juridical matters facing the assembly.[42]

Nenni's criticisms of both the form and the focus of De Gasperi's addresses to the assembly on June 25 and July 15 have already been noted. Togliatti repeatedly took De Gasperi to task on the same two grounds. On July 3, Togliatti's depiction of the prime minister was both cautious and condescending:

> I have heard many say that De Gasperi is an honest democrat. I have reservations; I would define him rather as an honest conservative. He still lacks some qualities which I hope he could acquire when stimulated by friendly criticism from our side of the assembly.[43]

In one of several lengthy articles published in the party paper *Rinascita* the year following the Christian Democrat's passing, Togliatti recalled that:

> De Gasperi abstained, deliberately and ostentatiously, from whatever participation in the work of the assembly for the formation of the new Constitution, making an exception only for the vote on article 7. His duties directing the activity of the government do not justify this absence, if one bears in mind the entire months spent, later, on propaganda tours across the country at election times. Prevalent in him, in this period, was true indifference for debates dedicated to an organic and programmatic solution to the major questions surrounding the construction of the new State. He preferred, from time to time, to devote himself to convenient partial solutions dictated by contingent necessities of the moment, thus revealing his political empiricism—another trait of his political personality—and perhaps the most important of all.[44]

Article 7 affirmed that:

> The State and the Catholic Church are, each in its own sphere, independent and sovereign. Their relations are regulated by the Lateran Pacts. Modifications of the Pacts, accepted by the two parties, do not require the procedure for constitutional amendments.

Over the preceding two years, the Vatican had pressed unremittingly for this outcome. The autonomy provided by the 1929 pact had enabled the Church to carry out its *magisterium* with considerable latitude, proclaiming Catholicism Italy's official religion of state. Henceforth, instruction in religion became mandatory in all public elementary and secondary schools, along with private and parochial institutions. Instruction in the catechism had in fact been included in the nation's elementary curricula since the period of the Liberal Monarchy; the Church was now able to extend that compulsory presence at the secondary level.[45] Catholic-sponsored youth organizations were also permitted—though Mussolini and Pius XI clashed two years later when the Fascist regime tried to shut them down because they had become too political.

Upon its signature in 1929, the pact had received severe criticism from the anti-Fascist underground. Togliatti then scorned the pact as officially codifying the alliance of throne and altar in defense of the capitalist interests of the Italian bourgeoisie. Alberto Cianca, writing in the newspaper of the Paris anti-Fascist Concentration, spoke of a "return to the theocratic middle ages and the temporal power of the pope."[46]

Vehemently opposing article 7 when it arose in the *Costituente* were the Socialists, Actionists, and Liberals. The terms of article 7, they noted, contradicted the freedom of religion guaranteed elsewhere in the text of the constitution. More broadly, article 7 exonerated the Church from the Faustian bargain it had struck with Mussolini's regime.

It was a great shock to his leftist compatriots when Togliatti decided to support article 7. He now argued the continuing necessity for establishing religious peace in Italy. In his calculation, the overriding benefit of this concession was that it buttressed his party's all-important ongoing dialogue with Catholics, both within and outside of the DC. Dutifully following their leader's wishes, on March 25, all members of the Communist delegation save one voted to include the Lateran Accords in the new constitution.[47]

Nenni opposed the formal inclusion of article 7 in the new constitution on the grounds that a tolerant spirit was already taking root in the hearts of most Italians. On April 1, the Socialist party leadership collectively denounced article 7's recent approval. The Catholic Church certainly deserved "sovereignty" in the specific areas of society which directly concerned it, but that did not negate the fundamentally secular nature of the State. The deeply religious dimensions of Italian society did not and should not be allowed to compromise "the moral values of the individual conscience."[48]

Over the next half year, the delegates of the *Costituente* turned their attention to many other articles, none of which were as controversial as article 7. Finally, on December 22, 1947, the assembly ratified the constitution by a margin of 453–62. On January 1, 1948, the republic was formally inaugurated.

Notwithstanding its overwhelming endorsement, however, the republican constitution had its flaws. Pressed to provide the nation with much-needed juridical direction, the members of the *Costituente* left many implementational provisions open. In February 1948, the Court of Cassation established a distinction between portions of the constitution which were immediately valid (*norme precettizie*) and those that were programmatic and would only come into effect with separate, subsequent enabling action (*norme programmatiche*). This delayed the realization of key features of the constitution. The Constitutional Court was formed only in 1956, the

Supreme Council of the Magistracy only in 1958, and full implementation of regional governance for all twenty of the nation's regions not until 1970. Other progressive articles, such as article 4 recognizing "the right to work," remained dead letters.[49]

For all of the inconsistencies and delays encountered in the implementation of the republican constitution, it has weathered seventy years of tumultuous history, continuing to serve as an essential political benchmark. June 2 is a major civic holiday, marking as it does the anniversary of both the referendum on the monarchy and the election of members to the Constituent Assembly. Prior to June 2, the major holiday following the fall of Fascism had been June 4, commemorating the liberation of Rome. Not all Italians were comfortable with this earlier ceremonial watershed. Had the government of Ivanoe Bonomi had its way, the first anniversary would have passed with little fanfare, for fear of excessive demonstrations by former partisans. From a different direction, youthful members of Catholic Action embraced the memory of June 4, associating in with the Pope's role as *defensor civitatis*.[50] This development in turn prompted the State to get more involved, in order to preserve adequate focus on the civil side of the event.[51] Successive governmental leaders have dealt with civil holidays in different ways. For his part, De Gasperi preferred to downplay the theatricality of these anniversary events, and consequently kept his own remarks brief and low-keyed.[52]

A Punitive Peace

As the elaboration of the constitution proceeded, another pressing task faced De Gasperi's government. Painful negotiations dragged out in Paris over the peace treaty among the Allied powers, with the United States and the Soviet Union clashing over the latter's insistence on a draconian settlement. At last a text was finalized, and an Italian delegation headed by De Gasperi came to the Parisian capital. De Gasperi demonstrated his remarkable sense of State in his measured, thoughtful presentation to the Allied powers on August 10, 1946. The latters' hostility was painful to him, if not unexpected.

"As I begin my remarks before this international assembly," he said, "I feel, notwithstanding your personal courtesy, that everything is against me: above all, my identity as an ex-enemy."[53] Notwithstanding that reality, the prime minister continued:

I feel the responsibility and the right to speak also as a democratic anti-Fascist, as the representative of the new Republic which, harmonizing within itself the humanistic aspirations of Giuseppe Mazzini, the universal principles of Christianity and the internationalist hopes of the workers, turns whole heartedly to that lasting and reconstructive peace which you seek, and towards that cooperation among peoples which it is your duty to fashion.[54]

At the conclusion of the Italian prime minister's speech, American Secretary of State James Byrnes spontaneously stood to shake De Gasperi's hand as he departed the silent hall. This handshake was consistent with Byrnes' independent spirit: historian James Miller has described the American secretary of state as a "moderate conservative with great political skills, including a superb negotiating technique."[55] Nevertheless, this gesture did not sit well with Byrnes' fellow Allied officials, who had agreed to keep the Italian leader at arm's length.

Byrnes' compassionate gesture may have touched the Italian prime minister, but it did not mitigate a very harsh settlement. Despite American efforts to soften its terms, the treaty was quite punitive, dispersing Italy's navy and imposing economic reparations totaling $360 million to Greece, Albania, the Soviet Union, and Ethiopia, amongst others.[56] In addition, Italy was forced to renounce her African colonies, and to cede the Dodecanese Islands to Greece, major parts of Venezia Giulia to Yugoslavia and several Alpine valleys in the northwest to France. Trieste became an international city pending further negotiation. The predictably destabilizing effects of such a treaty on Italy's neophyte democratic regime did not enter into the calculations of the Allied victors.

Togliatti complicated De Gasperi's already difficult task when he and several party colleagues showed up unannounced in Paris. The Communists took exception to De Gasperi "over-ambitious" push to have the prospective treaty respect Italy's territorial claims and permit Italian entry into the United Nations. Instead, the prime minister should have focused on more modest issues. The prime minister was taken to task for postponing resolution of the Trieste's status, which at the time was claimed by both Italy and Yugoslavia. Postponement of this question, it was argued, would only impede Italian-Yugoslav relations, prolong the presence of Allied troops in Italy, and exacerbate relations between the Great Powers. De Gasperi and much of the Italian press denounced the Communists' "inopportune" interference on this matter. Pietro Nenni tried to play peacemaker in this situation, acknowledging the Communists' right to criticize. At the same time, Nenni stood resolutely behind the efforts of De Gasperi and his delegation and praised the prime minister for his address of August 10.[57]

The Italian public reacted with bitterness when the terms of the treaty were announced. De Gasperi's political prestige suffered a major blow. Again, demonstrating his instinct for political timing, De Gasperi requested that the victorious powers ratify the treaty on their end before it came to a vote in Italy. Moving slowly, he hoped, would also permit public resentment at the terms of the treaty to abate. He hoped as well that, in time, the Allies themselves would soften and rethink some of that document's provisions. This strategy met with a measure of success when in early 1948, the Allies did remove the most painful clause of the treaty by conceding that Trieste was an Italian city.[58]

Influential American journalists empathized with the embattled prime minister. Writing in the *New York Times,* Anne O'Hare McCormick praised De Gasperi's remarks for elevating the tone of the conference. "How ironic," she continued, "he should suffer punishment for sins that he had fought against his entire life." In his syndicated column, Walter Lippman voiced similar sentiments. "Mr. De Gasperi is no ex-enemy statesman." Instead, he has been "always our ally and the partisan of the civilization which the war was fought to defend."[59]

A month before the treaty ratification, De Gasperi visited the United States at the invitation of *Time/Life Magazine* editor Henry Luce. The plane trip across the Atlantic encountered such fierce headwinds that it had to backtrack as far the Azores for more fuel. Finally approaching American shores, De Gasperi had a telling exchange with his daughter Maria Romana, whom he had invited to assist him. "Papa," she said to him, "it seems like you have to pass a test." Apprehensively, he agreed:

> It is true; I will have to present myself to a group of men unfamiliar with my history, my language or my life, whom I must convince that I merit their trust. This is all I may ask for: trust in my personal and political sincerity, faith in my commitment to the democratic method, and consequently hope for the support they may offer to help sustain my government. The Americans will ask, who can guarantee that this De Gasperi will still be in office six months from now? In Paris and in London I am treated as an ex-enemy; but I have been invited to Cleveland simply as a member of the human race. Still, I must be accepted as a friend if I am to win points in Italy's favor.[60]

During his twelve-day tour, he delivered widely heralded addresses in Cleveland, Chicago, and New York. His speech to at the Cleveland Council of World Affairs was particularly memorable. De Gasperi began by asking his listeners to forgive his halting English. He assured them that his intention was not to address unfavorable international decisions. Acknowledging that the council's basic purpose was to inform American public opinion, he presented himself "as a free man talking to free citizens." He promised to

> speak frankly, as I know that is this is what you expect from me. I speak as an Italian, an Italian who has never been to America but who has always believed firmly in the principles which undergird American democracy. I draw inspiration from an ancient and humanistic tradition (*civiltà*) which you all know.[61]

Upon his arrival in New York five days later, De Gasperi was

> treated as a conquering hero. The city's political establishment, the Catholic Church's hierarchy and the entire range of Italian-Americans turned out to toast democratic Italy and its prime minister. De Gasperi made a trans-Atlantic broadcast to Italy and another special broadcast to Italian-Americans.[62]

In New York as well, Cardinals Stricht and Spellman offered cordial help, organizing dinners and receptions and facilitating contacts. Especially useful were the introductions they arranged with men of finance, some of whom had flown in from as far away as San Francisco.[63]

By the end of his American sojourn, De Gasperi, ably assisted by Italy's ambassador to the United States Alberto Tarchiani, won three key concessions from the Truman administration. America would allow Italy to purchase—on favorable terms—fifty liberty ships. On January 8, the American treasury secretary presented De Gasperi a check for $50 million, and on January 13, the Export-Import bank offered an additional $100 million credits in reconstruction aid.[64]

The prime minister's successful American trip did not, however, offset the profound disappointment and rancor which the peace treaty provoked across the Italian political spectrum. After months of vituperation directed at the Allies—and at De Gasperi himself for not having secured more concessions from those powers—the Constituent Assembly debated the document's ratification between July 23 and 31. Among others, Orlando, Croce, and Togliatti harshly criticized the treaty. Nevertheless, the treaty was ratified on July 31.[65]

De Gasperi next faced the task of cajoling a sullen Enrico De Nicola to sign the text of the treaty. From the moment De Nicola had assumed the role of provisional head of state, he had made no secret of his deep aversion to the punitive nature of the treaty. He was outraged that his nation had virtually been treated at Paris on par with Nazi Germany, a fact that shamefully disregarded Italy's contribution as a cobelligerent to the defeat of that enemy.

In preparation for what was sure to be a tense solicitation with De Nicola, De Gasperi took the unusual step of penning, in his own elegant script, a letter to his executive counterpart, the better to make absolutely clear every clause of that document. This gesture was the more meaningful given the temperamental distance separating the two men. A stickler for decorum, De Nicola was respected for his objectivity and impartiality in legal and constitutional matters. Proper in his own way, De Gasperi was far more pragmatic in pursuing his chosen political ends.

Accompanied by Foreign Minister Sforza and several others, including his advisor, the University of Rome professor Mario Toscano, De Gasperi visited De Nicola at his office in the Palazzo Giustiniani. Speaking on behalf of the prime minister, it was Toscano who repeatedly invited De Nicola to sign. The latter repeatedly asked in reply, "so you insist?" On the third such exchange, De Nicola burst out, face flushed, shouting, "If it is like this, I shall not sign," grabbing the document and throwing it to the floor. It fell to Toscano to calm De Nicola, and finally to obtain his consent.[66]

Notes

1. My fundamentally sympathetic take on these two milestones cuts against considerably more critical assessments by many Italian historians. See in this regard P. Vercellone, "The Italian Constitution of 1947–48," in Stuart J. Woolf, ed., *The Rebirth of Italy* (New York: Humanities Press, 1972) 121–134, as well as Pietro Scoppola's survey of Italian historiography on the constitution in *La repubblica dei partiti*, 161–173. On the peace treaty, see Roberto Faenza and Marco Fini, *Gli Americani in Italia* (Milan: Feltrinelli, 1976), 170–172, and Norman Kogan's detailed analysis of the peace treaty negotiations in his *Political History of Postwar Italy*, 13–27.
2. Ginsborg, *History of Contemporary Italy*, 99–100.
3. Tamburrano, *Pietro Nenni*, 181.00
4. The latter party had been excluded from the first De Gasperi coalition on the grounds of its doctrinaire anti-monarchism.
5. Ginsborg, *History of Contemporary Italy*, 95.
6. Agosti, *Palmiro Togliatti*, 172–176.
7. Thus replacing De Gasperi, who had reluctantly agreed to take on the post at the height of the institutional referendum crisis, as noted above in chapter 4.
8. Francesco Barbagallo, *Storia dell'Italia repubblicana: La costruzione della democrazia dalla caduta del fascismo agli anni cinquanta* (Turin: Einaudi, 1994), 19–20.

9   Gambino, *Storia del dopoguerra*, 257.
10 Ibid.
11 Ginsborg, *History of Contemporary Italy*, 99.
12 Typescript summary prepared by Francesco Bartolotta, Istituto Luigi Sturzo Archivio Storico (hereafter ILSAS), and fondo Francesco Bartolotta, and busta 1946 XVII.
13 De Gasperi, "Intervento all' Assemblea Costituente," June 25, 1947, in *SDP*, III, I, 219.
14 Paolo Pombeni, "De Gasperi costituente," *Quaderni degasperiani* I (2009), 99.
15 De Gasperi, "Intervento all' Assemblea Costituente," June 25, 1947, in *SDP*, III, I, 219.
16 Nenni, *Tempo di Guerra Fredda*, 234.
17 Ibid., 234.
18 See in this regard David Kertzer's remarks on political ceremony and legitimation in *Ritual, Politics and Power*, 37–38.
19 Norberto Bobbio, *Dal fascismo all democrazia. I regimi, le ideologie, le figure e la cultura poltica* (Milan: Baldini and Castoldi, 2002), 310.
20 SDP, III, I, 271.
21 Described below in chapter 6.
22 Cited in Bocca, *Togliatti*, 413.
23 Ibid.
24 Leopoldo Elia, Lectio, *2005: Alcide De Gasperi e l'Assemblea Costituente* (Rome: Istituto Luigi Sturzo, 2005).
25 Ibid., 42–43.
26 Ibid.
27 See Calamandrei's three essays on this topic appearing in his newly founded journal *Il Ponte*, issues II and III. Calamandrei was one of the Action Party's few delegates to the *Constituente*.
28 Nicola Occhiocupo, "La Corte costituzionale," in Silvano Labriola, ed., *Valori e principi del regime repubblicano 3. Legalità e garanzie* (Bari: Laterza, 2002), 474.
29 Palmiro Togliatti, *Discorsi parlamentari*, I (Rome: Riuniti, 1984).
30 http://www.miglioriaforismi.com/2012/04/palmiro-togliatti-aforismi-e-frasi.html, accessed November 5, 2018.
31 Parri, "In memoria di Palmiro Togliatti," 89.
32 Renzo Martinelli, "La politica del Pci nel periodo costituente. Il rapporto di Palmiro Togliatti al Comitato centrale del 18–19 settembre 1946," *Studi Storici* 32:2 (April–June 1991), 494.
33 Ibid., 58–59, 63.
34 For a cogent analysis of this, for Italy, unprecedented institution, see Kogan, *Political History of Post-War Italy*, 117–119.

35 Another significant shift in the direction of enhanced democratic sovereignty was a provision for the direct election of senators, with the exception of a few life senators, such as ex-presidents of the republic.
36 Bobbio, *Dal fascismo alla democrazia*, 310.
37 Agosti, *Palmiro Togliatti*, 186–187.
38 Sandro Guerrieri, "*Il PCI e il processo constituente*," in Monina, ed., *1945–1946*, 51.
39 D'Angelo Bigelli, *Pietro Nenni*, 245–246.
40 Maurizio Degl'Innocenti, "*I socialisti*," in Monina, ed., *1945–1946*, 128.
41 Ibid., 133.
42 The full text of each of these presentations is reproduced in SDP, III, I, 218–511.
43 Bocca, *Togliatti*, 401.
44 Palmiro Togliatti, "È possible un giudizio equanime sull'opera di Alcide De Gasperi?" in *De Gasperi il resaturatore*, 99.
45 White, *Progressive Renaissance*, 25.
46 Alberto Cianco, "Il medioevo che ritorna," *La liberta'* (February 17, 1929), cited in Malgeri, *Alcide De Gasperi*, vol. II, 298.
47 Ginsborg, *History of Contemporary Italy*, 101.
48 Degl'Innocenti, "*I socialisti*," in Monina, ed., 1945–1946, 134, 195.
49 In Piero Calamandrei's deft formulation, "to compensate the forces of the left for a *rivoluzione mancata* [unrealized revolution], the forces of the right were not opposed to incorporating into the Constitution a *rivoluzione promessa* [promised revolution]. On the constitution, see Ginsborg, *History of Contemporary Italy*, 100–101.
50 Literally, "savior of the civilization that Rome represented." Logan, "Pius XII," 241.
51 Yuri Guaiana, *Il Tempo della Repubblica. Le feste civili in Italia (1943–1946)* (Milan: Unicopli, 2007), 69–71.
52 Ibid., 157.
53 Alcide De Gasperi, "Discorso al forum di Cleveland" (January 10, 1947) in Capurso, ed., *Discorsi*, 198.
54 Ibid.
55 Miller, *United States and Italy*, 170.
56 Hughes, *United States and Italy*, 148–152; Matt Frei, *Italy, The Unfinished Revolution* (London: Mandarin, 1996), 51; Miller, *United States and Italy*, 146–149, 193–205.
57 Sale, *De Gasperi gli USA e il Vaticano*, 36–37.
58 Frei, *Italy: The Unfinished Revolution*, 52.
59 Steven White, "De Gasperi through American Eyes: Media and Public Opinion, 1945–1953," *Italian Politics and Society* 61 (Fall/Winter 2005), 15.
60 Catti De Gasperi, *De Gasperi uomo solo*, 242.
61 Alcide De Gasperi, "Speech to the Cleveland forum" (January 10, 1947), in Capruso, ed., *Discorsi*, 211–212.

62 Miller, *United States and Italy,* 218.
63 Sale, *De Gasperi gli USA e il Vaticano,* 62.
64 Iuso, *Lezioni sul secondo dopoguerra (1945–1960),* 134; Craveri, *De Gasperi,* 271–277.
65 Malgeri, *Alcide De Gasperi.* vol. II, 246–254; Iuso, *Lezioni sul secondo dopoguerra,* 134.
66 Toscano's account of this dramatic episode was subsequently published in the journal *Nuova Antologia.*

6

Toward April 18, 1948

The years leading up to the April parliamentary elections saw the United States and the Vatican drawn ever deeper into Italian politics. American Ambassador to Italy James Dunn orchestrated a multipronged economic, political, and diplomatic intervention to help defeat the Communist-Socialist Popular Front. For its part, the Vatican attacked "Godless" communism, in contradistinction to venerable Catholic customs and values vouchsafed above all by the Holy Father. Implicitly and explicitly, the intended beneficiary of these efforts was the Christian Democratic Party.

De Gasperi evidenced his exceptional political ability in fashioning four successive governing coalitions between December 1945 and April 1948, thereby bringing much-needed stability to Italian political life. The first three De Gasperi governments incorporated representatives of the Socialist and Communist parties along with members from smaller lay parties. The fourth De Gasperi government was a *monocolore* [literally "single color"] one entirely composed of Christian Democrats, plus the "independent" Foreign Minister Sforza and Finance Minister Luigi Einaudi. Under De Gasperi Italy's economy regained its footing after surmounting the severe dislocation, which immediately followed the war.

Accompanying these accomplishments, however, were difficult political and societal developments. Togliatti's "insider" parliamentary strategy was discredited by his party's May 1947 exclusion, along with the PSI, from the government coalition—a shock that resulted in the party's censure by the newly constituted Cominform. The Socialist Party was weakened from within when, at the beginning of 1947, one-third of its members left it to join Giuseppe Saragat's new Italian Socialist Labor Party (soon to become the Italian Democratic Socialist Party). The *élan* of the broad-based anti-Fascist Resistance now seemed like a distant dream.[1]

The Demise of the Anti-Fascist Alliance

Parliament's ratification of the peace treaty fulfilled one of the two conditions that De Gasperi felt needed to be accomplished before he would be prepared to eject the Communists and their Socialist allies from his governing coalition. The other precondition was the incorporation of the Lateran Accords into the republican constitution, which, as already noted, occurred in late March of 2017.

In mid-July of 1946, De Gasperi, Togliatti and Nenni met at Castelgondolfo[2] to discuss the distribution of ministries in De Gasperi's newly formed second government. Already the relationship between De Gasperi and his two Marxist interlocutors was fraying. When Togliatti asked De Gasperi whether the latter wished him to stay in the government, the Christian Democratic leader replied: "If you are asking me to respond personally, no, because of everything you have done up to now." Togliatti then rephrased his question: "But we asked if you wanted the two of us, physically, to participate in the next government?" De Gasperi then said: "If your parties need (*dovranno*) to participate in the government, it is better that you enter as leaders, rather than remaining outside to molest us." Togliatti chose not to enter the new government, while Nenni stayed in as minister without portfolio and (once the peace treaty had been signed) foreign minister.[3]

Contributing to the looming crisis of the anti-Fascist alliance was the fundamental incompatibility between economic policies favored by the leftist coalition parties and those carried out by Budget Minister Luigi Einaudi. Rather than boosting the public's buying power by introducing progressive taxation, as proposed by Communist Finance Minister Mauro Scoccimarro, Einaudi imposed classical deflationary policies. These policies temporarily slowed inflation, but at the cost of crippling credit restrictions, which hit small- and medium-sized businesses very hard, provoking an overall decline investment and thus the demand for labor. The beginning of 1947 saw Italy's debt load continuing to escalate, as did inflation. This was fed by a variety of causes, including a growing demand for consumer goods and widespread hoarding by wholesalers and industrialists. Unemployment soared, and the average monthly jobless figure rose to an average monthly figure of over 2 million.[4]

Meanwhile American willingness to continue relief and reconstruction aid to Italy waned. Already in late May of 1946, Chief Allied Commissioner Stone reported that the Italian government would have to cut the daily grain ration in half unless the United Nations Relief and Rehabilitation Administration (UNRRA) could deliver on its food commitments. US and UNRRA officials responded by ensuring that food supplies would be available, but only until the end of the year. Politically, too, confidence in De Gasperi's ability to manage the situation sagged. In the first few months of 1948, the American embassy issued several of pessimistic predictions about the upcoming parliamentary elections. In mid-February, the Americans anticipated that the Popular Front would garner at least 40 percent of the vote, while the Christian Democrats could expect to tally not much more than 35 percent. During the same period, a series of American journalists:

> delivered dire warnings about the outcome of the vote, suggesting that … the Christian Democrats were not doing more to alleviate poverty, unemployment and the social and economics that the journalists found were being masterfully exploited by the Communists and Socialists.[5]

Such concerns appeared to be validated by the results of Sicily's regional elections on April 20–21, 1947. In these elections the *Blocco del Popolo* (comprising the Communists, Socialists, and some representatives of the Action Party) won just over 30 percent of the vote, while the Christian Democrats were able to capture only some 20 percent.[6]

In the meantime, longstanding divisions within the Socialist Party came to a head in January 1947, when the party formally split when Giuseppe Saragat[7] and his moderate faction walked out of the PSI and proceeded to establish a new reformist socialist party.[8] As summarized by James Miller:

> After emerging as the largest mass party of the left in the June 1946 elections, the Socialists … fragmented. The party comprised two distinct currents: a social democratic minority and a more radical majority … Pietro Nenni, who incarnated the intellectual confusion and radicalism of the left, presided over the party as its secretary. Although a skillful political tactician, Nenni was unable to conciliate the various currents of the majority with the social democrats. Moreover, Nenni was an orator of power who could never resist a bit of demagoguery. As a government minister, Nenni was prudent and restrained, but he was unwilling to commit the PSI to play within the bounds of the new democratic system. Nenni believed that the PSI must exploit any opportunity for a revolutionary transition to socialism, and maintain the wartime unity of action pact with the PCI.[9]

Saragat had stood shoulder to shoulder with Nenni during the interwar years. Still, he had always harbored reservations about the Socialists' tactical alliance with the Communists. In Spencer Di Scala's judgment, Saragat's strengths as a leader rested on:

the power of his ideas and the force of his personality rather than bureaucratic structures… Skilled in compromise, with a philosopher's aura and at the height of his prestige, this born leader, "tall, elegant, courteous… measured," with his winning personality, enchanted the Italian public, especially the newly enfranchised ladies of Rome's most chic neighborhoods. His clear and powerful defense of democracy and his courageous repudiation of the dictatorship of the proletariat commanded the attention of middle-class groups suspicious of growing communist prestige.[10]

In his swan song at the January Congress, Saragat rejected the Socialists' unity pact with the Communists, asserting that only a truly autonomous party could serve—from within the governing system—as a mediating factor between the Communists and the Christian Democrats. He added:

> Socialism needs be the directed by the working class itself and not be sterilized by bureaucratic apparatuses, which, perhaps with the best of intentions, lead the workers toward objectives which are not the ones the workers themselves have the right to chart.[11]

Both De Gasperi and Togliatti had "encouraged the split in the Socialist ranks; the former sought a more moderate socialist ally, the latter a Socialist Party rid of its anti-Communist elements."[12]

Controversy still surrounds the United States' possible hand in the fracturing of the Socialist Party. There is no question that the American Federation of Labor's (AFL) Luigi Antonini encouraged the split and poured AFL money into the new party. However, no evidence exists that the American government was directly involved in the split.[13] Nevertheless, 1945 State Department officials had hoped that moderate leftist, non-Communist parties might gain in political strength, the better to promote progressive reconstruction policies. The Republican Party, led by Ugo la Malfa and Randolfo Pacciardi, and the right wing of the Socialist Party under Giuseppe Saragat, attracted particular attention both before and, more intensively, after the Socialist split.[14]

The *coup de grace* for the now tenuous anti-Fascist coalition began with former Under Secretary of State Sumner Welles' May 18 call for increased American aid to Italy explicitly to stem growing Communist power there. Flush with Soviet financial assistance, the PCI was—Welles charged—preparing to launch a civil war. Incensed by Welles' charges, Togliatti published a blistering reply in the pages of *L'Unità*, entitled "What Cretins They Are!." The Communist boss heaped scorn on Welles personally and on American culture in general.[15] Welles, he said, "has little learning, little understanding, low political and moral sense—

representing the great majority of those who mold American public opinion in a rigid direction." The American people as a whole were "slave drivers," "less than intelligent," and lacking in "cultural and historical awareness." To illustrate this last point, he turned his sights on American film, scorning it for its "mechanical repetition of situations and techniques."[16]

De Gasperi then summoned Togliatti to the Viminal, dispensing with formalities when the latter arrived. The prime minister "found very little pleasure in the need to bring up" the justice minister's controversial comments. A witness to the face-off recalled that, as De Gasperi spoke, his voice betrayed tension, his face stretched with strain, and his eyes half-closed behind his lenses. Togliatti in turn became increasingly agitated but did not reply. The prime minister concluded that "it was his duty to inform the country what had occurred," adding that "the country had a right to know why," as he put it, Togliatti "opposed further foreign aid."[17] At the end of their face-off, Togliatti departed from the Viminal—and from the governing coalition.

The Communist leader did not at first take his summary dismissal from the governing coalition as seriously as might have been expected. Perhaps De Gasperi, he said, had temporarily lost his senses. Leaving the Viminal after being relieved from his ministerial position, he murmured that his absence would be a short-lived one.[18] Togliatti continued to believe that the tide of history was moving in his party's direction. After all, the Italian Communist Party was distinctive. While its base was composed of workers and peasants:

> [its] leaders came from every level of Italian society, with relatives and friends at the highest levels of the bureaucracy, of the cultural and educational worlds, of the Church, of the Vatican, and of the Armed Forces. Such a party could not regard itself as marginalized, isolated in one day… it believed itself to still have a role to play within the sphere of government.[19]

For their part, left-leaning members of the Christian Democratic Party did their best to reassure Togliatti and Nenni that the rupture would not be permanent and that relations between the three mass parties could "return to normal once Italy, which had needed American aid, recovered from its economic difficulties."[20] Togliatti did not understand that De Gasperi regarded the three-party alliance as but a temporary expedient. It was only a matter of time before the international Cold War, and intractable domestic economic and political differences, would shatter the anti-Fascist governing coalition. As the permanence of his political exile sank in, Togliatti would turn harshly against his new nemesis.

Togliatti versus De Gasperi

Before detailing that *volte-face*, let us pause to recapitulate the shifting valence of the Communist and Christian Democratic leaders' exchanges over the three years leading up to the fateful rupture of May 1947. Beginning in Rome during July 1944, the two leaders engaged in a series of carefully calibrated political exchanges. In an address delivered on July 23, 1944, at Rome's Teatro Brancaccio, De Gasperi said:

> Colleague Togliatti, we have appreciated your... declaration of respect for the Catholic faith observed by the majority of Italians. The mutual tolerance underlying our civil coexistence, which you propose we readily accept. As compared with the past, this tolerance represents noteworthy progress, which might bring us together more often, along the bitter road which we must take for the redemption of the Italian people... Yet there high up on the meadow, I see with my eyes of faith... another Proletarian, an Israelite like Marx; two thousand years ago he founded his International based on equality, on universal brotherhood, on the fatherhood of God.[21]

Symbolically, De Gasperi was willing to associate Marxism, with its compassion and commitment to the downtrodden, with Catholicism in the founding of a new Italy.

Remarks like these gave Togliatti hope. On several occasions he reassured skeptical party colleagues that he and De Gasperi could and would work together. Responding to doubts expressed by comrade Camilla Ravera, Togliatti said:

> But no, believe me, De Gasperi and I are in agreement on *un sacco di cose* (a host of things), from agrarian reform to trade union solidarity.... You'll see, *faremo insieme del buon lavoro* (we will accomplish a lot together).[22]

Interviewed in *L'Unità* on December 11, 1945, the day after De Gasperi formed his first government, he stated:

> De Gasperi is the leader of a party with mass support. This in itself makes him more acceptable than those so-called 'independent' politicians who only answer for their behavior to their cronies and their own vanity.[23]

Three months later, speaking to the *Direzione* [leadership body] of the PCI, he quipped that De Gasperi was working "for a republic with a crucifix, with the Pope as president," which would be "although small, a step forward."[24]

The Christian Democratic leader respected his Communist counterpart's intelligence, political ability, and realism, but he never cared for—and indeed came to fear—him. What lay at the heart of this animus? Was it Marxist philosophy? The Italian Communist Party per se? The Christian Democratic statesman rejected the harsh, class-based logic of Marxism even as he begrudgingly acknowledged the PCI's dedication and even its (in his view) misguided idealism. He dreaded the conformist, mass emphasis of the Italian Communist Party. In early postwar years he was reticent to tar them as totalitarian, however. Disciplined, self-righteous, even authoritarian, yes; totalitarian, no.

Already in the late war years, and consistently thereafter, De Gasperi did tar the Socialists and Communists alike for their "Jacobinism." This attribute, as employed in his writings and speeches, carried the following four negatives. The French revolutionaries of 1793–1794 were compulsive centralizers. They were rabidly anticlerical to the point of overthrowing the Christian calendar. They were fanatics, capable of even "The Terror." In addition, perhaps most disturbing of all, they were perfectionists, swept away by a utopian vision at odds with human possibility itself.

In an April 1946 letter to the Communist leader, De Gasperi firmly delimited the extent of the two leaders' cooperation in the following terms:

> We have never deluded one another that we might possibly exchange our doctrines, our tendencies and, I would add, our roles: that is that you might play the Christian and I the Marxist. Every person is born with his own attributes, and while evolutions are always possible, and indeed desirable, it is not legitimate to confound tactical reasoning with underlying conviction: those must be one thing or the other.... Thus it is, my dear Togliatti, one is not dealing with you or with me, but with an antithesis which supercedes our persons.[25]

The measured civility of this letter would not endure. Prior to the rupture of their governing alliance, the two leaders had on occasion addressed one another using the informal *tu*. Togliatti now stopped exchanging greetings with his Christian Democratic counterpart. When the two statesmen's paths crossed at the Chamber of Deputies' coffee bar, he pretended not to see De Gasperi. By contrast, De Gasperi recalled, "Nenni always greeted me, indeed expressed affection, often asking after my daughters."[26]

In 1948, De Gasperi would characterize his Communist adversaries in the following terms: "They are at our borders, and since I know them well, even having had them in my governments, I know that there is no possibility of dialogue with them. We speak mutually incomprehensible languages."[27] In turn, in his memoir dating from the same period, journalist Vittorio Gorresio cites the following harsh appraisal by the Communist chief of De Gasperi:

> He is a cold man who has no communicative warmth, lacks a contagious smile, has little faith in Italy and in the Italian people, has amassed multiple failures in foreign policy, has sold Italy's independence, lacks direction in his internal policies, is bought and owned by his worst collaborators, lacks systematic expression, accepts all of the requests made of him, indeed seems offended that others might already have reached conclusions on their own, he therefore earns the trust of no one.[28]

Still more caustic was the following charge:

> The abyss calls forth the abyss. The weight of betrayal oppresses our society. The shadow of this betrayal obscures the entire horizon…. It is the shadow of the government of De Gasperi, of Pacciardi—the shadow of Judah. Within this shadow all manner of crimes can grow.[29]

Togliatti's own, enduring sense of betrayal at De Gasperi's hands is unmistakable here. To paraphrase William Shakespeare, "hell had no fury like a Togliatti scorned."

On May 30, De Gasperi formed his fourth ministry, a minority government composed of Christian Democrats in all ministerial posts save Carlo Sforza as foreign minister and Luigi Einaudi, whose ministerial portfolio encompassed treasury, finance, and budget. American diplomats urged De Gasperi and the members of the Little Entente (Republicans and Social Democrats) to compromise their differences and form a Center-Left ministry with a social reform program. But the Republicans and Social Democrats at first refused to join the new coalition, only relenting in December.[30]

Even so, De Gasperi's government had to rely on the votes of the right wing in parliament—including neo-Fascists. This was a source of acute embarrassment to the United States and to the Christian Democrats. In a journal entry dated May 30, Nenni recorded a conversation of his with Sforza, in which he urged the latter to decline De Gasperi's invitation to become foreign minister. The "cousin-count" (a derogatory nickname applied to Sforza by Italian monarchists, presumably to scoff at his relationship with the Christian Democrats) offered a two-fold reply. In the first place, he needed to remain in the government to play his role in the "high international politics" of the day. In the second place, he hoped that his presence might free De Gasperi from his dependence on ten or so right-wing monarchist votes.[31]

The Socialist leader's response to the breakup of the anti-Fascist alliance was initially restrained. But the announcement of the rightward complexion of the new De Gasperi government prompted this comment: "Thus tomorrow we will have a government doubly guaranteed by the Vatican and America—a fact, it seems to me, of unprecedented gravity."[32]

The American Connection: Round I

The United States' influence on Italy at this critical juncture, and more broadly during and immediately following the Second World War, has prompted a great number of commentaries and analyses, written both by contemporaries and by historians. A particularly helpful account of this "American Connection" is James Miller's work *The United States and Italy 1940-1950: The Politics and Diplomacy of Stabilization.* As Miller's study makes clear, American intentions and actions were often improvised—products of a nation whose protean impact was disproportionally greater than its initial understanding of Italian realities. Driven by military necessity during the war, and by reconstructive initiatives in the mid-1940s, it was only in 1947 and early 1948 that "stabilization" of a society evidently imperiled by communism became America's overarching concern.[33]

A variety of American strategies jostled with one another under the banner of anti-communism. John Harper, another historian of Italian-American relations following the Second World War, has identified three such strategies. The first strand was a recycled social liberalism, which centered on the improvement of Italian living standards, especially for Italian peasants and workers. Overlapping but also competing with this strand was a classical liberal approach, determined to stoke the engine of Italian economic recovery, focusing especially on the needs and prospects of Italian entrepreneurs. The third strand placed less faith in economics and more on political and, potentially, military measures explicitly aimed at curbing Communist strength.[34] To this strategic trio, a fourth strand, christened "rollback," emerged by the early 1950s.[35]

All four approaches figured in the diplomacy of America's key player in this Cold War drama: James Clement Dunn, US Ambassador to Italy between February 1947 and March 1952. A deft bureaucratic insider, Ambassador Dunn combined an early reliance on economic aid with feel-good cultural diplomacy and, increasingly, an emphasis on the more tough-minded approaches noted just above. This staunch Episcopalian and business-minded conservative had married into the powerful Armour meatpacking family. Dunn understood and embraced the transformative potential of American capitalism. He approached Italy's communist threat in characteristically

American motivational and managerial terms.[36] Dunn's punchy memoranda to Washington were models of can-do realism. He fretted that the Italian Communists were more adroit than the Christian Democrats in packaging their political program. Steadfast in his appreciation for Prime Minister De Gasperi,[37] Dunn nevertheless lamented the partisan jockeying and self-interestedness of other members of De Gasperi's party and government. Such shortsightedness only aided the Communists with their subversive propaganda and had produced a "psychological malaise" in Italy, which only vigorous public relations initiatives, additional (and, if necessary, covert) economic and even military assistance could offset.[38]

Dunn's faith in De Gasperi supplanted earlier American uncertainty regarding the Christian Democratic leader and his party. As military victory over the Germans and their neo-Fascist associates drew closer, many American policymakers[39] had looked first to secular, middle-of-the-road Italian leaders as potential interlocutors. The moderate Carlo Sforza, for instance, was among the most respected and influential Italians who had fled Fascism for exile in the United States. American support for Sforza's mid-1945 candidacy as Italy's foreign minister foundered, due most of all to intractable British hostility.[40]

It was De Gasperi who wound up obtaining that ministerial brief. His firm but respectful manner as Parri's foreign minister between June and December of 1945 had registered favorably with the Anglo-Americans. Still, Christian Democracy as a political force was unfamiliar in Great Britain and the United States. The very name of the party, Christian Democracy, sounded suspicious to some. Why should a genuinely democratic political entity require such a modifier? And how did the adjective "Christian"—understood to mean Catholic—relate to the American liberal focus on political process and procedural fairness as democratic hallmarks? Would Christian Democratic preeminence bring undue Vatican influence in Italian domestic affairs?

The latter concern reflected Protestantism's traditional near monopoly of State Department officialdom.[41] By the war's end, however, reservations about political Catholicism waned.[42] Already in December 1943, Myron Taylor, FDR's personal envoy to the Vatican, met secretly with Cardinal Domenico Tardini to discuss potential post-Fascist leaders in Italy; in response, the cardinal offered only one name—Alcide De Gasperi. Tardini qualified that endorsement in a subsequent conversation with Taylor's associate Harold Tittman, characterizing De Gasperi's political abilities as "conspicuous, though not excessive."[43]

Doubts about De Gasperi in both Vatican and American circles surfaced more directly in late 1946 and early 1947, when the De Gasperi government struggled to address mounting economic problems. The prime minister's faltering popularity with the Italian public raised questions about the prime minister's and his party's political capabilities. Dunn countered those concerns by emphasizing not Christian Democratic doctrine, but the bounty of American foreign aid, and the resourcefulness and determination of De Gasperi in securing that bounty. The Italian prime minister and the American ambassador were both consensus builders, solicitous of the interlocking institutional health of Italy's government and of the United States Department of State.

As the April 1948 parliamentary elections drew nearer, Dunn threw himself into a frenetic, tough-minded public relations campaign:

> He traveled the length of the peninsula many times over. He seemed to be everywhere during the course of the campaign: there to greet every hundredth ship bringing relief supplies and foodstuffs from the United States, there at the official openings of bridges, hospitals and homes built using U.S money, public and private. He delivered literally dozens of addresses to Italian voters, reminding them that the U.S. aid was conditional on continued Italian participation in "free and democratic" Western bloc.[44]

Complementing these efforts were a plethora of independent public and private initiatives. Sympathetic labor leaders like Generoso Pope invited leading democratic Italian politicians to tour the United States, as well as broadcasting from Italy speeches by De Gasperi, Sforza, and others. A particularly colorful initiative prompted thousands of Italian-Americans to write letters to relatives in Italy, underscoring the importance of voting for anti-Communist parties.[45]

Several international developments in the year leading up to the April 18, 1948 vote bolstered the electoral prospects of the Christian Democrats and their partners. The Marshall Plan, announced by the American Secretary of State on June 5, 1947, offered Europeans the opportunity to regain control of their national destinies through a cooperative program of economic reconstruction embracing both loans and outright grants. Eight months later, on February 24, 1948, the Czech Communist Party seized power in that Eastern European country through a violent coup. This shocking act galvanized anti-Communist forces in Italy, thrusting Communist aggression into the heart of the parliamentary contest. Finally, on March 15—the Ides of March—the State Department formally announced that the United States would cut off Marshall Plan aid to Italy in the event the Left prevailed in the election.[46]

Pius XII, Gedda, and the Civic Committees

> Who is the Pope? What must he be for you?...an unknown, an authority meaning as little to you as he does to Protestants or schismatics...or Vicar of Christ, Teacher, Mentor and Father?.... [D]o you have faith (*fiducia*) in him befitting a Christian, and an Italian?
>
> —*Stella mattutina* (1942)[47]

Watching from the Vatican, Pius XII was also alarmed at the Popular Front's strength and at the Christian Democrats' inadequate response to that threat. Beginning in the mid-1947, he enlisted the efforts of an indefatigable and dynamic layman, Dr. Luigi Gedda. A Piedmontese physician by profession, he had first made his mark within Italian political Catholicism in 1934, when he assumed the presidency of the Young Men of Catholic Action (*Gioventù Italiana di Azione Cattolica* [abbreviated GIAC in Italian]). Already in the later 1930s, Gedda had envisioned a Catholic political movement, which, unlike emergent Christian Democracy, would devote itself entirely to carrying out the papal will in all sectors of society, including the sphere of politics.[48] Such devotion, he believed, was the only viable way to surmount the moral and material disarray of an increasingly war-ravaged nation. The weakened stature of the Italian army, the monarchy, and other societal bulwarks of law and order at the war's conclusion made matters worse. In view of this disarray, it was all the more important to buttress the Church's presence everywhere on the peninsula.

Afraid to simply allow the political chips to fall where they might in the coming 1946 elections to the Constituent Assembly, Gedda pressed Catholic Action in its entirety to sanction reliably orthodox candidates. Beyond that, he believed that Church needed to throw its full organizational and propaganda apparatus into the electoral fray, though Catholic Action itself was officially to remain outside of the political arena. This ban had been a key stipulation of the 1929 Lateran Accords and Concordat. Gedda's response to that prohibition, as we will see, was to create "Civic Committees," which unabashedly intervened in the run-up to the April 1948 vote.

A prominent Catholic opponent of Gedda's activity was the liberal, pastorally oriented Vittorino Veronese. Their rivalry, dating from mid-1943, bears closer examination here, as Veronese's standoff with Gedda prefigured De Gasperi's later hardships vis-à-vis Gedda and the Pope during the 1952 Sturzo Operation. A native of Vicenza, as a young man, Veronese had fallen under the sway of

Monsignor Gian Battista Montini (the future Paul VI) within the fold of the Federation of Catholic University Graduates. By 1939, he was deeply involved in the reorganization and revitalization of the *Istituto Cattolica di Attività Sociale* (ICAS). This organization afforded Veronese a platform in 1943 to call on his fellow Italian Catholics to become a "creative presence within the social fabric of the Nation," offering an indispensable contribution to Italy's civil progress from the bottom up rather than (as in the past) "formally intervening as an *instrumentum regni* [instrument of power]."[49] Veronese's choice of words in this last phrase is very interesting, critiquing as it does the imperious manner which had characterized all too many of the Vatican's interwar political and diplomatic initiatives.

The most significant document reflecting Veronese's role in this Italian Catholic effort of sociocultural explication and *aggiornamento* [literally "bringing up to date"] was the *Codice di Camaldoli*. In July of 1943, Veronese discretely invited a group of some sixty Catholic intellectuals to gather for a week-long retreat at the monastery of Camaldoli, situated in the hills of eastern Tuscany. The charitable spirit of the code is ably conveyed by its formal title, "*Per la comunità cristiana: Principi dell'ordinamento sociale a cura di un gruppo di studiosi amici di Camaldoli*" ("For the Christian Community: Principles of Social Organization Elaborated by a Group of Learned Friends of Camaldoli"), known as the "Code of Camaldoli" for short. The "Code" synthesized a series of ninety-nine propositions, grouped sequentially in the following functional categories: the Spiritual Foundation of Social Life; the State; the Family; Education; Work; Property, Production and Exchange; Public Economic Activity and International Life.

In his editorial preface to the code upon its 1945 publication, Veronese invited not only to his fellow Italian "Christians," but "all men of good will" to reflect on the work. Perhaps this dialogic sensitivity helps explain the fact that this code refers only occasionally to earlier encyclicals, instead casting the insights of the *magisterium* within a colloquial idiom and seeking to persuade the reader through the serene, logical sequence of its assertions. Veronese anticipated a central insight of the Vatican II Council, e.g., that Christian values did not need to be shouted from rooftops in order to be heard by a people earnestly seeking answers to their own questions. More immediately, the Camaldoli Code provided many principles which De Gasperi incorporated into his 1943 essay *Idee ricostrutive della Democrazia Cristiana* (Reconstructive Ideas of Christian Democracy), perhaps the key intellectual and ideological foundation of the nascent Christian Democratic Party.[50]

Building on the Camaldoli Code in a series of high-level meetings of Italian Catholic lay and clerical leaders in late 1945 and early 1946, Veronese urged that Catholic Action undertake a "program of cultural enrichment (*approfondimento*) and civil education from which all Italians might benefit, preparing them to conscientiously exercise their rights and fulfill their duties in sound democratic coexistence with their countrymen."[51] Acknowledging that the appropriate societal subsoil for the proper functioning of democratic institutions could not be built up overnight, Veronese asserted that Catholicism had an indispensable societal role—arising out of the Church's millennial grassroots presence—to play over the long haul. Confident in his countrymen's intelligence and adaptive capability, Veronese counseled a patient, pastorally oriented profile for Catholic Action.

Consequently, during the 1946 municipal elections, the vote for the Constituent Assembly, and the 1948 parliamentary elections, Catholic Action was to play a complementary (but not directly overlapping) role vis-à-vis the Christian Democratic Party. Behind the scenes, Veronese and Gedda sparred repeatedly, as the latter pressed continually for closer integration between lay movement and political party. In nominating candidates for the Constituent Assembly, Gedda urged Catholic Action to put together its own list of "reliable" persons, which would be "associated with" the Christian Democratic Party slate—a move that Veronese predictably, and successfully, opposed on the grounds that it would exceed Catholic Action's fundamentally religious and moral scope.[52] Gedda, in turn, took Veronese to task for the uneven nature of Catholic Action's mobilization across the peninsula. As late as the fall of 1949, Catholic Action would have a presence in only half of the parishes in Italy. To remedy this situation, the Pope would back Gedda over Veronese in a power struggle for the leadership of Catholic Action, as is detailed below in chapter 7.

In his memoir *18 aprile 1948*, Gedda traced his inspiration to form the Civic Committees back to Pius XII's address to the GIAC (Young Men of Catholic Action) of September 9, 1947. "His voice vibrant and solemn," the Holy Father spoke to an overflowing audience of 70,000, gathered at St. Peters square. Looking ahead to April 18, the Pope invoked "three words, arising from its annals" (dating, that is, from its founding by Pius XI) that defined the members of GIAC:

> Men of "prayer," possessing a rich inner religious life; men of "action," engaged in tireless activity on behalf of the Catholic cause; men of "sacrifice," generously dedicated to Christ, to the Church, to the Papacy.[53]

Inspired by these words, the Civic Committees harnessed the activities of "hundreds of preexisting lay organizations, including three hundred diocesan committees and dozens of other local committees in some 18,000 of Italy's 27,000 parishes." At the national headquarters in Rome, four different offices were established, each with its own task or target audience. Especially important was the "'Mary, Jesus and Joseph Agency," also known as the psychological office, which oversaw the production of the propaganda material, whether paper, radio or film. An "international bureau" was tasked with "analyzing and reporting the propaganda activities of the Popular Front." By the end of March 1948, the Civic Committees had enlisted some 300,000 volunteers.[54] Powerfully facilitating this remarkable achievement:

> In the weeks and months before the vote, statues and icons of dozens of Marian entities, from the world-renowned Lady of Fatima to obscure Marian figures particular to smaller towns and villages in every corner of Italy, made their way through the peninsula. The Virgin carried with her, as in centuries past, the promise of eternal salvation of souls, to be sure. But within the context of the pending national vote, she could also be seen as the portent of an uncertain future and a warning sign of celestial displeasure with the prospect of a communist Italy.[55]

Complementing such processions, the Civic Committee distributed fliers like one entitled "The Vote and Sin," which asserted,

> that it was a sin to either abstain or to vote for the Popular Front: If you were to go to confession, for example at Easter, with the intention of voting for the Popular Front, you would not give a good confession.... on the contrary, you would commit a sacrilege because you did not have the requirements needed for a valid confession but (instead) having the will to commit a sin. *Reflect, therefore, and decide to vote, but in such a way as not to commit a sin* (italics in original).[56]

The Christian Democrats' party posters were equally blunt. One showed a giant Stalin trampling on the "Wedding Cake," the oversized white marble monument in the center of Rome commemorating King Victor Emmanuel II and Italian unification. On a lighter note, one Christian Democratic poster proclaimed:

> Don't think that you'll be able to flavor your pasta with the speeches of Togliatti. All intelligent people will vote for De Gasperi because he has obtained free from the Americas the flour for your spaghetti and the sauce you put on it.[57]

In the last month of the campaign, Pius XII piloted the elaborately stage-managed, almost theatrical kind of public appearance that would become the hallmark of Pacellian populism in the years to come.[58] Easter Sunday of 1948—some three weeks before the elections were to take place—offered a particularly dramatic such occasion. The Pope's message on this day was notably "Roman" in its content, delivery, and setting.

While refraining from endorsing the Christian Democratic Party by name, Pius XII exhorted the faithful gathered in St. Peter's Square on Easter Sunday not to shrink from taking sides at the polls, citing Christ's own "terrible verdict: he who is not with me, is against me." "My beloved children," the Pope continued, "you can well appreciate what a crossroads we face, with what consequences for Rome, for Italy, for the world." In its final paragraph, the Christian Democratic paper *Il Popolo*'s article on the Pope's Easter address noted the "presence in the crowd of the President of the Council of Ministers Alcide De Gasperi on the right near the colonnade."[59]

The prime minister's low-profile position in the audience that day reflected his Catholic devotion on the one hand, and on the other the appropriate space separating state and Church. De Gasperi's discrete presence during this event was also in keeping with his general discomfort with Roman theatricality. The Trentine statesman avoided *la vita salottiera romana* [Roman high society]. Ever the provincial bourgeois, he found respite and rejuvenation the circle of his immediate family. While on vacation in the Valsugana he sometimes joined older gentlemen in the nearby town for a game of *bocce*; in Rome he rarely partook of public entertainment. As De Gasperi's disciple Giulio Andreotti (himself a polished performer within Rome's social whirl) remarked, with a rare note of reproof, the prime minister's domesticity deprived the latter of "opportunities to broaden his circle of contacts among men of diverse experiences (here it is enough to think of Rome's intellectual milieu and of its diplomatic one)."[60]

Further reinforcing the Church's preelection crusade were the broadcasts of Jesuit Father Riccardo Lombardi, the zealous radio announcer who came to be known as "the Microphone of God." In an address broadcast one week before the election, Father Lombardi ridiculed Italy's Communists as immoral hypocrites; PCI claims of respect for the family were contradicted by Marxism proclamation that the family should be abolished.[61] He went on to assert that "there are foreigners among us who have come to spread the germs of the barbarity what rules over their land. But I tell you with the utmost certainty that they will fail. Mary will win!"[62] Lombardi explicitly linked the danger from within with a danger from without: "Many have said that Italy is poor and undefended. And from the East—cowards!—They amass troops at our borders." But these Oriental foes would also be defeated, for Italy was the home of the papacy, the "spiritual head of all humanity."[63]

Here the PCI was feared less for its socio-political ideology than its possible collusion with a national enemy, both following orders emanating from Moscow. The eruption of the Tito-Stalin split between January and May of 1948[64] was widely dismissed in Rome as a mere ruse; if it were real, it would be short-lived, since the Soviet Union could not allow such a blatant challenge to its power to grow. The PCI's detractors had long accused the party of engaging in a *doppio gioco* (literally, "playing double game"), acquiescing in the formulation of sometimes unpopular government policies, which its rank and file attacked in the streets. A more serious charge leveled by De Gasperi now was their purported *doppio lealtà*—a double loyalty to Moscow as well as to Rome.

On Election Day itself, *Il Popolo* featured a column by Fortunato Bellonzi under the dramatic headline "Life or Death of Our Civilization." At stake in the election was "the survival or end of *romanità*, of Christianity and of European unity." As Bellonzi elaborated, "European man" still, as in past centuries, depended on a bedrock of "Roman and Christian unity," which was the fruit of "Rome's purely spiritual and human empire."[65]

De Gasperi's personal image differed from the triumphalism surrounding the Pope. The dust jacket of Leo Valiani's 1949 book *L'avvento di De Gasperi* depicted De Gasperi posed in front of the Vatican, appearing "modest and bourgeois ... wearing a Homburg hat and the big, dark overcoat which he wore, as was his habit, draped with an indifferent alpinist's air over his shoulders." Novelist Italo Calvino also noted the political resonance of De Gasperi's "modesty." Leftists like Calvino himself had "failed to understand that a majority of Italians saw themselves in De Gasperi."[66] The Italian electorate found reassurance in the very modesty of his person and the sensibility of his aims. What after all was wrong with focusing on the immediate prospect of a bit of tranquility and a bit of happiness—goals that the Christian Democrats, and behind them the Americans, were most likely to deliver?

Notes

1   Upon his return to Italy from the United States near the end of the 1940s, the irrepressible Gaetano Salvemini was discouraged by the apolitical lassitude which he encountered among young people, including university students. Even at his advanced age, Salvemini felt "younger at heart" than they were. Killinger, *Gaetano Salvemini*, final chapter.

2   This picturesque town situated on the shores of Lake Albano is also the site of the papal summer residence.
3   Sale, *De Gasperi gli USA e il Vaticano*, 18n.
4   Ginsborg, *History of Contemporary Italy*, 112-113.
5   Robert Ventresca, *From Fascism to Democracy: Culture and Politics in the Italian Election of 1948* (Toronto: University of Toronto Press, 2004), 228.
6   Ginsborg, *History of Contemporary Italy*, 111; Ventresca, *From Fascism to Democracy*, 142-143.
7   Already identified in chapter 5 as the first president of the Constituent Assembly.
8   As noted above, Saragat's new party was initially named the Italian Socialist Labor Party.
9   Miller, *United States and Italy*, 219; On Nenni's comments at this time, see Peter Nichols, "On the Italian Crisis," *Foreign Affairs* 54 (April 1976), 511-526. Miller's characterization here merits a word of clarification. By the beginning of 1947, Nenni had served more than a year as an "insider," first as minister for the *Costituente* and High Commissioner for Sanctions against Fascism Epuration in Parri's government and then as foreign minister in De Gasperi's second government. In these capacities he had, in fact, grown more comfortable in playing within the bounds of the new democratic system. But, on the stump, his soaring rhetoric often romanticized a revolutionary transition to socialism.
10 Spencer Di Scala, *Renewing Italian Socialism: Nenni to Craxi* (London: Oxford University Press, 1988), 60-61.
11 Introduction to Giuseppe Saragat, "Discorso al II congresso del PSIUP," January 11, 1947 in Capurso, ed., *Discorsi*, 220.
12 Ginsborg, *History of Contemporary Italy*, 104.
13 Miller, *United States and Italy*, 220.
14 Faenza and Fini, *Gli americani in Italia*, 196-225.
15 Agosti, *Palmiro Togliatti*, 184-185.
16 Togliatti, "Ma come sono cretini!" *L'Unità*. May 7, 1947, 20; Agarossi and Zaslavsky, *Stalin and Togliatti*, 228.
17 "Per l'oro di Mosca e la parole 'cretini' il PCI fu costretto a uscire dal governo," *Il Giornale d'Italia*, January 8, 1967, "Ritagli di stampa sul PCI."
18 Interestingly, De Gasperi himself hinted that the breach might be overcome in the not too distant future. Gambino, *Storia del dopoguerra*, 392.
19 Norman Kogan, *La politica estera italiana* (Milan: Lerici, 1965), 88.
20 Pietro Nenni, *Intervista sul socialismo italiano*, ed. Giuseppe Tamburrano (Bari: Laterza, 1977), 79.
21 Cited in Malgeri, *Alcide De Gasperi*, vol. II, 35-36.
22 Paolo Spriano, *Storia del Partito communista italiano*. vol. II (Turin: Einaudi, 1875), 383.
23 Agosti, *Palmiro Togliatti*, 167.

24 Ibid., 168.
25 De Gasperi letter to Togliatti, April 16, 1946, in *De Gasperi Scrive* II, ed. Maria Romana De Gasperi (Brescia: Morcelliana, 1972), 213–215.
26 Gorresio, *Carissimi nemici*, 100.
27 Catti De Gasperi, *De Gasperi, uomo solo*, 267; Nassi, *Alcide De Gasperi*, 284.
28 In a lighter, jocund mood, he added that he "realized that De Gasperi had become even more diffident in that mountain-bound head of his. He is fearful in any case." Gorresio, *Carissimi nemici*, 99.
29 Franco Andreucci, *Falce e Martello. Identità e linguaggi dei communisti italiani fra stalinismo e guerra fredda* (Bologna: Bononia University Press, 2005), 54.
30 Ibid., 239.
31 Nenni, *Tempo di Guerra Fredda*, 365.
32 Ibid., At the end of July, Nenni took a much-needed vacation. Just before that leave-taking, he had a cordial and candid conversation with Acting Head of State De Nicola. De Nicola admonished Nenni to "moderate his polemical ardor … the agitator needed to give way to the man of State." In effect, De Nicola encouraged the Socialist leader and his party to take on the role of "loyal opposition." Nenni was not so inclined.
33 Here I draw on the four successive parts of Miller's work: involvement, occupation, reconstruction, and stabilization.
34 John Harper, *America and the Reconstruction of Italy, 1945–1948*.
35 Mario Del Pero, "American Pressures and Their Containment in Italy during the Ambassadorship of Clare Boothe Luce, 1953–1956," *Diplomatic History* 28:3 (2004), 407–439.
36 For the wider salience of such thinking in American popular views of De Gasperi and his party, see White, "De Gasperi through American Eyes."
37 Steven White, "Anti-Communist Duet: Alcide De Gasperi and James Clement Dunn," paper delivered at Leuven, Belgium Workshop on European Christian Democracy, November 14–15, 2013.
38 Kaeten Mistry, "The Dynamics of Postwar US-Italian Relations, American Interventionism & the Role of James C. Dunn," paper delivered at the Society for Historians of American Foreign Relations meeting, Madison, Wisconsin, June 26, 2010.
39 Representative of this group was OSS analyst H. Stuart Hughes, whose judgments have been noted already in Chapter 2.
40 Miller, *United States and Italy*, 100–101.
41 George Q. Flynn, *Roosevelt and Romanism. Catholics and American Diplomacy, 1937–1945* (Westport: Greenwood, 1976).
42 Steven White, "Soft on Catholicism: Secular-Clerical Rapprochement and American Policy in Italy, 1943–1948," paper delivered at Society for Historians of American Foreign Relations meeting, Charlottesville, March 23, 1993.

43 Ennio Di Nolfo, *Vaticano e Stati Uniti. 1939–1952 (dalle carte di Myron C. Taylor)* (Milan: Angeli, 1978), 61.
44 Ventresca, *From Fascism to Democracy*, 79.
45 Miller, *United States and Italy*, 242.
46 Ibid., 230–247.
47 Title of a weekly Roman Marian newspaper: May 17, 1942 issue. The year 1942 was Pius XII's Episcopal Jubilee Year, and the parishes of Rome observed this date as the "day of the Pope," stressing the need for devout Catholics to sustain a strong and personal *fiducia*—confidence in and reverence for—the Holy Father.
48 Embassy hand Llewelyn Thompson devoted an 11½-page report to Gedda in mid-1952, noting his nondemocratic tendencies with some concern but concluding that, on the balance, he remained "a good risk" for democracy in Italy because of his organizational abilities and his wholehearted loyalty to the Church. See also the earlier memo, Thompson to Secretary of State, October 26, 1950. Both in NARA, State Department, RG 59, Box 3942.
49 This robust assertion comes from an article entitled "Unità e carità," which Veronese published in the summer of 1943, both in *Studium* and in *L'Osservatore romano*. See Carlo Felice Casula, "L'impegno sociale di Vittorino Veronese," in *Vitttorino Veronese dal dopoguerra al Concilio: un laico nella Chiesa e nel mondo*. Atti del convegno di studi, Roma, 7–8 maggio 1993 (Rome: A.V.E., 1994), 66.
50 Craveri, *De Gasperi*, 131.
51 Francesco Malgeri, "La presenza di Vittorino Veronese nell'ACI e la rinascita democratica del dopoguerra," in *Vitttorino Veronese*, 20.
52 Ibid., 21.
53 Gedda, *18 aprile 1948*, 107.
54 Ventresca, *From Fascism to Democracy*, 178, 187.
55 Ibid., 105.
56 Ibid., 210.
57 Frei, *Italy: The Unfinished Revolution*, 52. The PCI countered such attacks by emphasizing Togliatti's patriotism. The PCI distributed pictures of their leader as an Alpine soldier during his First World War military service. Marsili, "De Gasperi and Togliatti," 253.
58 Holmes, "Pope Pius XII: Impressions of a Pontificate," *Clergy Review* LXI (1976), 438; Steven White, "Christian Democracy or Pacellian Populism? Rival Forms of Postwar Italian Political Catholicism," in Thomas Kselman and Joseph Buttigieg, eds., *European Christian Democracy: Historical Legacies and Comparative Perspectives* (Notre Dame: Notre Dame University Press, 2003), 199–227.
59 *Il Popolo*, March 30, 1948.
60 From a commemorative article appearing in *Il Tempo*, August 18, 1974, now in Giovanni De Capua, ed., *Processo a De Gasperi* (Rome 1976), 110.

61 Frei, *Italy: The Unfinished Revolution*, 50.
62 Riccardo Lombardi, "L'Italia a Maria: Il discorso di padre Lombardi a Napoli," *Bollettino bimestrale del Santuario della Madonna di Divino Amore* (April 11, 1948), 3–4, as cited in Ventresca, *From Fascism to Democracy*, 100.
63 Ibid., 115.
64 Adam Ulam, *Stalin: The Man and His Era*, expanded edition. (Boston: Beacon, 1989), 664–666.
65 This empire's divine provenance set it off from other (French, German, English, etc.) empires, "which were merely the accidental offspring of political happenstance or crude incarnations of the Caesarian ideal." *Il Popolo*, April 18, 1948.
66 Valiani, *Avvento di De Gasperi*, 159–162.

7

Cold War Stasis, 1948–1954

During the period of 1948–1954—the so-called years of centrism—the domestic Italian and international Cold War imposed severe strains upon the Italian republic. The country's new constitutional order was bent but did not break. The Christian Democrat-led government delayed implementation of key constitutional provisions for fear that these would unduly strengthen the leftist opposition. Eager to recover from the Popular Front's April 1948 parliamentary defeat, the Communists and Socialists wrapped themselves in the mantle of principled constitutional guardians without, however, relinquishing the possibility of revolutionary action in extremis. Despite deep animosity between De Gasperi and Togliatti, the Christian Democratic leader regarded the Communist Party as a *justis hostis*, "a legitimate enemy to be defeated rather than eliminated."[1] His goal remained that of excluding the Communist Party from the nation's government, while still containing them within the parliamentary arena. The Left exercised a moderating influence on a number of occasions when the country might have descended into civil war. Even so, the rhetorical war between De Gasperi's successive coalition governments and the leftist opposition escalated relentlessly as Italy entered the Cold War's coldest era.

Vatican, American, and Soviet interference in Italian affairs reinforced such domestic tensions. The Church began to deny communion to openly Socialist and Communist parishioners. On July 15, 1949, the Sacred Office decreed that voting for the Italian Communist or Socialist parties would henceforth constitute grounds for excommunication. Some sources attribute the excommunication proclamation to Cardinal Ottaviani[2] and like-minded officials within the Sacred Office. Other sources suggest that it was the Pope who, rather impulsively, issued the edict.[3] Between 1949 and 1951 the Vatican and the United Sates pressed De Gasperi to outlaw the PCI, emulating the precedent set by Konrad Adenauer's government in West Germany. The prime minister refused on the grounds that such a step would disenfranchise a quarter of the Italian voting public. But in the

Roman municipal elections of 1952, the Vatican applied heavy political and even personal pressure on De Gasperi to join forces with the far Right—including the neo-Fascist Italian Social Movement (Movimento Sociale Italiano—MSI for short). Unsuccessful in the end, this effort, which has come to be known as the Sturzo Operation, represented the high-water mark of overt Vatican intervention in domestic Italian political life. A disillusioned Pope Pius XII later told former British Field Marshall Mongomery that "he liked the first part of the [Christian Democratic] party's name, but not the second."[4]

In 1952 newly elected President Dwight Eisenhower and his Secretary of State John Foster Dulles promulgated the goal of "rolling back Communism," not only in the Eastern Bloc countries but in countries such as Italy as well. Yet this proved unwieldy as a foreign policy objective. James Dunn was replaced as American Ambassador to Italy by Ellsworth Bunker for a year, paving the way for the controversial ambassadorship of Clare Boothe Luce between 1953 and 1956. In the name of "rollback," Luce brought a more heavy-handed, and in key respects, less persuasive brand of anti-communism to the fore.[5] Luce questioned De Gasperi's effectiveness and castigated his party for faint-heartedness, incompetence, and opportunism: it began to seem that the Christian Democratic Party was doing little actual good against the Communist threat, even as it was manipulating the United States for continuing economic assistance. In Luce words, the DC's ongoing invocation of the Communist threat constituted "Italy's most profitable business." Parallel to this, Ambassador Luce pushed for her own version of an Italian "opening to the Right," which would bring in Big Industry as a direct interlocutor as well as more conservative and even Monarchist political formations.[6]

From the East, the Soviet Union also upped the ante for the young Italian republic. At the September 1947 founding meeting of the Communist Information Bureau (Comintern for short), the PCI was excoriated for the Popular Front's failure to overtake the Christian Democrats as Italy's dominant political force. Both the Italian and French parties had failed to show sufficient vigilance against "cosmopolitanism" (by now a stock Stalinist accusation), excessive "parliamentarism," and coalitional politics.[7] In view of the Popular Front's exclusion from Italy's government, the Soviet dictator conceded that "in the American sphere of influence Marxists could not build socialism but only prevent reaction."[8] As the 1940s drew to a close, a hardening Soviet party line, conveyed directly and through the Cominform, induced the Italian Communist Party to ratchet up its own policies of political and economic obstructionism. The PCI dutifully hewed to the new party line, loudly denouncing the Marshall

Plan, stepping up its grassroots mobilization efforts, and unleashing boycotts and strikes in key industries. At the same time, Togliatti cast his party as a stalwart champion of the constitution and of civil liberties against repressive, fear-mongering DC-led governments.[9] De Gasperi's governments, he said, perniciously conflated the roles of state and party. "Anti-communism might be an objective of the DC," he said, "but had no business becoming... the ideology of the State."[10]

Socialists joined Communists in denouncing NATO and American assertiveness in foreign affairs, as well as "clerical authoritarianism" in domestic Italian life. Nenni travelled to Moscow to receive the Stalin Peace Prize in 1951. At the same time, the Socialists grew increasingly restless at having to play second fiddle to the PCI within the Popular Front. Thus, after years of barbed exchanges in the halls of parliament and in the press, in 1952, Nenni and De Gasperi resumed person-to-person conversations, faintly echoing the frank, respectful exchange of views, which had characterized their wartime cohabitation within the sanctuary of St. John Lateran Seminary. The Christian Democratic leader tried valiantly, but unsuccessfully, to convince the Socialists to break with the Communists and to explore the formation of a Center-Left coalition. Nenni in turn appreciated his interlocutor's personal probity and statesmanship, while lamenting his dogmatic anti-communism. As the Socialist leader noted in a July 1953 diary entry, De Gasperi still "remained prisoner of American and Vatican vetoes and of his own anti-communism." Nenni regarded De Gasperi's view of Togliatti as excessively pessimistic—an aversion based "more on terror than on hate."[11]

An Ambiguous Mandate

On April 18, 1948, the governing parties swept to victory in the republic's first national parliamentary elections. Despite early polls intimating a leftist triumph, the elections garnered the Christian Democrats alone over 48 percent of the popular vote. Because of the preferential voting system used in the election, the Christian Democratic Party actually netted an absolute majority within the Chamber of Deputies: 305 out of 574 seats belonged to Christian Democratic deputies.[12] The Social-Communists gained 31 percent of that combined vote; the Communists increased their number of parliamentary seats (as compared to the June 2, 1946 Constituent Assembly election) from 104 to 141 deputies, while the Socialists dropped from 115 to 42 seats. The Social Democrats fell from 52 to 33 seats.[13]

Pius XII and De Gasperi drew very different conclusions from this watershed triumph. To the Pope, the Christian Democrats' electoral success heralded a broader crusade on behalf of integral Catholic values, radiating out from *la città sacra* (sacred city) of Rome, encompassing Italy and aiming, ultimately, at the "re-Christianization" of a Europe spiritually bankrupt by war and totalitarianism. The Pope expected the Christian Democrats to form a single-party government, the better to participate in his grander crusade.

Frustrated in that goal, Pius XII hosted a series of spectacular celebrations, either centered in or radiating out from the Eternal City.[14] The Pope envisioned these ritual undertakings as affirmations of *cristianità*—modern manifestations of "Christendom" in the double sense of Christian civilization and Christian order. Here the Pope was evoking something grander than mere *cristianesimo* (Christianity), a term with which De Gasperi was more comfortable.

For his part, De Gasperi read the 1948 election results in liberal, pluralist terms—as a mandate to renew multiparty rule among the Christian Democrats and the smaller, centrist Social Democratic, Republican, and Liberal parties. Thus, he formed a governing coalition composed of eleven Christian Democratic ministers, along with three Social Democrats, two Liberals, two Republicans, and two Independents. This arrangement reinforced the republic's foundational, two-fold consensus of anti-Fascist commitment and determination to leave behind the peninsula's centuries-old divide between the forces of clericalism and anti-clericalism. As parties to this consensus, even the Socialists and Communists formed a constitutional, if angry, parliamentary opposition.[15] For De Gasperi, Togliatti and his colleagues were dangerously mistaken—which meant that they had to be handled firmly but prudently. For Pius XII, by contrast, communism was "intrinsically perverse."[16]

De Gasperi's commitment to sustained coalition governance was not mere pragmatism, but reflected years of reflection dating back to the late interwar period. The Christian Democratic leader understood democratization as an organic, gradual process, necessarily engaging all Italy's major political forces. De Gasperi well knew that the nation's *retroterra cattolico* (Catholic hinterland) would need time and guidance to grow into the responsibilities of democratic citizenship.[17] As he saw it, political Catholicism, as represented by Christian Democracy, would have a double role to play in the public life of the republic—weaning Italy's largest political subculture from its longstanding suspicion of the Italian State and also expressing humanistic values essential to democracy itself. As he noted in a January 1952 letter to Pius XII, such humanistic values were shared by many non-Catholic statesmen of the day and offered a crucial, if tenuous, basis for republican praxis. But this praxis necessarily expressed itself best in parliament, not the piazza, as the former remained, for De Gasperi, the most modern and fitting arena for organized ideological competition.[18] As the Trentine statesman pronounced at a June 1949 Christian Democratic national Congress: "It was important to distinguish roles: the party was to stimulate and prepare; Parliament was to deliberate; and the government was to execute."[19] This formula view exposed him to criticism from younger Christian Democrats, as well as Vatican observers, on the grounds that it unduly subordinated the policy-shaping vocation of the party.

At a press conference held two days after the election, De Gasperi reflected briefly on the significance of his party's victory. Going into the election, he had been confident that the Christian Democrats would garner a plurality of the votes cast, but he never dreamed that they would achieve an absolute majority. What might explain this outcome? Though he had lacked sufficient time to prepare formal addresses, De Gasperi had spoken "simply and frankly at the hustings," finding people everywhere "attentive, thoughtful, and convinced of the facts" presented.[20] Already, in his 1947 New Year's Day radio address, De Gasperi had acknowledged the lingering *miseria* of so many of his countrymen by launching a campaign of national solidarity. "The Republic," he proclaimed, "is to be made in one's heart and in one's habits, based on the moral duty of those who have more to share with those who have less, and of those who are strong to carry the load of those who are the weakest." "We are calling," he added, "for a celebration of justice, of generosity, of sacrifice and of spiritual unity among all Italians."[21] This inclusive, uplifting language certainly appealed to a broad cross section of Italians in the months leading up to the April elections, but it did not accord with the Vatican's increasingly chiliastic orientation.

The Shadow of the Vatican

As the 1940s drew to a close, and the Pope's disappointment in De Gasperi and his party deepened, Pius XII turned to two key lay lieutenants to help promote his crusade for a new Christendom in Italy. The first and most important was Luigi Gedda; the second was Father Riccardo Lombardi. As noted in chapter 6, both men had figured prominently in the lead-up to the 1948 parliamentary elections. Gedda's Civic Committees faded in importance for the time being, as the Pope increasingly focused on Catholic Action in its entirety, determined to reorient it in a more conservative direction.

Standing in the way of the Pope's politicization of Catholic Action was Vittorino Veronese, the respected lawyer and disciple of (future Pope Paul VI) Giovanni Battista Montini who had led Catholic Action as general president since early 1946. Veronese's differences with the Holy Father resembled those of De Gasperi, noted above. The prime minister and the Pope disagreed over the appropriate relationship between religious engagement and political action. Within Catholic Action, opinions diverged as to the kind of spirituality, which should motivate the apostolate.

Veronese framed the choice in the following terms: should the apostolate's efforts be shaped in "problematic[22], spiritualistic, and profoundly formative terms, or in more assertively activist and collective terms, focused especially on re-shaping public opinion?"[23] Veronese championed the former, which privileged the conscience of the individual believer over the crusading group mentality of the latter. Here his spirituality resembled the private, meditative wellsprings of De Gasperi's faith. Each operating in their own sphere, the two men had consulted frequently during the lead-up to the April 1948 elections.

But in Pius XII's eyes, the times required a different approach. Veronese came under papal fire on the grounds of administrative inefficiency and political complacency. In September 1949, Veronese's nemesis Gedda was named to the newly created post of Catholic Action organizational vice president. This move threw Veronese on the defensive, as his rival was given a sweeping mandate to tighten up Catholic Action's decision-making and administrative implementation.[24] The beleaguered general president correctly read this as an indication of declining papal confidence in his own leadership. In a heartfelt letter to a highly placed cleric, Don Sergio Pignedoli, Veronese begged for clarification of his responsibilities. Surely, he wrote, "The faith which the Church requires of me is not that of a simple material instrument, but instead that of a person in full possession of his human dignity and his thoughtful generosity."[25] Nevertheless, two and a half years of behind-the-scenes struggle culminated with Veronese's abrupt deposition as Catholic Action president in favor of Gedda in January 1952.

In response, Christian Democratic Party Secretary Guido Gonella, speaking for the party's leadership, urged Veronese to remain firm in confronting Gedda's challenge.[26] But the sharpening of the domestic and international political (and, in Korea, even military) Cold War confrontation between West and East did not bode well for Veronese's gentle, pastoral stewardship of Catholic Action. For the Pope, the mortal threat posed by "Godless Marxism" and materialism—internationally and domestically—called for a militant Catholic response far more robust than anything a Veronese or a De Gasperi could inspire. In the Italian municipal elections of 1951–1952, Italy's Socialist and Communist parties, already in control of many northern cities, had threatened to gain control, in part or in full, of more, including Rome herself. It was this news which finally catalyzed the leadership shake-up in Catholic Action. Gedda's organizational and persuasive talents were now unleashed at the apex of Catholic Action to prepare her engagement in the pending round of the municipal elections.

The crestfallen Veronese was placed at the head of the far more peripheral Apostolate of the World Laity. At the first World Congress of that body, organized by Veronese in October 1951, Pius XII elaborated on the reciprocal interpenetration of the religious apostolate and political action:

> Politics, that is, in the elevated sense of the word, signifies nothing other than collaboration for the good of the State…. In such political terrain, laws with the widest significance, such as those touching on marriage, the family, the child and the school, are discussed and promulgated…. And how can a true apostole [sic] remain indifferent or apathetic to problems such as these?[27]

Still more florid was the Pope's "Exhortation to the Faithful of Rome" broadcast on February 10, 1952. "The time has come to set aside baneful lethargy," Pius proclaimed; "It is time for all good souls, all those who care about the destiny of the world, to acknowledge one another and close ranks … the whole world needs to be refashioned, the savage made human, and the human divine." Referring to Rome herself by the Latinate term *l'Urbe*, Pius XII proclaimed the Eternal City "the promoter of salvation." All prior ages had left traces of their glory on the city, and "within a brief period of time," this latest crusade might also transform "the exterior face of Rome."[28]

The Sturzo Operation

The timing of the papal exhortation (on the eve of the twenty-third anniversary of the Lateran Accords) reminded the Pope's audience how much the Church's evangelical mission depended on the Vatican's physical and political security. Three days before the papal broadcast, Rome's municipal election campaign of 1952 had commenced. The Italian capital figured in the second round of municipal elections across the peninsula. In the first round, held the previous spring, the Christian Democrats and their centrist allies had done poorly. During August 1951, his star now in the ascendant with the Pope, Gedda publicly belittled the parliamentary gymnastics of "the De Gasperi virtuosos."[29] Echoing a growing sentiment in conservative Vatican and Catholic lay circles, Gedda insisted that the time had come for Italian Christian Democracy to pursue a new course: from Rome southward, the party should forge a "sacred union" with the Monarchists and the Italian Social Movement—both of which now claimed to be confessional parties.[30]

On December 5, 1951, Pius XII directed Monsignor Pietro Pavan to visit De Gasperi personally at the latter's apartment, located not far from the Vatican on Via Boniface VIII. In a "frank, but still respectful" exchange, Mons. Pavan voiced papal preoccupations that the vigorous political "proselytizing" of the "Extreme Left" threatened to overtake the excessively cautious and complacent approach of the Christian Democrat-led government. Should the Left gain the upper hand, either on the national political stage or in the approaching Rome municipal elections, "the Supreme Pontiff would find himself in the greatest difficulty in his Governance of the Universal Church." Pavan's choice of language here bears underscoring, for he was deliberately casting the Pope in the role of a fellow political leader alongside (but also superior to) the prime minister, possessing a mandate whose scope superseded De Gasperi's own.[31]

In Rome, De Gasperi and his colleagues faced a special challenge. A united opposition list of candidates, including the Socialists and Communists, had emerged, placing at the head of its list the elderly Neapolitan radical and former Prime Minister (from June 1919 to June 1920) Francesco Saverio Nitti. To counter Nitti's appeal, senior Vatican officials prevailed upon Don Luigi Sturzo, the founder and head of the Italian Popular Party (during its relatively brief existence from 1919 to 1926) to abandon political retirement and head up a unified "anti-Marxist" list incorporating a broad spectrum of centrist and right-wing politicians.[32] Fairly or not, this entire electoral enterprise has come to be known as "the Sturzo Operation."

The provenance of the Sturzo Operation—even the identity of the person who first approached the Sicilian priest about heading up the proposed "civic list"—remains open question to this day. Gedda, Monsignor Roberto Ronca, Rector of the Sanctuary of Pompeii, and Undersecretary of State Domenico Tardini each figure prominently in published accounts of the affair. Based on Augusto D'Angelo's careful recent assessment, Tardini's role is not to be minimized.[33] By contrast, the Holy Father himself remained oddly detached at critical junctures throughout the drama, particularly considering the immense stakes in his own eyes.

The major turning points in this intricate affair may be briefly summarized. Queried in early April as to whether a danger existed of the Socialist-Communist bloc winning the Romanocentric municipal elections, Christian Democratic secretary Guido Gonella demurred, saying that "in elections, there is always risk." The DC had already begun secret negotiations with the Monarchists about case-by-case cooperation in some municipalities of the Mezzogiorno. But the neo-Fascists were another matter. An April 14 meeting between Lombardi and Gonella turned into shouting match between the two men, with the latter insisting that his party would never "dirty itself" by allying with the neo-Fascists.[34]

Three days later the Pope upped the ante, directing Lombardi to visit De Gasperi at the latter's via Boniface VIII apartment. Instructed by papal housekeeper Sister Pasqualina, on behalf of Pius XII, to "speak forcefully, even reprovingly," Lombardi found the prime minister obdurate. "There is no danger of Rome becoming officially Communist," De Gasperi asserted. He would enter a coalition including neo-Fascists only "if the Pope were to command it," and even then, against his own political judgment.[35] During this critical period, party colleague Amintore Fanfani asked the prime minister why he had not gone to the Pope directly. De Gasperi responded, "No, I won't go; as a Christian I don't want to find myself in a position where I will have to ignore his counsel. No, I will reflect and then decide within the limits of my responsibility."[36]

During this period, De Gasperi received letters and visits from many supporters, including the presidents of several branches of Catholic Action, entreating him not to abandon his centrist politics. The prime minister's daughter, Maria Romana, recites how the bearer of one of these appeals "allowed himself in his enthusiasm to accuse the Head of the Church of interference in Italian politics." Her father stopped him with a gesture, saying "If it is imposed on me I will break my life and my political work, but I can do no other than bow the head." The man saw that the eyes of De Gasperi were heavy with tears.[37]

Lombardi came away from his April 17 visit to the De Gasperi apartment flush with the belief that he had "succeeded" with the Italian governmental leader. Upon receiving word of this, Pius XII is reputed to have said that the Jesuit father was "the only one to have succeeded."[38] Yet the Holy Father was also uneasy about applying such pressure on De Gasperi. As Lombardi recorded in his memoirs, "the Holy Father felt it would not do to issue commands in cases such as these to a prime minister."[39]

Ideally, De Gasperi should experience a change of heart—be converted, in a sense—from what Pius XII saw as an overly rigid ideological stance. One can't help but be struck by the restraint and sensitivity of the two leaders towards one another, even as their disagreement escalated. How either figure might prevail or, if need be, honorably disengage or (in De Gasperi's case) belatedly submit was tremendously important to these two proud and stubborn men. Employing a new tactic to break the stalemate, Sister Pasqualina now directed Lombardi to intervene with De Gasperi's wife Francesca. On Saturday, April 19, the Jesuit paid a visit to De Gasperi's small villa overlooking Lake Albano.[40] In an interview lasting an hour and a half, Lombardi announced that he had come in obedience to a clear mandate from the Holy Father, adding

> if Rome elected a Communist mayor democratically, that would be a shame and a scandal (*vergogna*) for the Church, for the Pope, for the whole anti-Communist world and also for Christian Democracy and for the government…. The Pope would rather see Stalin and his Cossacks in St. Peter's Square than the Communists victorious in the elections to the Campidoglio. Take care, for if the elections go badly we shall make him [De Gasperi] resign.[41]

Mrs. De Gasperi agreed only "to pass on the Pope's opinion" to her husband.[42]

The next evening, Monsignor Montini was the dinner guest of Emilio Bonomelli, manager of the papal villa at Castelgondolfo. As an ex-member of the Popular Party and longtime friend of the family, Bonomelli often hosted both the De Gasperis and Montini at his residence on weekends. Over dinner, Montini underscored the extent of the Holy Father's dissatisfaction with the Christian Democrats. Bonomelli asked Montini if the Pope really meant to repudiate the Christian Democratic leadership in this way. "It is just what they (e.g., the conservatives in the Vatican) want," Montini replied. "They have done nothing but repeat for a long time that the Party is carrying us to ruin, and they think that Gedda and his Catholic Action is the only efficient force capable of replacing the Party and standing up to Communism." When Bonomelli passed this news on to De Gasperi, the latter replied, "Only now do I realize you were right when you painted such a black picture of the state of mind nourished towards us in the Vatican."[43]

The tide began to turn in De Gasperi's favor on Monday, April 21 and Tuesday, April 22, as several intermediaries took action on his behalf. Bonomelli convinced Count Enrico Galeazzi, the architect in charge of Vatican business affairs, of the dangers of the proposed operation. Galeazzi, an influential man for whom the Pope's door was always open, then went to see the Holy Father, accompanied by the Pope's brother Prince Francesco Pacelli.[44] Half an hour later Galeazzi offered Bonomelli general reassurances that the Pope was coming around and that, in extremis, he would not forsake the Christian Democrats. Bonomelli telephoned the good news to De Gasperi, who was anxiously awaiting developments back at Castelgondolfo; the prime minister, however, was afraid to put much stock in what he heard.

Several scholars have concluded that the decisive intervention was that of Giulio Andreotti, whose forceful memo reached the Pope's desk, with the help of a sympathetic monsignor Quirino Paganuzzi and of Sister Pasqualina, on Monday afternoon, April 20. The memo, entitled "On the Roman Elections," outlined eight likely repercussions of the proposed operation. These consequences ranged from the collapse, locally and nationally, of alliances with the other centrist political parties to adverse responses "in America and in the Atlantic world." Uniformly, the Social-Communists stood to gain from these foreseeable complications. Having already campaigned victoriously against communism in Italy, De Gasperi deserved to be given credit in the present, difficult situation. "No less than others," Andreotti concluded, De Gasperi "feels the need for a jealous defense of the city of Rome, episcopal seat of the Pope himself."[45] Tired of being pulled in different directions, and anxious to extricate himself from his deepening entanglement, the conflicted Pius XII seems to have been swayed by Andreotti's Romanocentric argument.

However, none of the other principals in the affair yet realized this. The next day, the embattled De Gasperi and Gonella attended a secret summit with Gedda and several "exponents of the Vatican Secretariat of State" at Grottaferrata, not far from Castelgondolfo in the Alban Hills. The Catholic Action leader threatened to run a separate list of Catholic Action candidates in the Rome elections if the Christian Democrats did not reach an agreement with the rightist parties. Later, Gedda shifted tactics, threatening to withdraw Catholic Action members from the centrist coalition list. Worn out and fearful at the prospective collapse of the "political unity of Catholics," De Gasperi agreed to renew his party's efforts to find a solution within the framework of the Sturzo Operation. Conversing again with Bonomelli by telephone late in the morning of April 22, De Gasperi said wearily, "*Consummatum est*" adding that the party had signed what could only be called surrender with discretion.[46]

Ironically, Gedda's own position was undercut just two days later at a meeting of Catholic Action's five branch and movement presidents whom Gedda had gathered to enlist their support. Unwilling to see Catholic Action play so conspicuously political role, four of the five presidents (the leaders of the Catholic Action Youth Movement, the Catholic Elementary Schoolteachers Federation, the Catholic Women's Movement, and Catholic University Graduates) refused. Only the head of the Catholic Men's Movement (Gedda's one-time power base) endorsed his plan.[47]

Tuesday and Wednesday morning, frenetic negotiations continued between Sturzo and top centrist and right-wing party leaders, with Gedda advising and encouraging the latter. Running short on patience, Sturzo set a deadline of midday Wednesday for the conclusion of a definitive agreement. Last-minute hair-splitting prevented the Monarchists and neo-Fascists from meeting this deadline, and at 2:00 p.m. April 23, Italian State Radio announced that Sturzo was withdrawing from the campaign. The Sicilian priest took this step in consultation with the DC leadership, but without obtaining clearance from the Vatican. One would like to think that Sturzo's decision here reflected not only a willful disposition, but also the reassertion of his anti-Fascist conscience.[48]

How accurately was Father Lombardi conveying the Pope's sentiments in the stormy confrontations of April 14 (with Gonella), April 17 (at De Gasperi's in-town apartment), and April 19 (at the De Gasperi villa in the Castelli Romani)? As William Purdy has noted, it was an "old Roman trick to make free with the Pope's name for tactical purposes." Regardless of whether Lombardi was taking liberties of this kind, Pius XII's general remoteness and indecisiveness may well have abetted such presumption by the Jesuit father.[49]

Pius XII was very irritated with Don Sturzo and the Christian Democrats for "brusque manner" in which negotiations had finally been cut short. News of the Catholic Action majority's rebuff of Gedda, conveyed by Tardini, further distressed the Pope.[50] The disarray and public discord among the Italian Catholic leaders made a mockery of papal hopes for a harmonious, resolute joining together of Christian "crusaders for a better world."

On April 27, the Pope granted an audience to a group of young Catholics gathered in Rome for a national St. Vincent De Paul conference. Among this group were Wladimiro Dorigo, then head of propaganda of Catholic Action's youth organization (*Gioventù italiana dell'Azione Cattolica*) and Giorgio La Pira, the idealistic, left-wing Christian Democrat who was later to become Mayor of Florence. Immediately after kissing the Pope's hand, La Pira rose to offer his own high hopes that "the enemy would not prevail" in the upcoming municipal elections and that "Rome would be preserved." Surprised by these remarks, Pius XII responded with stony reserve. "Let it be, professor," the Pope said, turning his shoulders, "certain refusals and certain forms of ostentation should never have occurred!" There was little question in La Pira's or Dorigo's minds that the Holy Father's remark was directed particularly toward De Gasperi.[51]

On Election Day, the specter of an "atheist administration" on the Campidoglio, which had so alarmed the Vatican and Roman conservative circles, was dispelled. When the ballots were tallied after the May 25 municipal elections, the centrist list (embracing candidates from the governing coalition Christian Democratic, Liberals, Republican, and Social Democratic parties) turned back a strong challenge mounted by the Socialist and Communist parties, along with their secular left-of-center allies. Some 384,000 voters backed the centrist list, while the leftist "Peoples' Bloc" list tallied some 314,000 votes and a separate rightist list received some 206,000 votes.[52]

A month after the Rome municipal elections, De Gasperi and his wife Francesca requested an audience with Pius XII on the dual occasion of their thirtieth wedding anniversary and of their daughter Lucia's having taken her perpetual vows as a nun. On two prior occasions, the Christian Democratic leader had been granted private audiences. The first had come in 1949, on the occasion of the twentieth anniversary of the signing of the Lateran Accords. The second had come the following year, after the prime minister had officially assisted in the ceremony proclaiming the Dogma of the Assumption of the Virgin Mary.

But on this occasion, to De Gasperi's shock and chagrin, he and his wife were refused. The papal snub brought home the depth of the Pope's disaffection with Christian Democrats, particularly in the wake of the Sturzo Operation. De Gasperi responded bluntly to the Holy Father. "As a Christian," he wrote:

> I accept the humiliation, although I can't understand how it could be justified. But I am also Italy's President of the Council of Ministers and Minister of Foreign Affairs. I cannot divest myself of the dignity of these offices even in my personal relations. For this reason, I am bound to express my stupefaction as such an exceptional refusal and must insist on clarification from the Vatican Secretariat of State.[53]

Maria Romana De Gasperi has testified to the lasting pain which this breach with the Pope cost her father. Initially he sought to conceal the rift from public view, suffering further sorrow when it became generally known.[54]

For his part, Pius XII intended the refusal of the papal audience as a rebuke of De Gasperi the Catholic, rather than De Gasperi the Prime Minister. The Pope's keen sense of protocol had prevented the Pontiff from imposing a specific political strategy on a sovereign head of government—even during the height of the Sturzo crisis. His intense disappointment in the Christian Democratic leader seems to have lessened somewhat after De Gasperi fell from power. Shortly after De Gasperi's death, Pius XII praised the former as an exemplary Christian, wistfully adding his regret that De Gasperi had never come to him for advice.[55]

Philosophically, as well as personally, the Sturzo Operation both dramatized and began to resolve the breach which had long existed within Italian political Catholicism. Though weakened, Gedda continued to criticize De Gasperi.

In mid-October 1952, youthful "green berets" of Catholic Action gathered in Rome for an address by the Holy Father, paraded loudly past the Palazzo Chigi, where De Gasperi was meeting with Pietro Nenni. In his dairy for that day, Nenni recorded how De Gasperi had exclaimed, "Gedda is doing this against me."[56] Father Antonio Messineo, editor of the authoritative Jesuit journal *Civiltà Cattolica*, joined the chorus of right-wing criticism of the prime minister in a series of articles between mid-1952 and mid-1954.

Father Lombardi's peremptory visitations to De Gasperi in Rome and to his wife at Castelgondolfo had subjected Italy's head of government to extraordinary personal pressure—pressure which, in extremis, the devout De Gasperi could hardly withstand. That pressure, originating as it did from the head of another state, infringed upon Italian sovereignty. The substance of Pius' diktat, in the case of the 1952 Roman municipal elections, could also be said to be "antidemocratic" since it demanded that the DC embrace, however tactically, the Monarchists and neo-Fascists—avowedly anti-republican political formations of the far Right. If, in the end, Pius XII wavered, this reflected less a crisis of political conscience than a cool recalculation of partisan odds.[57]

The "Swindle Law"

Outside of Rome, the Christian Democrats and their centrist allies experienced mixed success in the two-stage 1951–1952 administrative elections. In comparison with the 1948 national elections, the Christian Democrats lost ground but remained the strongest single party.[58] The party's share of the vote in the two rounds of local elections was 38.4 percent, a drop of some ten percentage points from the 1948 national elections. Their centrist allies, the Liberals, Social Democrats, and Republicans, suffered major reversals. The leftist, and especially Communist, opposition registered modest gains, obtaining 31.9 percent, an increase of some two percentage points in comparison to 1948. The biggest breakthrough, however, came on the right end of the political spectrum. The neo-Fascist Italian Social Movement tripled its 1948 tally, jumping to 15.1 percent of the vote. Concentrated in the Mezzogiorno, this groundswell came almost exclusively at the expense of the Christian Democrats. The Monarchists and neo-Fascists won control of Naples, Bari, and Foggia, doubling their nationwide share of the vote of five years earlier. The "democratic forces" of the governing coalition had garnered a mere 51 percent across the peninsula. Should this pattern recur during the upcoming 1953 parliamentary elections, Monarchist and MSI forces would hold the balance of power in parliament[59]—an unacceptable situation. Nevertheless, right-wing Vatican sources continued their drumbeat that the Christian Democrats were too weak to contain communism without reaching out to the nation's *uomini sani* ["sound forces"] to their right. Such rhetoric betrayed persisting sentiment that a second, unabashedly conservative Catholic party would be preferable to Christian Democracy.

As 1952 drew to a close, the unity of the party came increasingly into question, with conservative factions paying closer heed to the Church in areas like public morality, while progressives like Giovanni Gronchi called for more extensive social reforms. In order to strengthen the party's position in the national parliamentary elections scheduled for the summer of 1953, two new prospective coalition partners were approached. Overtures were made to the Monarchists on the condition that they break with the neo-Fascists. Though attractive to conservative Christian Democrats, such an opening to the Right was rejected by the Social Democrats and Republicans. A potentially bigger electoral *coup* would be an opening leftward to Nenni's Socialists. Such a potential realignment attracted widespread media coverage through the late spring and early summer of 1953. But De Gasperi would entertain such a move only if the Socialists formally renounced their unity pact with the Communists—a step Nenni was unwilling to take.[60]

Facing this problematic electoral landscape, the prime minister and his interior minister Mario Scelba turned to the highly explosive expedient of modifying the electoral law prior to the upcoming parliamentary elections. Extrapolating from the results of the recently completed administrative elections, De Gasperi judged that his own party in tandem with its current centrist partners—the PSDI, PRI, and PLI—had little prospect of gaining a stable governing majority. Instead, he feared that the majority of the vote nationally would be split between Italy's two "undemocratic" extremes: the Social-Communists to the Left and the neo-Fascists and Monarchists to the Right. The two extremes would have great difficulty in forging a coalition government—and could not be trusted with power in any case. The nightmarish prospect that the 1922 stalemate between Socialists and Populists might repeat itself drove the prime minister and interior minister to propose a dramatic and immediately controversial electoral reform.

The proposed election law modified the system of pure proportional representation that had prevailed heretofore in the republic.[61] The law would award a two-thirds majority in the Chamber to any coalition garnering 50.1 percent of the vote. This meant that recipients of even a bare majority of votes cast would be entitled to 380 out of 590 seats. Bearing the cumbersome title of "Modification to the Uniform Code of Law for the Election of the Chamber of Deputies, previously approved by Presidential Decree Number 5, February 5, 1948," the proposed reform was quickly and effectively dubbed "the Swindle Law" by Communist leader Gian Carlo Pajetta.[62]

The proposed reform repelled Nenni and many of his fellow politicians; for them, tampering with the republic's pure system of proportional representation was tantamount to undermining democracy itself. In their view, the proposal disturbingly resembled the 1923 Acerbo Law, which had helped smooth the Italian Fascist Party's path to power. After weeks of exceptionally bitter parliamentary debate and protest, the law passed the Chamber in late January 1953 and the Senate in late March. The Socialist and Communist parliamentary delegations boycotted both votes.[63]

From the outset, this proposal proved highly problematic. The Christian Democrats' Liberal and Republican allies' support for the reform was lukewarm at best, while the Social Democrats waivered, at first rejecting the proposal in favor of the purely proportional status quo. When the party subsequently, and reluctantly, came around in support, seven eminent dissenters, including Parri, Calamandrei and historian Carlo Arturo Jemolo, broke away and formed a new party: *Unità Popolare* (Popular Unity). As expressed by several of the new grouping's most trenchant leaders, the Christian Democratic Party "was aiming solely at ensuring for itself in both Houses of Parliament that *fictitious* exclusive majority which it well knows it no longer commands in the country." More broadly, in words of British Italianist Muriel Grindrod, "People had grown tired of the Christian Democrats with their rather humdrum and pedestrian virtues," reproaching the party for

> the Government's slowness in initiating much needed social reforms and in implementing the legislation required by the Constitution; their alleged tendency to plant their own supporters in all the best jobs; their too strongly marked clerical associations; the swollen bureaucracy; the repressive methods of Signor Scelba's police, and above all, the general feeling that they were becoming too high-handed, too *prepotente* [arrogant] and were seeking to perpetuate their predominance by means of the *legge truffa* [swindle law].[64]

Of all of the critics of his proposed electoral law, De Gasperi was most disturbed by the opposition posed by Luigi Sturzo. While acknowledging the dispersive effective of pure proportional representation, as demonstrated in the administrative elections of 1951, Sturzo opposed the awarding of "bonus seats" as anti-democratic and in fact reminiscent of the Acerbo Law. The proposed legislation would transform elections from freely fought contests for political supremacy to rearguard, retrograde defenses by governing coalitions against their opponents.[65] The prime minister responded to Sturzo in a lengthy letter, in which he acknowledged that constitutional revisions were to be undertaken only under exceptional circumstances but added that the combined threat of the extreme Left and Right was so great that the proposed electoral reform was justified. The two extremes, he asserted, could not be counted on to honor the rules of democratic politics.

In the end, the law was narrowly endorsed in parliament but only applied to the Chamber of Deputies. In the June 7, 1953 national parliamentary elections, conducted according to the controversial law, the governing coalition prevailed but fell just short of the majority necessary to garner the bonus. The governing coalition garnered 49.8 percent of the valid votes. The total of invalid votes, including blank ballots, was 4.6 percent. De Gasperi might have appealed the result, given the narrow margin of his coalition's defeat. Indeed, some members of his party, as well as American Ambassador Luce, pressed him to do just that.[66] But De Gasperi declined, convinced that the remote chance of reversing the outcome did not merit the suspense and controversy that it would certainly prompt.[67] The disheartened De Gasperi then tried, and failed,[68] to obtain parliamentary support for an eighth government, and thus he was forced to step down as prime minister.

The American Connection: Round II

Compounding De Gasperi's trials was Clare Boothe Luce's appointment as US Ambassador to Italy in February 1953. Even before her appointment had been formalized,

> Alberto Tarchiani, Italy's ambassador in Washington, was asked [by his Italian superiors] to intercede to prevent it. While it was "obvious that officially or even unofficially" it was not possible to oppose the candidacy of Luce, the Foreign Ministry stressed that it would have been better "not to be confronted by such a question." In Italy "feminism" was an "imported plant," which had difficulty in "taking roots" and "had not yet entered the mental habit of the Italian public," the bulk of which "would hardly understand the nomination…. It might well be interpreted as a slight, as sign of the scant importance of Rome."[69]

Cognizant of these reservations, Luce must have appreciated her husband Henry Luce's different take on her prospects:

Personally, while I try to be very objective, I can see no objection from a specifically Italian point of view to the appointment. The "woman" angle could be a nine-day wonder in diplomatic circles. I even dare to believe that being a woman would help in a country where the women's vote will be decisive in the forthcoming [national parliamentary] elections.[70]

De Gasperi was less concerned at Luce's gender than at her inexperience in foreign affairs, which did hold the potential of enfeebling Italy's diplomatic clout in Washington.[71] In this respect he missed ex-ambassador Dunn's worldly, old-school diplomacy. Skeptical of the sweeping emotionalism of "rollback," Dunn had countenanced targeted steps to curb Communist influence in the police, armed forces, civil service, and educational system. These were discrete, pragmatic, mutually sanctioned steps, not manifestations of a pell-mell crusade.

Fortunately for Italian sovereignty, American intrusions in the domestic affairs of the peninsula were hobbled by conceptual blind spots, rooted in American political and socio-intellectual history. The first of these has been alluded to just above. This was the tendency in modern American diplomacy for identifying and then concentrating, perhaps even fixating, on one key interlocutor. Henry Luce played a noteworthy stateside role in De Gasperi's case, inviting him to the Cleveland forum in January 1947 and then featuring him in the cover story of the magazine's issue published right before the 1948 elections. This "personalization" of the new republic clearly strengthened De Gasperi's hand, though arguably at the expense of a deeper portrayal of Italian political life at the time. After De Gasperi fell from power, American policymakers lamented the absence of anyone of comparable stature and authority among his successors. True, the stock of Amintore Fanfani (briefly prime minister in early January and February 1954, and again from mid-1958 to early 1959) did rise for a period in American eyes. Though disparaged by Claire Booth Luce as an "Italian Kerensky," Fanfani was able to earn American trust for a period because of his apparent mastery of troublesome DC Party factions and government coalitions. For a brief period, the US policymakers felt it had found in Fanfani[72] their "man in Rome."

A related outlook bearing on Italo-American relations during the Cold War was American unfamiliarity with coalitional parliamentary systems of governance. When addressing the American Congress in 1951, De Gasperi described democracy in Italy as a young, and in some ways tender, plant. It was in good measure the Italian parliamentary tradition that he had in mind. The prime minister had never forgotten how excessive partisan polarization had paralyzed parliament following the First World War, opening the door to Fascism. The revival of parliamentary governance after the Second World War required the cooperation of extremely diverse parties, including even the Communists. The Italian parliamentary tradition, battered though it was, carried forward vital Risorgimento and anti-Fascist values. For De Gasperi and other leaders of the young republic's political elite, the free ebb and flow of political dialogue and the patient forging of compromises were inherently valuable at this stage of the nation's history.

A third relevant factor was modern American political culture's suspicion for anything smacking of elaborate "ideology," coupled with an almost instinctive pragmatism. "Let's get the job done and get out" was the virtual creed of the average GI during the Second World War. The overarching aim of containing or even rolling back Italian communism resonated much more readily in Washington than deliberation over the ins and outs of Italian coalitional governance. In a 1948 memo to Secretary of State George Marshall, the usually perceptive James Dunn implausibly envisioned the emergence of a bipolar Italian party system, which would bring together Socialists and Communists on the one hand against one all-encompassing Center-Right party based specifically on anti-communism.[73] But the Cold War as it dragged on in Italy did not lend itself to such logic. As a result, American policymakers became increasingly anxious to hit upon the right technique or methodology: Political intervention? More economic development? Psychological warfare? Covert or even overt military action?

A number of other recent scholarly studies have suggested a greater measure of autonomy by De Gasperi vis-à-vis both the Vatican and the United States than presumed during the fiercest years of the international and Italian domestic Cold War. Much as he valued American and Vatican assistance in Italy's domestic Cold War, his brand of anti-communism differed from that of Pius XII or the American policymaking establishment. In Mario del Pero's felicitous phrase, this was a *matrimonio di interessi*, a "marriage of convenience" for both partners. This marriage was consummated through a lengthy, laborious process. The marriage was the offspring of repeated compromises by both partners. For De Gasperi it was the offspring, less of deeply rooted political, cultural, and programmatic convergences than of unavoidable historical necessities.[74]

Overall, Italian responses to American initiatives in this period combined cooperation in some areas with a strategy, which Del Pero has termed "containing containment." To Italians, relief aid and longer-term economic assistance were of paramount importance. Political intervention and what the Americans dubbed "psychological warfare" were another matter however. De Gasperi had welcomed official and unofficial American backing during the spring 1948 parliamentary elections but distanced himself from the bellicose tone of American foreign policy rhetoric during the Korean War. Writing during the Korean War, De Gasperi characterized the Americans as "grown-up children" (*fanciulloni*), judging that a "more balanced and experienced (*esperta*) Europe needed to step forward and provide a very firm word of peace."[75] Nevertheless, De Gasperi backed Italian rearmament as a corollary to the nation's entry into NATO, though this permitted the leftist parties to mount an effective peace campaign and to present themselves as champions of neutrality and national sovereignty.

The Fall of De Gasperi

The final acts in De Gasperi's calvary of public service played themselves out in 1953 and 1954. He delivered his last address to the Chamber of Deputies in July 1953 before a "hostile, gloating audience," composed not only of politicians, but also "the select of journalism and Roman society who had gathered to witness the old man's fall."[76]

When Nenni visited De Gasperi at the Viminal Palace on July 6, he found the Christian Democratic leader

> practically at the limits of his physical strength, speaking disjointedly of "tragedy," "drama," "conscience," "responsibility to God," "Christian soul" and so forth—expressions better suited to the confessional booth than [the seat of government] ... I have always been inclined to believe that De Gasperi's mystical-religious foundation limited his capacity for comprehension and action.[77]

Nenni tried to convince his counterpart that it was unreasonable—indeed "ahistorical"—to view the problem of communism in Italy in the same light as communism in Bulgaria or Czechoslovakia, where it had been imposed "at Soviet sword point." The PCI was different, "supported by large portions of the Italian people," and demonstrably "adaptable and unbiased [*dutile fino alla più assoluta spregiudicatezza*]."[78] Nenni was not about to insist on full collaboration with the Communists but added that his party could not enter

> a new governing coalition without the confidence and support of the entire working class, without which we would be worn down [*logorato*] shy of obtaining the minimum broadening of the base of the republican State.

But De Gasperi refused to "relinquish his prejudices."[79]

Months after his departure from the prime ministership, De Gasperi was elected secretary of the Christian Democratic Party, succeeding Guido Gonella in that office. But De Gasperi's election was a tainted one, as the forty-nine yes votes he received were accompanied by twenty-two blank ballots. Most commentators on the election suggest that the majority of the blank ballots were cast by members of the party's "old guard," unhappy with their leader's recent opening to Amintore Fanfani's *Iniziativa democratica* [Democratic Initiative] faction. At the conclusion of the reunion, Fanfani approached a visibly embittered De Gasperi, asking where he was going and why he was departing alone. Bound for Castelgandolfo, De Gasperi responded that the driver's company would suffice, though he then agreed that Fanfani and Mariano Rumor might accompany him.[80]

At the beginning of 1954, the former prime minister found himself the object of scathing public criticism in the pages of the periodical *Candido*, written by right-wing satirist and journalist Giovannino Guareschi. In January 1954, Guareschi revived a story, which had circulated late in the Second World War, that De Gasperi had urged the Allies to bomb the outskirts of Rome and, in particular, the aqueducts in order to provoke an anti-German, anti-Fascist popular uprising. To buttress this inflammatory claim, Guareschi cited two incriminating letters dated January 19 and 26, 1944. The first of these, addressed to English Lieutenant Colonel Bonham Carter, was typed on Vatican letterhead and seemingly signed by De Gasperi. The second was a short note, appeared to be written entirely in De Gasperi's hand. In an acerbic commentary accompanying the letters, Guareschi vilified De Gasperi actions as "not only unconscionable and blind, but...a sacrilege. Not a simple act which betrays hospitality, but the execrable act of a Catholic who betrays the Holy Father."[81]

De Gasperi felt he had no choice but to defend himself in court; above and beyond his personal honor, the legitimacy of the Resistance itself had been called into question.[82] The letters cited by Guareschi had circulated in for some time in some circles and had been hawked, unsuccessfully, to private dealers in 1951 and 1952. Compromising the longer, first letter's credibility was the fact that the numbered stationery used for the letter did not correspond with any stationery used by the Vatican during the year 1944. Furthermore, then retired Col. Bonham Carter asserted that it was not until after the war that he had ever heard of De Gasperi. Interestingly, the prosecution opted not to call in a calligraphy expert, given the inexact nature of such appraisals and the importance of ruling expeditiously. Following a three-day trial in mid-April, Guareschi was found guilty of libel and sentenced to a year in prison.

Painful though it was in personal terms for De Gasperi, the Candido Affair seems to have catalyzed a fundamental shift in his image among his countrymen. The tenor of the final verdict, and of the coverage afforded by the mainstream media, suggested that Guareschi's attack on the former prime minister had besmirched the dignity of the State itself. Half a year before his death, De Gasperi began to be seen as an icon of the republic, not a superannuated politician.

In June 1954, De Gasperi delivered his political swan song. This remarkable address was cordially received, but the Trentine statesman, now seriously ill, was unable to complete his prepared remarks. Only now did the Christian Democratic statesman more directly acknowledge and articulate some of the logical implications of his breach with Catholic integralism. De Gasperi rejected a Vatican-backed effort to make the party become an officially confessional emanation of ecclesiastical authority.

> To operate in the … political sphere, neither faith nor virtue is enough: what is required is to create and nurture an instrument suited to the times: the Party, a political organization with its own program, its own method, its own autonomous responsibility and democratic method. It is not possible to conduct a 20th century democratic regime with the paternalism of a Bossuet.[83]

It is interesting to speculate as to what else De Gasperi might have realized and written had, like Machiavelli or Dante before him, he lived on for many years after being exiled from the political activity, which had been his life's blood. Clearly he had more to say; in a letter to Fanfani, written ten days before his death, De Gasperi defended his own, unflagging efforts to overcome Italy's age-old "Guelph-Ghibelline divide" and alluded to "secret episodes," which he wished to pass on to his successor at the helm of the party.[84]

On August 19, Alcide De Gasperi died. The last words on his lips were "Gesù" (Jesus).[85] In a meditative diary entry dated August 23, 1954, Nenni commented on the "solemn and moving" state funeral for De Gasperi, held that day at San Lorenzo Church in Rome. Yet he added, "How much better it would have been to have left him among his mountains and his woods, where he always must have imagined that he would sleep for the last time."[86]

Notes

1   Mario Del Pero, "The United States and 'Psychological Warfare' in Italy, 1948–1955," *The Journal of American History* (March 2001), 1333.

2 Ottaviani went so far as to boast (referring to "sacrilegious" opposition voters), "You can say whatever you like about the divinity of Christ but if, in the remotest village of Sicily, you vote Communist, your excommunication will arrive the next day." Sandro Magister, *La politica vaticana in Italia 1943–1948* (Rome: Studium, 1979), 52.
3 See Derek Holmes' discussion of this step, and of Pius XII's anti-communism in general, in his "Pope Pius XII," 434–435. See also Barbara Taverni's introduction to *SPD*, IV, 211–212.
4 White, "Christian Democracy or Pacellian Populism?" 218. To the extent that the Pope acknowledged democracy as a form of governance, it had to ground itself on the transcendent value of the "human person" as distinct from secular championing of the "rights of the individual."
5 Del Pero, "American Pressures and Their Containment in Italy during the Ambassadorship of Clare Boothe Luce", 408–439.
6 Ibid.
7 Agarossi and Zaslavsky, *Stalin and Togliatti*, 232–233.
8 Di Scala, *Renewing Italian Socialism*, 45.
9 Agosti, *Palmiro Togliatti*, 209.
10 Alessandro Natta, *Togliatti in parliamento* (Rome: Riuniti, 1988), 25.
11 Nenni, *Tempo di Guerra Fredda*, 586.
12 In the Senate, the electoral outcome was less clear cut; 106 Senators held their seats by nomination, not election.
13 Miller, *United States and Italy*, 249.
14 The most important of these events were the 1949 Crusade for the Great Return, the 1950 Holy Year Jubilee, the Better World Movement of 1952, and the Marian Year of 1954. See Steven White, "A Modern Schism: Alcide De Gasperi, Pius XII and the Meaning of Christian Democracy." American Historical Association Annual Meeting, Washington, DC, January 9, 1999.
15 One of the reasons advanced for this coalition was to guarantee the government support in the Senate, where the Christian Democrat senators fell short of a majority.
16 Phrasing previously used by Pius XI in his encyclical *Divini redemptoris*. Di Nolfo, *La guerra fredda e l'Italia (1941–1989)*, 513.
17 Scoppola, *La repubblica dei partiti*, 30–31.
18 De Gasperi's entire career as a political actor and thinker had expressed his sense of the bonds mutually sustaining democracy and Christian social commitment. Again and again he invoked the Christian-inspired values of human solidarity, social justice, and compassion as the shared historical grounding of all of Italy's anti-Fascist parties. For a fuller discussion of De Gasperi's tolerant attitude toward non-Catholic Italian political traditions, see Nassi, *Alcide De Gasperi*, 290–291. See also the stirring spiritual manner in which De Gasperi framed his relationship with his own public in his November 3, 1946, speech at Rome's Teatro Brancaccio. See Aldo Tenaglia, *Religione e politica in Alcide De Gasperi* (Reggio Emilia: Pozzi, 2001), 29–30, 34.

19 De Gasperi, *SDP* IV, I, 227.
20 "La testimonianza più evidente del nostro popolo," *Il Popolo*, SDP IV. II, 1116.
21 Innocenti, *L'Italia del 1948*, 26.
22 For Veronese a mark of intellectual honesty and inquisitiveness.
23 Malgeri, "La presenza di Vittorino Veronese," 36–37.
24 Domenico Settembrini, *La Chiesa nella politica italiana (1944–1963)*, 2nd ed. (Milan: Mondadori, 1977), 220–221; Magister, *La politica vaticana e l'Italia 1943–1978*, 162.
25 Veronese to Pignedoli, September 1, 1949, ILS, Fondo Vittorino Veronese-Azione Cattolica Italiana, B. 4, f. 37.
26 Malgeri, "La presenza di Vittorino Veronese," 45.
27 Pius XII, *Discorsi e radiomessaggi*, vol. XIII, 300–301, as cited and discussed in Augusto D'Angelo, *De Gasperi, le destre e l'"Operazione Sturzo"* (Rome: Studium, 2002), 20.
28 Ibid.
29 This phrase appeared in a column of Gedda in the Catholic Action daily *Il Quotidiano*, August 7, 1951. Cited in Jean-Guy Vaillancourt, *Papal Power: A Study of Vatican Control over Lay Catholic Elites* (Berkeley: University of California Press, 1980), 200.
30 Ibid. On the confessional claims of the Monarchists, see Ruggero Orfei, *L'occupazione del potere. I democristiani "45/"75* (Milan: Rizzoli, 1976), 128. On the political dialogue and entente, which Monsignor Ronca and other Catholic conservatives were undertaking in this period with both the Monarchist and neo-Fascist parties, see Riccardi, *Il "partito romano*," 143–176.
31 Mons. Pietro Pavan, "Colloquio con Alcide De Gasperi sul mandato di Sua Eccellenza Tardini a nome del Santo Padre," reproduced in Riccardi, *Pio XII e Alcide De Gasperi*, 71–79. It is significant here that Pavan reported not to Montini (who generally coordinated Vatican relations with the Christian Democratic Party and with the Italian government) but to the more conservative, Romanocentric Domenico Tardini.
32 Magister, *La politica vaticana*, 195, n. 22.
33 D'Angelo, *De Gasperi, le destre*, 75–78.
34 Giulio Andreotti, "Montini e la politica italiana," *30 Giorni*, n. 6 (June 1999), 58; Magister, *La politica vaticana*, 164; Giancarlo Zizola, *Il microfono di Dio* (Milan: Mondadori, 1990), 298–299.
35 Zizola, *Microfono di Dio*, 300–301; see also Andreotti, *De Gasperi visto da vicino*, 209.
36 Scalfari, interview with Amintore Fanfani, August 10, 1978, published in Scalfari, *Interviste ai potenti*, 242.
37 Catti De Gasperi, *De Gasperi, uomo solo*, 328.

38 D'Angelo, *De Gasperi, le destre*, 74.
39 Zizola, *Microfono di Dio*, 301.
40 The small villa had been presented to the premier by the Christian Democratic Party on the occasion of his seventieth birthday.
41 Zizola, *Microfo di Dio*, 302–304.
42 Catti De Gasperi, *De Gasperi, uomo solo*, 327–328.
43 Vaillancourt, *Papal Power*, 201–202.
44 Commemorative article by Bonomelli cited in Di Capua, ed., *Processo a De Gasperi*, 198; Vaillancourt, *Papal Power*, 202.
45 Orfei, *Occupazione del potere*, 22–135; Giorgio Galli, *Storia della democrazia cristiana* (Bari: Laterza, 1978), 144–147; Aurelio Lepre, *Storia della prima repubblica. L'Italia dal 1942 al 1992* (Bologna: Il Mulino, 1994), 152. Andreotti's Cassandra-like memo is reproduced in Magister, *Politica vaticana*, 170–172. Significantly, it was Tardini who called Andreotti later on the afternoon of the 20th in order to convey to him the Pope's response.
46 Zizola, *Microfono di Dio*, 305; Catti De Gasperi, *De Gasperi, uomo solo*, 330. In his journal entry dated April 23, Nenni underscored the alarm and anger which Pius XII's tactics now prompted among Socialists and Social Democrats. Perhaps the Socialists and Social Democrats should consider reuniting, he noted, in view of the deepening crisis.
47 Undersecretary Montini, also in attendance at this meeting, conveyed its outcome back to the Vatican. Gedda, *18 aprile 1948*, 153; D'Angelo, *De Gasperi, le destre*, 90.
48 See Domenico Settembrini's thorough summary of the Sturzo Operation, incorporating the sometimes inconsistent recollections of Sturzo himself, DC Interior Minister Mario Scelba and GIAC veteran Wladimiro Dorigo, in *La Chiesa nella politica italiana*, 253–269.
49 On the Pope's increasingly retiring disposition, see Tardini, *Pius XII*, 52, 77–78.
50 Gedda, *18 aprile*, 153.
51 Wladimiro Dorigo's recollections of this group audience, published originally in *Questitalia* (January–February 1959), are reproduced in his *Polemiche sull'integrismo* (Vicenza; La Locusta, 1962), 35. See also Galli, *Storia della Democrazia Cristiana*, 457, footnote 10 and Settembrini, *La Chiesa nella politica italiana*, 268–269. In an October 1952, papal audience, *Corriere della Sera* editor Mario Missiroli praised both De Gasperi and Gedda to the Holy Father. Pius XII remained conspicuously silent at the mention of De Gasperi, but the Pope's face lit up, however, when the Catholic Action leader's name came up. Of Gedda, Pius XII said, "He is a saintly man." For an account of Missiroli's audience, see Nenni, *Tempo di Guerra Fredda*, 545.
52 The Christian Democrats' and their centrist allies' success in Rome was a bright spot in a generally forbidding political landscape: nationwide, the party's aggregate

share of the vote had fallen from 48.5 percent in the 1948 parliamentary elections to 35.1 percent in the 1951–1952 administrative elections. Gianni Baget-Bozzo, *Il partito cristiano al potere: la DC di De Gasperi e Dossetti* (Florence: Le Monnier, 1974), 398; Kogan, *A Political History of Postwar Italy*, 74.

53 Catti De Gasperi, *De Gasperi, uomo solo*, 335. See also Jean-Dominique Durand, "Alcide De Gasperi ovvero la politica ispirata," *Storia Contemporanea* 15:4 (1984), 590. According to Maria Romana, after May 1952, her father never again referred to these "deeply hurtful" events—yet "the sorrow of not having been fully appreciated and supported by the Pope remained etched in the furrows of his brow" (336). Within a year of the appearance of Maria Romana's biography, other principal actors in the Sturzo Operation sought to downplay the significance of Pius XII's refused audience. Emilio Bonomelli, who as manager of the papal summer villa at Castel Gandalfo and a longtime friend of the De Gasperi family had opened his private diaries to Maria Romana, asserted that Pius XII's refusal was only consistent with the Pope's having resolved "for years not to receive Italian political figures." See his commemorative article from *Concretezza* X, 16 (August 16, 1964), cited in Di Capua, ed., *Processo a De Gasperi*, 197. Giulio Andreotti, De Gasperi's devoted, but very clerical, junior colleague, has construed the prime minister's note of protest as being essentially pro forma. See Andreotti's *Intervista su De Gasperi*, ed. Antonio Gambino (Bari: Laterza, 1977), 116.

54 Maria Romana De Gasperi, interview by author, March 24, 2011. Tellingly, the single portion of the De Gasperi papers, which remains closed to researchers, is the series on Pius XII and De Gasperi. Also revealing is De Gasperi's statement from the late 1940s that "I am the first Catholic to serve as President of the Council. I believe I have fulfilled my duty toward the Church. Yet I am merely tolerated there." De Gasperi's daughter sister Lucia offered her father much-appreciated spiritual solace throughout this difficult period. See Suor Lucia De Gasperi, *Appunti spirituali e lettere al padre* (Brescia: Morcelliana, 1964).

55 On Pius XII's volatile relationship with De Gasperi, see Andrea Riccardi, *Pio XII e Alcide De Gasperi: Una storia secreta* (Bari: Laterza, 2003).

56 Nenni, *Tempo di Guerra Fredda*, 545. See also Gedda's refutation of this charge in his *18 aprile 1948*, 159–160.

57 Relative newcomers to Rome, both Lombardi and Gedda were regarded as loose cannons by some members of the curia—a judgment that may now have begun to influence the Pope. Riccardi, *Pio XII e Alcide De Gasperi*, 5–26.

58 Ginsborg, *History of Contemporary Italy*, 141.

59 Alfredo Canavero, *Alcide De Gasperi: Cristiano, democratico, europeo* (Soveria Mannelli: Rubbettino, 2003), 105.

60 Tamburrano, *Pietro Nenni*, 226.

61 Canavero, *Alcide De Gasperi*, 114.

62　Donald Sassoon, *The Strategy of the Italian Communist Party* (New York: St. Martin's, 1981), 96.
63　Ballini, critical introduction to *DSP*, IV, I, 239–240.
64　Grindrod, *The Rebuilding of Italy*, 87.
65　D'Angelo. *De Gasperi, le destre*, 124–125.
66　See Henry Luce letter to Clare Boothe Luce, June 10, 1953, Clare Boothe Luce papers, box 738, folder 9, held at Periodicals Room, Library of Congress.
67　Craveri, *De Gasperi*, 602.
68　By a margin of 263–283.
69　Del Pero, "American Pressures," 415.
70　Clare Boothe Luce diary entry for January 23, 1953. Clare Boothe Luce Papers, box 56, folder 10.
71　Eisenhower's decision to nominate Boothe was largely a reward for her husband's support of the 1952 Republican ticket. Del Pero, "American Pressures," 414; An ex-congresswoman and novelist, the glamorous and outspoken Boothe had converted to Catholicism in 1946. Her zeal for the Church and especially for the Pope (who welcomed her as a friend and acolyte) was another source of concern. According to a popular joke at the time alleged that Luce urged Pius XII to be tougher on communism in defense of the Church, prompting the Pontiff to reply, "You know, Mrs. Ambassador, I am a Catholic too." *L'Osservatore Romano*. www.chiesa. espressonline.it, accessed September 14, 2011.
72　See Giorgio Galli's penetrating political biography *Fanfani* (Milan: Feltrinelli, 1975).
73　*Foreign Relations of the United States*, 1948, III, 832–835.
74　Mario Del Pero, *L'alleato scomodo. Gli Usa e la DC negli anni del Centrismo, 1948–1955* (Roma: Carocci, 2001).
75　Guido Formigoni, *La Democrazia Cristiana e l'Alleanza Occidentale 1943–1953* (Bologna: Il Mulino, 1996), 370.
76　Hughes, *United States and Italy*, 201.
77　Nenni, *Tempo di Guerra Fredda*, 584.
78　Ibid., 584–585.
79　Ibid., 585.
80　Ballini, *Alcide De Gasperi*, vol. III 628 n.
81　G. Guareschi, "Il Ta-pum del cecchino," *Candido* 4 (January 24), 20.
82　Catti De Gasperi, *De Gasperi, uomo solo*, 490–491.
83　Speech at Naples' Teatro San Carlo, June 27, 1954, in P. G. Zunino, ed., *Scritti politici di Alcide De Gasperi* (Milan: Feltrinelli, 1979), 444.
84　Romana De Gasperi, ed. *De Gasperi scrive*, vol. I, 334.
85　Catti-De Gasperi, *De Gasperi, uomo solo*, 418.
86　Nenni, *Tempo di Guerra Fredda*, 635.

8

Aftermath

This chapter will look at the legacies of De Gasperi, Togliatti, and Nenni as they unfolded over three successive periods: 1954–1964, 1964–1980, and 1980–1994. During each of these periods, developing events and trends conditioned the way these statesmen were remembered by their countrymen, as well as the extent to which their party heirs followed in their footsteps. No successive leader within the DC, PCI, or PSI matched the deference with which De Gasperi, Togliatti, and (to a degree) Nenni were viewed within their respective parties or—more broadly—across Italian society. Italy's age-old divide between *paese legale* (in the form of elite political gymnastics) and *paese reale* (the tribulations of ordinary daily life) re-emerged and deepened, as the country's political order struggled to keep pace with rapidly changing socio-economic developments.

1954–1964

For six months following De Gasperi's passing, Nenni refrained from writing in his diary. The Socialist leader needed time to take stock of an altered political landscape, gauging its domestic and foreign implications. He returned to the diary on December 5. As the year 1954 drew to an end, Nenni was sobered by what he saw as generally "negative developments for us"—referring here to the Popular Front. Yet he was encouraged by the "distension" at last setting in between East and West.[1]

Had De Gasperi lived longer, would he too have taken comfort in the incipient East-West thaw? Would De Gasperi's retirement from government responsibilities and from party leadership have allowed this inveterate cold warrior to reconsider his aversion to communism, both at home and abroad? There is little reason to think so. In Pietro Scoppola's words, De Gasperi's anti-communist remarks "could fill an entire volume."[2] As the Christian Democratic leader observed to a friend following the 1948 elections:

Togliatti does not know how to lose... after April 18, he ceased to greet me; even when we crossed paths in the Chamber of Deputies' canteen, he moved away, pretending not to see me. He is cold, metallic. Russia made him a perfect Bolshevik; a machine for receiving and transmitting messages from which the human essence/soul had disappeared."[3]

By the end of the 1940s, anti-communism became the common ideological denominator among all segments of the Christian Democratic Party. For the next quarter century, the Christian Democrats held firm to a policy of *conventio ad excludendum*—a "compact of exclusion" designed to permanently exclude the PCI from power—even as factional DC leaders bickered among themselves over privileges and perks accrued as governing insiders.

From the other side of the ideological divide, Togliatti recalled that "De Gasperi, for the rest, fought us sparing no blows, rebuffing any sense of humanity whatsoever."[4] Addressing the PCI's central committee on December 7, 1954, he characterized the DC as "solely the enemy we have to face in a frontal attack." If anything, he disparaged the short-lived Giuseppe Pella and Mario Scelba governments even more forcefully than he had De Gasperi's preceding ones. He singled out Scelba as more dangerous than De Gasperi had ever been, condemning the hardline former interior minister's government for its "out-and-out McCarthyism."[5]

It is true that, in a column appearing the day after De Gasperi's passing, the Communist leader acknowledged the Christian Democratic statesman's commitment and conduct in support of "the grand coalition of popular forces," lasting from March 1944 (the time of Togliatti's Salerno Turn) to May 1947 (when the Socialists and Communists were expelled from the governing coalition). As long as it lasted, Togliatti said, the anti-Fascist coalition played an absolutely decisive role in successfully launching the postwar Italian state. In the words of Togliatti's biographer Aldo Agosti:

> The *post mortem* homage to his great opponent that appeared in *L'Unità* was not only full of respect, it was also a political message that dwelt above all on "what we had in common, what we experienced together in a common aim, even if only temporarily."[6]

Yet a year and a half later, in a series of *Rinascita* articles provocatively entitled "*È possibile un giudizio equanime sull'opera di Alcide De Gasperi?*" ("Is a Balanced Assessment of the Record of Alcide De Gasperi Possible?"), he denounced De Gasperi's capacities and actions in areas ranging from economics and post-Fascist politics to clericalism and the menace of a new theocracy.[7] For the next twenty years, the Communist Party would continue to lambast the Christian Democratic Party on all of these grounds, each linked to its shameful subordination to "American imperialism." In light of such rhetoric on both sides, it is not surprising that the images of De Gasperi and Togliatti conveyed in the press and in political circles remained trapped in the partisan stereotypes of the *secondo dopoguerra*.[8]

Even as De Gasperi's immediate Christian Democratic successors echoed his anti-communist rhetoric, they abandoned elements of his brand of party leadership.[9] De Gasperi was faulted for neglecting the party's organizational structure. Under his aegis, the party had been too dependent at election time on the capillary presence of Catholic Action and Gedda's Civic Committees. De Gasperi's characteristic appeal to the conscience of the individual voter now seemed overly moralistic and schematic. His mentality struck many in the party as outmoded, more suited perhaps to the liberal Catholicism of the Risorgimento era than the socio-economic exigences of a modern nation.

De Gasperi's profound sense of State, powerful though it was, had in their view prompted him too often to privilege the dictates of his coalition governments over the particular interests of his party. De Gasperi's successor as party secretary, Amintore Fanfani (1954–1959) criticized the amorphous ("artisanal" and "pre-modern"[10]) organizational structure which had heretofore typified the DC. In order to make the party more "agile" (*scattante*) and less reliant on Church bodies such as Catholic Action, he reorganized and energized the party's internal structure. But Fanfani's forceful and sometimes authoritarian style drew criticism from many quarters. Giovanni Guareschi satirized Fanfani in the pages of his weekly *Candido*, depicting him as "the anti-De Gasperi: Napoleonic [i.e., short] in stature but Stalinist in mentality."[11] Under Fanfani distinct party "currents" became formalized, as did the process of *lottizazione* (the parceling out of power and resources)—both trends De Gasperi had resisted.

Prominent among Fanfani's rivals was Giulio Andreotti, now the head of his own party current. Unapologetically embracing the mantle of Degasperianism, Andreotti launched a journal bearing the title *Concretezza*, a tribute to his mentor's sober empiricism.[12] Andreotti was regarded earlier by many as De Gasperi's *dauphin*, his heir apparent. Yet De Gasperi had reservations about this precocious Roman politician. Asked by a journalist his opinion of his youthful protégé, De Gasperi said that Andreotti's qualities were admirable save one— that he "had the prudence of an old man. In politics one should be ready to take action even if one burns oneself—only on one finger though." Another contemporary recalls De Gasperi having chided Andreotti more forcibly: "if you are so cynical in your twenties, what will you be like in your fifties?"[13]

Neither "second generation" leaders like Fanfani nor "third generation" figures like Andreotti could command the party-wide devotion which De Gasperi had enjoyed. Emblematic of a wider crisis of trans-generational legitimacy is the following 1953 lament penned by Catholic activist Mario Rossi:

> Old people today shake their heads and ask just what do these young people want?.... They want to be sustained by the understanding of their fathers. Yet today's world is a world without fathers and where fatherhood is lacking, paternalism takes over.[14]

Rossi was dismayed at the acquiescence and even complicity of prior generations[15] in the rise of Fascism: "Dictatorships," he wrote, "came from paternalism gone wrong." Rossi had supported De Gasperi during the Sturzo Operation (discussed in the previous chapter) in no small measure because the Trentine statesman balked at conservative integralist pressure to link up with neo-Fascists in the 1952 Rome municipal elections. In place of DC party figures, however, many young, idealistic Catholics like Rossi preferred to look to Monsignor Giovanni Battista Montini (the future Pope Paul VI), as a "non-suspect, non-threatening father."[16]

Like De Gasperi, Togliatti confronted factionalism within his party. Already as "Ercole," exiled in distant Moscow, and throughout his twenty years of leadership following the war, Togliatti enjoyed strong support among the party's rank and file. The party closed ranks behind him during the coldest Cold War years. His stature peaked in 1953. As Marzia Marsili has put it:

> The cult of Togliatti... took shape within a context of institutional charisma, where the 'gift of grace' is attributed to the institution of the party (like the Pope in the case of the Church) rather than to any single personality. Togliatti, protected by Gramsci[17] and Stalin, was considered as *the* father by the militants: sometimes too strict, occasionally friendly, always paternal.[18]

In his 1956 secret speech to the Soviet Communist Party, Nikita Khrushchev denounced Stalin's "cult of personality" and promulgated a new doctrine of "peaceful coexistence." This *volte face* forced a major reconsideration of PCI ideology. Togliatti struggled to come to terms with Khrushchev's new line, concerned lest it undermine party unity and discipline. Beneath the surface, the PCI had for years experienced clashes between its hard line or "leftist" wing, led by Pietro Ingrao, and its moderate or "rightist" wing, headed by Giorgio Amendola.[19] These differences came to the fore in late 1961.[20] Ingrao now bemoaned the "degenerations of Soviet monotheism" deriving from Khrushchev's revelations, while Amendola defended Khrushchev's "passionate denunciation." The new Soviet leader's language "possesses a certain iconoclastic fury indeed, but it destroys the myths and icons of Stalinism. It is a liberating fury; it is a moralizing fury." Taking aim at Ingrao, and Togliatti too, Amendola claimed that "before criticism...self-criticism is needed for the tentativeness, caution, timidity and reticence which have slowed down our march."[21]

During his twilight years, Togliatti began to distance the PCI from the Soviet Communist Party (even though the party continued to covertly accept Soviet funds until well into the 1980s[22]). In a *Rinascita* article in December 1961, he promulgated a new doctrine, dubbed "polycentrism," affirming the right of each national communist party to define its own path.[23] In early August 1964, Togliatti and his partner Nilda Iotti travelled to Moscow and then to Yalta on the Black Sea. Two days after arriving at that resort city, Togliatti suffered a massive brain hemorrhage. Eight days later, the storied Italian leader died.[24] On the eve of his departure for Russia, Togliatti penned a secret memorandum which came to be known as the "Yalta Testament." In it he wrote:

> It is not right to talk about socialist countries (the Soviet Union included) as if in those countries everything was always fine ... The problem which poses major attention, as relates both to the USSR and to other socialist countries, is that of overcoming the regime limiting and suppressing personal and democratic liberties installed by Stalin.[25]

Notwithstanding Khrushchev's softening of Soviet Cold War rhetoric in his secret speech of February 1956, the USSR and its Warsaw Pact partners violently suppressed the anti-communist uprising in Hungary in October of that year. Togliatti and his PCI colleagues dutifully supported the Soviets' brutal actions. An unsigned editorial appearing in *L'Unità* (written by the paper's editor Ingrao but expressing the view of the party secretariat) asserted that "when the weapons of the counter-revolutionaries are rattling, you take one side of the barricades or another. There is no third way."[26]

The repression of the Hungarian uprising and the accompanying PCI endorsement prompted the Socialists to break their unity pact with Togliatti's party. Nenni had championed the Popular Front pact ever since 1944. Forcefully, if painfully, he now abandoned that political line. In an October 24 journal entry, he wrote: "In Budapest they fight. In Budapest they die. And in the combat and the blood a system is extinguished...[communist] internationalism becomes colonialism." The facts spoke for themselves. On November 7, he added: "To do one's duty is difficult. To do mine this evening cost me a bitter address to the Chamber [of Deputies], an address rupturing with Moscow and the PCI."[27] Emblematic of Nenni's disenchantment was his decision to renounce and return the Stalin Peace Prize money ($25,000) which he had been awarded in 1951.

Nenni's long record of political reincarnation—at first an anarchist, then a radical Republican-turned revolutionary Socialist who, in the interwar period, first challenged Stalinist communism and then, between 1934 and the mid-1950s, championed a united front Socialist-Communist alliance, only to distance himself and his party from the PCI thereafter—exposed the Socialist leader to charges of incoherence and impulsiveness. Though he had served as party secretary from August 1943 to August 1945, and again from 1949 to 1963, his tactical twists and turns adapting to shifting political conditions sometimes obscured his long-term hopes of reconciling, and realizing, socialism on the one hand and democracy on the other. Between 1947 and 1956, he saw DC-sanctioned clericalism and integralism as the greatest threat to a democratic Italy—a threat necessitating the Socialist-Communist political bond. Relinquishing that bond in late 1956, Nenni slowly led the PSI into supporting NATO in addition.

Nenni's complicated relationship with Togliatti continued to fluctuate during this period of transition. In early September 1960, Nenni and Togliatti found themselves together at the same hotel at the alpine tourist resort of Cogne. Journalists present were, characteristically, curious about the tenor of the two men's rapport: on this occasion, Nenni informed them, they needed to content themselves with the knowledge that his exchanges with Togliatti were limited to "good day" and "good evening."[28] Yet as the Christian Democrats' 1963 "Opening to the Left" (detailed below) drew closer, Nenni confided in his journal that he welcomed the prospect of returning to the *stanza dei bottoni* (literally "the room with the buttons" of power). Togliatti encouraged the Socialist leader in turn with the words "you are fortunate to be able to *fare politica* [e.g., move from an oppositional stance and play a positive political role]."[29]

The chief Christian Democratic proponent of a DC-PSI rapprochement was Aldo Moro, who became party secretary in March of 1959. Moro acknowledged the legitimate democratic "citizenship" of Nennian socialism. The political trajectories of Christian Democracy and Italian Socialism, he said, represented "convergent parallels"—diverse in provenance and ideological orientation, yet destined to "converge inevitably toward a common direction."[30] In December 1963, the DC and the PSI, along with Saragat's Social Democrats and

La Malfa's Republicans,[31] launched the "Opening to the Left" forming a coalition government led by Moro as prime minister and Nenni as deputy prime minister.

The Opening to the Left did not extend as far as the PCI, which continued to be barred from the nation's governing coalitions due to the Christian Democrats' *conventio ad excludendum* doctrine. But Communists headed city governments in many other cities across northern and north central Italy. Bologna had been a PCI stronghold continuously since the end of the Second World War.[32] Indicative of the party's grassroots presence were the estimated one million people who attended Togliatti's funeral in Rome. In his diary, Pietro Nenni commented that this was "a show of strength rather than emotion…as everything was in the activity of Stalin's communist generation."[33] Carlo Levi saw the commemorations more generously, writing in the pages of *L'Unità*:

> [T]he numerous crowds were there… driven by a conscious and shared desire to bear witness… to affirm what Togliatti had represented, the profound symbolism of his name was in Italy a poignant expression. Their collective presence declared. "We are here, we are involved and we are not turning back, in the shadow of civic non-existence."[34]

Levi had been elected in 1963 to the Italian Senate as an independent on the Communist Party ticket. His testimony reflects the sympathy which Togliatti and his party enjoyed among many members of Italy's intelligentsia.

1964–1980

Facilitating the country's Opening to the Left were winds of change sweeping the Church. Popes John XXIII (1958–1963) and his successor Paul VI (1963–1978) transcended the aura of omniscience which had surrounded Pius XII and called for *aggiornamento* (literally "bringing up to date") in Catholic doctrine and practices. John XXIII relaxed Pius XII's (and his conservative, integralist Vatican entourage's) fixation on internal Christian Democratic affairs. In a private conversation with Amintore Fanfani, John XXIII said, "The two banks of the Tiber [the Vatican and the Montecitorio, seat of the Chamber of Deputies] [are] united in their respect for shared values, but aware that their areas of competence and objectives are very different."[35] The reformist Second Vatican Council (1962–1965) authorized the use of the vernacular in the mass. Moderating its clericalism,[36] the council recast the Church itself as "the body of the faithful."

Internationally, Pope John sought to restrain the escalating nuclear arms race between two superpowers, and the profound reciprocal paranoia which fed it. In his 1962 encyclical *Pacem in Terris* (Peace on Earth), the Pope—for the first time in Church history—addressed not only the Catholic faithful, but "all men of good will." Behind the scenes, the Vatican played a key mediating role between the Kennedy and Khrushchev governments, helping to pave the way to the Limited Nuclear Arms Test Ban Treaty between the United States and the USSR.[37]

The center-left governments of the years 1963–1968 faced a more variegated socio-economic landscape than had typified the era of the *secondo dopoguerra*. The "economic miracle" of the late 1950s and early 1960s alleviated much of the material hardship of the early postwar years. Large numbers of rural Italians, especially from the Mezzogiorno, moved to towns and cities, where they found both opportunity and disdain amidst their urban counterparts. Women entered the workforce in increasing numbers, challenging traditional familial gender relations. American-style consumerism found expression in many facets of Italian life, ranging from television to the automobile culture. The upper tiers of society partook of the *dolce vita* ("sweet life") evoked in Federico Fellini's 1960 film of that name. Such developments were welcomed by most Italians, even as they unsettled observers on the Marxist left and in some Catholic circles as well.

Among the center-left's accomplishments were the creation of the *scuola media unica*,[38] the reform of mental institutions, the establishment of state nursery schools, and pensions reform. The influential American journalist Walter Lippman, a good friend of Nenni's, wrote an April 1962 column which judged the new government coalition in very positive terms. President John Kennedy approved of the Christian Democrats' outreach to Nenni's Socialists, both to promote social reforms in Italy and to blunt the Communist Party's appeal there. Unfortunately, the nationalization of the country's electrical system turned out badly, provoking a serious economic contraction.[39] Ambitious initiatives in the area of economic planning were left unrealized, and the creation of regional governments (mandated initially in the 1948 constitution) had to wait until the beginning of the 1970s. The latter delay was particularly unfortunate, as a bloated central state bureaucracy was slow to carry out much-needed reforms.[40]

The disappointments associated with the center-left damaged the fortunes of both the PSI and the PSDI. In the 1963 parliamentary elections, the Socialists had garnered 13.8 percent of the vote and the Social Democrats 6.1 percent. The two parties then merged as participants in the center-left (the coalition created on the basis of the 1963 elections), under the banner of the Unitary Socialist Party (PSU). Together, Nenni and Saragat hoped to score gains in the 1968 parliamentary elections. But the ill-fated PSU managed only 14.5 percent of the vote that year, barely two-thirds of the total the two distinct parties had garnered five years before.[41] This electoral reversal, and the ensuing break-up of the PSU, left Nenni despondent.

His home life brought welcome respite from the vicissitudes of party politics. Deeply devoted to one another throughout their sixty-nine years of marriage, Nenni and his wife Carmen enjoyed spending evenings together during their latter years, he silently writing or reading at his desk as she sat knitting nearby. When visiting the Socialist leader one evening at his apartment on via Polonia, conservative journalist Indro Montanelli was bemused to see, stacked up on Nenni's desk, tomes by Bakunin, Stirner, and Enrico Ferri (all works recalling the anarchism of the youthful Pietro), but not a single book by Marx, Engels, or Lenin. As the visit drew to a close, a child's cry could be heard from the room next to the study. "These are our real tyrants," Nenni exclaimed. Montanelli left with the image of:

> [T]he honorable Pietro with the little tyrant, the daughter of his daughter, wrapped around his neck, intent on soothing her, bouncing her in his arms and saying "*Ecco nonno!... Ecco nonno!* (Here is grandpa!... Here is grandpa!)"[42]

The student militance confronting Italy in the late 1960s also drew Nenni's attention. Italian student protest was influenced by the transnational anti-Vietnam war movement and the ideological iconoclasm of figures such as Mao and Marcuse. Its material basis derived from the educational reforms of the 1960s: with the introduction of compulsory secondary education until the age of fourteen, the number of school students nearly doubled between 1959 and 1969. University enrollment subsequently exploded, yet the facilities, material resources, and, most ominously, the antiquated pedagogy prevailing in Italian higher education lagged far behind.[43] Student picketing, riots, and, by January 1968, thirty-six campus occupations were the result. Dovetailing with student unrest were labor protests, strikes, and lockouts which climaxed in the "Hot Autumn" of 1969. Nenni now engaged the student and labor rebels in candid and sometimes heated dialogue. Once an angry rebel himself, Nenni was maturing into a respected sage, eloquently defending the founding values and institutions of the republic he had helped to create.

Following the collapse of the center-left, he resigned as deputy prime minister. In December 1968, Christian Democratic Prime Minister Mariano Rumor named Nenni foreign minister, returning him to a post which he had occupied some twenty-two years in De Gasperi's third government (February–May 1947).

Of the many governmental hats he had worn during his career, this was one of the ones that fit Nenni best. Among his impressive achievements during the second Rumor government (December 1968–August 1969) were Italy's diplomatic recognition of Communist China, and his country's admission—at long last—to the United Nations.[44]

In 1970, he was named Senator for Life—a well-deserved honor for a statesman who had loyally served his party and country for nearly three quarters of a century. Three years later Nenni presided over the Senate's eighth legislature. Here Nenni the flamboyant orator yielded to Nenni the esteemed parliamentarian. As a longtime friend and fellow parliamentarian Giovanni Spadolini recalled, Nenni "was perfect for the position... . His style was impeccable: dry, essential, anti-rhetorical. the opposite of rhetorical," returning him, "beyond politics, to his native vocation—journalism."[45]

Notwithstanding the civic commitment and capabilities of individuals like Nenni, Italy's political system struggled to cope with a host of crises fraying of the social fabric of the nation. Unregulated, speculative urban development produced "concrete deserts." Whole neighborhoods were wracked by oppressive rents and by insufficient social services, conditions which went unremedied despite intense lobbying by tens of thousands of residents.[46] Divorce emerged as bitterly contested political issue: after years of parliamentary wrangling, it was legalized in 1974 via popular referendum.[47] Most traumatic of all was the eruption of political violence of the so-called *anni di piombo* ("Years of Lead"). Right-wing extremists shocked the nation by bombing Milan's Piazza Fontana in 1969. Even more brutal was their assault on the Bologna train station eleven years later, which claimed the lives of eighty-four persons. At the opposite end of the spectrum, a desperate far Left organization known as the Red Brigades, formed in 1970, carried out robberies, kidnappings, bombings, and assassinations.

Alarmed by the country's turbulent status and by the inability of the political status quo to surmount these challenges, Italians turned with renewed appreciation to the figures of De Gasperi and Togliatti. The twentieth anniversary of De Gasperi's death (August 19, 1954) coupled with the tenth anniversary of Togliatti's passing (August 21, 1964) occasioned a flurry of newspaper columns, periodical and journal articles, and books. These commemorative pieces offered homage to one or the other statesman while disparaging—or simply ignoring—the other. More systematic and increasingly sympathetic comparisons of the two would have to wait until the next anniversary round ten years later.[48]

Anticipating such explicitly comparative approaches was Pietro Scoppola's 1977 watershed work *La proposta politica di De Gasperi*, which focused on the years of the DC-PSI-PCI anti-Fascist coalition (1944 to 1947). Elaborating on the recollections of Maria Romana De Gasperi shared in her 1964 biography *De Gasperi, uomo solo*, Scoppola's study documented De Gasperi's reservations about Catholic integralism and the charismatic populism of Pope Pius XII.[49] Scoppola also detailed previously under-appreciated areas of consonance between DC, PSI, and PCI anti-Fascist ideals.[50]

Scoppola's study appeared in the context of a developing rapprochement between the DC and PCI.[51] Between 1972 and 1976, the PCI electoral strength grew 27.1 percent to 34.4 percent of the vote, while the DC held steady at 38.7 percent.[52] Prominent among the reasons for the Communists' gains was the leadership of the gentlemanly Enrico Berlinguer, elevated in 1972 to the post of PCI general secretary. Berlinguer was an eloquent advocate for Eurocommunism—a moderate alternative to the Stalinist orthodoxy still prevailing behind the Iron Curtain. In 1973 he called for a "historic compromise" between the PCI and the DC, promising to respect the Church and Italy's NATO commitments in exchange for long overdue social reforms.[53] Aldo Moro was the chief Christian Democratic advocate for renewed dialogue with the PCI. By 1976, even Giulio Andreotti, once an intransigent anti-communist, became receptive to a discrete "Grand Coalition" power sharing arrangement with the Communists.

On the morning of March 16, 1978, after leaving mass, Moro was kidnapped by the Red Brigades.[54] His five bodyguards were all killed in the ambush, while Moro was spirited away into hiding. His captors eluded a nationwide manhunt, finally killing Moro and leaving his body in the trunk of a car parked, symbolically, half-way between the Christian Democratic and Communist Party headquarters in the center of Rome. Moro's murder marked the ending of the historic compromise. More broadly, it represented the antithesis of the patient, dialogic vision that had animated his entire career—a vision eloquently articulated by the Christian Democratic statesman already in 1959 in the following terms:

> A great deal of the creativity of the democratic state is in fact education, persuasion, liberation of moral energies. Education and persuasion in fashioning law by means of political debate, and through the free choice of the electorate; education and persuasion in the implementation of laws; education and persuasion so that man's spiritual qualities may emerge.
> —Aldo Moro, October 1959[55]

Moro's death dealt the First Republic a blow from which it was never fully to recover.

1980–1994

On January 1, 1980, Pietro Nenni passed away at age eighty-eight. At his funeral, his younger party colleague Bettino Craxi concluded his eulogy saying: "Ciao Nenni... Ciao because you remain here with us. Your workers this day have remembered and spoken as you wished, affirming that the man who has just died has never abandoned us."[56] As Nenni's apparent *dauphin*[57] at the time, Craxi had assumed the secretaryship of the PSI in 1976. He would retain this post— at great cost to his party and his country—until 1993.

Even more than Nenni the partisan, it was Nenni the person whom his fellow Italians came to miss. As a politician he was much discussed and often criticized; as a man he was beloved. Nenni possessed a singular sense of history. He wrote in his journals (*diari*) as a way of making sense of experiences, day by day—but he also understood the value they would have in years to come, as their readers perused them the better to understand their country's recent past. He savored the immediacy of his political battles, deeply aware at the same time of the full historical meaning of these struggles.[58] With disarming modesty, he freely acknowledged his failures along with his successes—more freely, it must be said, than did either his Christian Democratic or his Communist counterparts. Whimsically speaking, Nenni managed to combine contrasting traits reminiscent of both protagonists in Miguel Cervantes' *Don Quixote*. In his continual pursuit of an elusive democratic socialist ideal, he recalled Don Quixote. Yet like Sancho Panzo, he remained firmly grounded in the companionship of family, friends, and comrades.

A longtime parliamentary colleague and friend of Nenni's was Florentine historian and journalistic commentator Giovanni Spadolini. The 1981 accession of this respected Republican Party member to the prime ministership was a sign of political health, ending as it did three and a half decades of continuous Christian Democrats occupation of that post. But Spadolini's tenure was a short one, soon followed by the prime ministership of Bettino Craxi (1983–1987). Nothwithstanding his glowing eulogy to Nenni, cited above, the opportunistic, unscrupulous, and venal Craxi was anything but a sincere Socialist. Corruption metastasized across the political spectrum during these years. In Roy Domenico's words, Craxi and his associates "flaunted the bounty of office in a fashion never witnessed by their predecessors. Christian Democrats may have been corrupt, but they usually veiled it well behind their staid and family-oriented presence."[59]

Even after the prime ministership returned to Christian Democratic hands in 1987, Craxi stayed on as a behind-the-scenes player. Then in early 1992, the *tangentopoli* ("bribesville") scandal broke, revealing far-reaching financial malfeasance by Craxi and associates within and beyond the PSI. State magistrates responded with far-reaching investigations in what came to be known as the "clean hands" inquest. More and more politicians from across the political spectrum now came under suspicion of corruption; by the end of 1993, 144 parliamentary deputies out of a total of 630 were under investigation.[60]

This dreary sequence of events deeply disillusioned the Italian electorate. Dramatic international developments further compounded the political crisis. The 1989 collapse of communism in Eastern Europe induced the PCI to rebrand itself as the Democratic Party of the Left (soon shortened to the Democrats of the Left). Softening its image, the new party dropped the hammer and cycle from its emblem. This ideological and organizational transformation offended more militant party members, who broke away and formed their own party, Communist Refoundation. The disappearance of the PCI, and rapid decline of the PSI, deprived the Christian Democratic Party of its traditional Marxist nemeses. In 1994, the DC dissolved in turn, succeeded by much smaller left- and right-leaning parties.

The pluralistic party system and bifurcated political culture of the republic were in tatters, leading some commentators to proclaim the end of what they now dubbed "The First Republic." The scene was set for the entry onto the political scene of Silvio Berlusconi, the charismatic Milanese real estate magnate and media mogul. The self-proclaimed "Cavalier" promised a complete break with the country's recent political past[61] (even though Bettino Craxi had been a close ally of his for many years). Beginning in 1994 and continuing for nearly the next two decades, Berlusconi was to dominate Italian civic life. In 2011, he lost a vote of no confidence in parliament and resigned. Two years later he was convicted of multiple charges of tax fraud and banned from political activity for six years. Sidelined from government, he continued to occupy the nation's political spotlight.

The likes of Craxi and Berlusconi fell far short of the standards set by the republic's major founders. Many of the commemorative pieces of De Gasperi, Togliatti, and Nenni written in August of 1984 enshrined them "within an ample constitutional pantheon" (*Nel Pantheon dell'arco costituzionale*). RAI television's channel one broadcast interviews with Nilde Iotti and Giulio Andreotti, in which they reflected on Togliatti's and De Gasperi's "parallel lives" during the *secondo dopoguerra*. Reviewing this telecast in the pages of the Roman daily *La Repubblica*, Miriam Mafai depicted the two statesmen—as noted in chapter 1— as *carissimi nemici* (literally "dear enemies"). Domenico Settembrini penned a shrewd variation on this theme, stating that De Gasperi's "master work was to neutralize the anti-democratic forces within the PCI and those within the Church angling for an authoritarian Catholic restoration, playing one off against the other"—an insight subsequently echoed by other commentators.[62]

The metaphor of the pantheon recurred ten years later in the next major round of commemorative articles, but with two important differences. First, given the collapse of the republic's major parties by 1994, the pantheon became an ensemble of worthy individuals more than an array of partisan icons. Second, many writers dropped Togliatti from the pantheon altogether. The fall of the Soviet Union and the opening of Soviet Communist Party archives there severely damaged Togliatti's reputation. Previously inaccessible collections in Moscow showed the PCI leader to have been fully subordinate to Stalin, willing and able to serve as a consummate Comintern apologist for the Soviet dictator. Other commentators who chose to retain Togliatti in a founding pantheon did so on the basis of his postwar record of relative restraint, with minimal reference to his interwar behavior.

De Gasperi garnered the lion's share of accolades in the 1994 round of commemorations—a pattern which would only accelerate in ensuing years.[63] Two years earlier the archbishop of Trento promoted a cause for the Trentine statesman's canonization (though it subsequently stalled due to family desires to protect their privacy). With typical irony, the iconoclastic left-wing paper *Il Manifesto* printed a piece about De Gasperi and Togliatti entitled "Il Beato e Il Migliore."[64] A more reverential, popular work about the Christian Democratic leader, entitled *Mussolini e De Gasperi: vite divergenti* (Mussolini and De Gasperi: Divergent Lives) had appeared a number of years earlier.[65] By the late 1990s, a new juxtaposition began to appear in the Italian media, one juxtaposing the modest, upstanding Trentine statesman to the charismatic but unscrupulous Berlusconi.[66]

Ten years after his passing, Nenni was honored in a colorful collection of essays by his former peers, as well as by historians. In one touching contribution, Republican Party luminary Randolfo Pacciardi celebrated his former Spanish Civil War comrade's lifelong devotion to the ideals of Giuseppe Mazzini.[67] Similarly affectionate were Giovanni Spadolini's recollections of Nenni published the same year in *Nenni sul filo della memoria, 1949–1980*. Thereafter, commemorations of the Socialist leader's life and work appeared less often. Even so, the celebrated writer Orianna Fallaci's *Interview with History*, incorporating the spirited interview she conducted with Nenni in his twilight years, continued to attract readers. In that interview, she asked whether the many trials of his political career had depressed him. Nenni's replied, 'If you ask me what's going to happen tonight, I'll say it will probably be something unpleasant. But if you ask what's going to happen in the years to come, then I become an optimist."[68]

Each of Italy's founding fathers possessed virtues vital to the nation's health as a democratic polity. De Gasperi's most distinctive asset was his commitment to the dignity and endurance of the Italian State. His personal rectitude, coupled with his ability to recognize and address political realities, steadied Italy's ship of state in the face of complex domestic and foreign challenges. Palmiro Togliatti too was a realist, resourceful and resolute in guiding his PCI, the West's largest communist party, from his interwar years of exile until his death in 1964. Togliatti's vision and fortitude were all the more necessary for a party relegated (after May 1947) to a position of permanent political opposition. Nenni's passionate, lifelong championing of republicanism contributed in no small measure to the republic's institutional confirmation in the referendum of 1946. Politically less adroit than his Christian Democratic and Communist counterparts, Nenni surpassed them in rhetorical flair, person-to-person warmth, and sheer zest for life. To return to the classical paradigm which opened this work, De Gasperi's *gravitas* (poise), Togliatti's *constantia* (resolve), and Nenni's *magnitudo animi* (generosity of spirit) each proved indispensable in the fashioning of Italy's resilient republic.[69]

Notes

1   Nenni, *Tempo di Guerra Fredda,* 636.
2   Scoppola, *La proposta politica di De Gasperi* (Bologna: Il Mulino, 1978), 253.
3   Catti De Gasperi, *De Gasperi, uomo solo,* 259.
4   Massimo Caprara, "Strategie togliattiane," cited in *Dovuto a De Gasperi: testimonianze & documenti nel 50. anniversario della morte,* ed. Nicola Guiso (Milan: Ares, 2004), 8.
5   Pella's government lasted from August 1953 to January 1954; Scelba's from February 1954 to July 1955. Iuso, *Lezioni sul secondo dopoguerra,* 210–212.
6   Agosti, *Palmiro Togliatti,* 226.
7   See Fabio Silvestri, introduction to Palmiro Togliatti, *De Gasperi il restauratore,* 3, followed by the full text of the *Rinascità* articles appearing from October of 1955 to June of 1956.
8   Marsili, "De Gasperi and Togliatti," 249–261.
9   Steven White, "Like Father, Like Sons? Alcide De Gasperi's Search for Christian Democratic Heirs." Paper delivered at American Catholic Historical Association Semi-Annual Meeting, Princeton, NJ, March 10, 2010.

10 Language he directed specifically at Guido Gonella, party secretary from 1950 to 1953. In his collection of political sketches *Visti da vicino* (Milan: Rizzoli, 1982), Giulio Andreotti stated that Gonella viewed the party as an "organizer of consensus rather than a rigid apparatus," 162.

11 On the Neapolitan satirist and politician, see Alessandro Gnocchi, *Giovanni Guareschi: Una storia itlaiana* (Milan: Rizzoli, 1998).

12 With a combination of modesty and presumption, Andreotti was quoted as saying "Don't ask me who today De Gasperi's political heir is. His heirs are all Italians who choose Democracy and Liberty." Cited in Giulio Andreotti, "La continuità dell'opera di De Gasperi." Amos Ciabattoni and Armando Tarullo, eds. *De Gasperi: Storia-Memoria-Attualità* (Soveria Mannelli: Rubbettino, 2004), 15–17.

13 Massimo Franco treats the De Gasperi-Andreotti relationship extensively in his *Andreotti visto da vicino* (Milan: Mondadori, 1993).

14 Mario Rossi, "Queste generazioni nuove" in *Gioventù* XXX (1953), 154, cited in Hebblethwaithe, *Paul VI: The First Modern Pope* (New York: Paulist Press, 1993), 242;

15 To cite one example, Amintore Fanfani had written enthusiastically about Fascist corporatism in the 1930s.

16 Hebblethwaite, *Paul VI*, 242.

17 On Gramsci's thought and legacy, so fundamental to his comrade Togliatti's postwar intellectual and cultural prestige, see Roberto Esposito, *Living Thought: The Origins and Actuality of Italian Philosophy*, trans. Zakeya Hanafi (Stanford: Stanford University Press), 157–216, and Agosti, *Palmiro Togliatti*, 158, 247–248.

18 Marsili, "De Gasperi and Togliatti," 259.

19 Bocca, *Togliatti*, 526–543; Agosti, *Palmiro Togliatti*, 272–278.

20 The immediate instigation of this exchange were the decisions made at the Soviet Communist Party's twenty-second congress to remove Stalin's remains from the mausoleum in Red Square and to change the name the city of Stalingrad to Volgograd. Agosti, *Palmiro Togliatti*, 273.

21 Ibid.

22 Domenico, *Remaking Italy*, 138.

23 An English language translation of this article, entitled "Diversity and Unity in the International Proletarian-Communist Movement," is available at marxists.org/archives/Togliatti/1961/unityanddiversity.htm.

24 Nilde Iotti's recollections of the couple's last voyage together are recorded in Corbi, *Nilde*, 181–185.

25 Bocca, *Togliatti*, 568. Togliatti's scholarly critics have questioned the import of this a last-minute conversion. In the view of such authors as Elena Agarossi and Victor Zaslavsky, Togliatti never relinquished the long-term goal of establishing hegemony in Italy. They characterize Togliatti's opportunistic and at times ruthless manner

of party leadership as Stalinistic. Agarossi and Zaslavsky, *Stalin and Togliatti*. While acknowledging the authoritarian quality of Togliatti's leadership, Paul Ginsborg offers a more balanced assessment of the Communist leader as a master of *realpolitik*. Ginsborg, *History of Contemporary Italy,* 291–293. See also Terzuolo, "Uncongenial Realism."

26 Agosti, *Palmiro Togliatti*, 241.
27 Nenni, *Tempo di Guerra Fredda,* 237.
28 Spadolini, *Padri della Repubblica,* 211.
29 Tamburrano, *Pietro Nenni*, 252.
30 Giovanni Di Capua, *Aldo Moro: il potere della parola* (Rome: EBE, 1988), 99–100.
31 La Malfa also "played an important part in fostering and facilitating the *rapprochement* between political and intellectual strands—social liberalism, social reformism and social Catholicism—that had been divided by the Cold War." https://www.oxfordhandbooks.com/view/10.1093/oxfordhb/9780199669745.001.0001/oxfordhb-9780199669745-e-21, accessed October 17, 2018.
32 That fact, coupled with the city's first-class cuisine and the historic prestige of its university, earned Bologna the nickname *La Dotta, la Grassa e la Rossa* ("The Learned, the Fat and the Red").
33 Nenni, *Gli anni di centro-sinistra. I diari 1957–1966* (Milan: SugarCo, 1982), 388.
34 Agosti, *Palmiro Togliatti,* 292.
35 Michele Marchi, "La DC, la Chiesa e 'l'asse vaticano', 1959–1962, *Mondo contemporaneo* 2 (2008), 39.
36 This trend was not lost on Nenni, who began to tone down his own anti-clericalism. Mauro Ferri, a younger party colleague of Nenni's, has related how the two of them attended religious services for a deceased party supporter late in the 1960s. Although Nenni refrained from participating in the mass, he listened respectfully. When it came time for the congregants to exchange a sign of peace, the officiating priest descended from the alter to offer his hand to the Socialist leader. How Nenni's receptivity on this occasion differed from that he had displayed at a pre-Vatican II mass for another deceased comrade: to Nenni, that mass, ornate and sung in Latin, was a "ridiculous anachronism." Mauro Ferri, "Un leader amato," in *Nenni dieci anni dopo,* 77–78.
37 See Norman Cousins, *The Improbable Triumvirate: John F. Kennedy, Pope John, Nikita Khrushchev* (New York: Norton, 1972).
38 The *scuola media unica* was an inclusive form of middle school which supplanted the earlier elitist three track structure. Subsequently Latin ceased to be a required subject in middle school, on utilitarian grounds and a widespread perception that it was inherently bourgeois. White, *Progressive Renaissance,* 169–172.
39 D'Angelo Bigelli, *Pietro Nenni dalle barricate a Palazzo Madama,* 348.

40 As of the early 1970s, 95 percent of senior civil servants had entered the service prior to 1943. Based on interviews with these officials, Robert Putnam concluded that, for them, "it was not so much Italian political life *in se* and *per se* that was uncongenial:" nearly half of them expressed reservations about universal suffrage. Putnam, "Attegiamenti politici dell'alta burocrazia nell'Europa occidentale," *Rivista Italiana di Scienza Politica* III: I (1973), 172–175.

41 https;//en.wikipedia.org/wiki/Elections_in _Italy, accessed November 6, 2018.

42 Montanelli, *Gli incontri*, 100.

43 Ginsborg, *History of Contemporary Italy*, 298–299.

44 Tamburrano, *Pietro Nenni*, 287.

45 Giovanni Spadolini, *Nenni: sul filo della memoria (1949–1980)* (Florence: le Monnier, 1983), 32, 50.

46 Ginsborg, *History of Contemporary Italy*, 323–325.

47 Domenico, *Remaking Italy*, 118.

48 Marco Messeri, "Decenni Paralleli. De Gasperi e Togliatti nella stampa italiana," *Ventunesimo Secolo* 7 (April 2005), 141–147.

49 De Gasperi's daughter Maria Romana made the same observation in her 1964 biography *De Gasperi, Uomo solo*, 315–339.

50 Scoppola subsequently fleshed out these observations in his *La repubblica dei partiti*.

51 Domenico, *Remaking Italy*, 125, 129, 138.

52 https://en.wikipedia.org/wiki/Elections_in _Italy, accessed November 6, 2018.

53 Domenico, *Remaking Italy*, 138.

54 This was the day that Andreotti was due to present a new government to the Chamber of Deputies which would have included the PCI in the "area of government." Ginsborg, *History of Contemporary Italy*, 384.

55 Aldo Moro, "Lo stato del valore umano," in Giovanni Di Capua, ed., *Aldo Moro: il potere della parola (1943–1978)* (Rome: EBE, 1988),107.

56 Tamburrano, *Nenni*, 293.

57 Santarelli, *Pietro Nenni*, 435.

58 Giorgio Benvenuto, "Quello che gli dobbiamo ancora oggi," in *Nenni dieci anni dopo*, 172.

59 Domenico, *Remaking Italy*,142.

60 Ibid., 143.

61 Paul Ginsborg, *Silvio Berlusconi: Television, Power and Patrimony* (London: Verso, 2004), ch. 5.

62 Messeri, "Decenni parallelli," 149. See also Gaetano Arfe, ed., *De Gasperi e togliatti: politiche a confronto* (Rimini: Maggioli, 1985).

63 In the first four years of 2000 the Christian Democratic leader was the subject of films and travelling exhibits as well as newspaper accounts, articles, and books. White, "In Search of De Gasperi," 466–467.

64 Messeri, "Decennali Paralleli," 155.
65 Braschi, *Mussolini e De Gasperi*.
66 Steven White, "Deconstructing Berlusconi: Another De Gasperi?" Paper delivered at the American Association for Italian Studies conference, Eugene, April 11, 2013.
67 Randolfo Pacciardi, "Ricordi di un amico mazziniano," in *Nenni dieci anni diopo,* 16–24.
68 Fallaci, *Interview with History,* 239.
69 Each of these humanistic attributes partakes of what Aristotle termed *ethos:* the character and credibility of a speaker or writer. In the sociological study *Three Bells of Civilization*, Sydel Silverman connects such attributes to the value Italians still place on being *civile* (a highly suggestive term implying eloquence, courtesy, education, and resourcefulness).

Chronology of Events

July 10, 1943. Anglo-Americans land in Sicily, launching their Italian Campaign.

July 25–26, 1943. Fascist Grand Council removes Mussolini from power. Victor Emmanuel III dismisses him as prime minister and has him arrested. Marshall Pietro Badoglio forms new government and outlaws Fascist Party.

July 26–Sept. 11, 1943. Rome's "45 Days." De Gasperi, age sixty-two, and other anti-Fascist leaders gather and adopt wait and see stance toward new Badoglio government.

August 6, 1943. Nenni, age fifty-two, returns to Rome after nineteen years of exile, primarily in France.

September 8, 1943. Anglo-American forces land at Salerno.

September 9, 1943. Armistice announced between Italy and the Allies. Flight of King Victor Emmanuel III, Marshall Badoglio, and skeleton government to Brindisi, forming the Kingdom of the South. Meanwhile representatives of six anti-Fascist parties meet, lay foundations for their Committee of National Liberation.

September 11, 1943. German troops occupy Rome.

September 23–28, 1943. Rescued by German paratroopers and flown north, Mussolini creates collaborationist Italian Social Republic (the "Republic of Salò").

October 17, 1943. Unity pact signed between Socialist and Communist Parties, forming the Popular Front.

November 1, 1943. Allied Control Commission established.

December 5, 1943–Feb. 5, 1944. De Gasperi, Nenni, and other major CLN leaders forced underground, finding refuge in the St. John Lateran Seminary.

January 29–30, 1944. CLN holds first open congress at Bari, calling for the king's abdication and formation of new government led by six CLN parties: Christian Democrats (DC), Liberals (PLI), Democracy of Labor, Action Party, Socialists (PSI), Communists (PCI).

March 27, 1944. Togliatti, age fifty-one, returns from Russian exile to Naples.

March 30, 1944. Togliatti announces his "Salerno Turn."

April 12, 1944. Victor Emmanuel III cedes his powers to his son Umberto II (now named Lieutenant General of the Realm), but keeps his crown.

June 4–10, 1944. Rome liberated by Allies, the day prior to D-Day in Normandy. New CLN-based government formed by Ivanoe Bonomi.

July 27, 1944. High Commission for Sanctions against Fascism established, beginning Italian government's purge efforts.

September 26, 1944. Allied Control Commission becomes the less-intrusive Allied Commission. FDR proclaims an economic "New Deal for Italy."

December 12, 1944. Second Bonomi government formed; Socialist and Action Parties refuse to participate.

April 1, 1945. Allies breach Gothic Line, initiate final push into Po Valley.

April 27–29, 1945. Mussolini captured trying to escape to Switzerland, is shot, then has body hung upside down in Milan.

May 2, 1945. Germans surrender in Italy.

June 21, 1945. Action Party leader Ferruccio Parri forms government, Nenni becomes vice premier, De Gasperi foreign minister, Togliatti minster of justice.

December 10, 1945. De Gasperi forms his first government: Nenni remains vice premier and Togliatti remains minister for justice.

January 1, 1946. Allied Commission grants Italian government sovereignty over northern Italy. De Gasperi replaces CLN appointees by career prefects and police chiefs.

March 10–April 7, 1946. Administrative (municipal) elections; women exercise right to vote for the first time.

May 9, 1946. Abdication of King Victor Emmanuel III in favor of his son Umberto II.

June 2, 1946. Referendum endorses Republic over Monarchy, 54 percent–46 percent. Concurrent elections to Constituent Assembly; Dc comes in first, PSI second, PCI third.

June 22, 1946. Togliatti dissolves purge commission, grants broad amnesty.

August 10, 1946. De Gasperi addresses Allies at Paris Peace Conference.

October 8, 1946. Nenni relieves De Gasperi as foreign minister.

January 3–15, 1947. De Gasperi's first trip to the United States; addresses Cleveland Council of World Affairs; secures reconstruction gift of 50 million dollars.

March 25, 1947. Article 7 adopted, preserving all terms of 1929 Concordat in republican Constitution.

May 5, 1947. Togliatti featured in *Time* magazine cover article.

May 27, 1947. De Gasperi expels PCI, PSI excluded from government.

November 1947. PCI joins newly created Cominform, which severely chastises it for excessive "parliamentarism" and coalitional politics.

January 1, 1948. Republican Constitution takes effect.

January 30, 1948. Constituent Assembly completes its work, having established special regions in Trentino-Alto Adige, Val d'Aosta, Sicily, and Sardinia to accommodate linguistic minorities or separatist movements.

February 1948. Court of Cassation distinguishes between *norme precettizie* (parts of Constitution to be put into effect immediately) and *norme programmatiche* (parts of Constitution to be realized at some indefinite future date).

April 18, 1948. National parliamentary elections: DC wins 48.5 percent of the popular vote, translating 305 out of 574 seats. Popular Front wins 31.0 percent.

April 19, 1948. De Gasperi featured in *Time* magazine cover article.

May 10, 1948. Parliament elects Luigi Einaudi first president of the Republic.

May 23, 1948. De Gasperi defies Vatican pressure for a single party DC government, instead forming a centrist coalition also including PLI, PSLI, and PRI ministers.

July 14, 1948. Togliatti shot and seriously wounded by right-wing extremist outside of the Chamber of Deputies.

July 1, 1949. Vatican issues decree excommunicating "those who hold to the materialistic and atheistic doctrines of Communism."

December 1951. Nenni awarded Stalin Peace Prize in Moscow.

Early 1952. De Gasperi resists American, Vatican pressures to outlaw PCI.

January 22, 1952. Pius XII names integralist Luigi Gedda head of Catholic Action.

March 22, 1952. Nenni and De Gasperi resume cordial personal contact.

April 19–24, 1952. "Sturzo Operation," pressuring DC to ally with right-wing parties including neo-Fascists in Rome municipal election campaign, is launched, then abandoned. A month later DC and centrist allies prevail over center-left slate.

June 1952. Pius XII denies De Gasperi and his wife audience on twentieth anniversary of their marriage, and of their daughter Lucia taking her vows as nun.

January 21–March 31, 1953. Protracted controversy over "Swindle Law," which provides for bonus seats (two-thirds of total) for party coalition receiving majority of votes. Narrowly passed by Chamber of Deputies and later by Senate.

March 5, 1953. Death of Stalin; the next day Togliatti eulogizes him "as a giant in thought and in action."

June 7–8, 1953. National parliamentary elections. Party coalition led by Christian Democrats, fall short of majority by 57,000 votes. De Gasperi chooses not to contest results.

July 6, 1953. De Gasperi refuses to pursue an "opening to the Left," declining Nenni's invitation to form a center-left coalition.

July 28, 1953. Failing to form a single-party DC government, De Gasperi falls from power. Though pleased, Nenni refuses to celebrate publicly, writing that "an adversary should be defeated, but not humiliated."

August 19, 1954. De Gasperi dies in Sella di Valsugna. Nenni writes sympathetically of De Gasperi, recalling however that his counterpart "always had his foot on the break, while mine was always on the accelerator." Togliatti writes a respectful tribute published the next day in the pages of *L'Unità*.

October 1955–June 1956. Togliatti publishes caustic series of articles entitled "*È possibile un giudizio equanime sull'opera di Alcide De Gasperi?*" (Is a Balanced Assessment of the Work of Alcide De Gasperi Possible?").

August 19, 1964. Togliatti dies in Yalta, USSR, having written the Yalta memorandum a few days before his passing. Nenni says his counterpart's death "struck him," though Togliatti had been "his enemy friend, if one could say that."

January 1, 1980. Nenni dies in Rome.

Bibliography

Archives

ITALY
   Florence
      European University Institute, Historical Archives
   Pieve Tesino
      Fondazione Trentina Alcide De Gasperi
   Rome
      Archivio Centrale dello Stato
      Archivio del Senato
      Fondazione Pietro Nenni
      Istituto Luigi Sturzo, Archivio Storico
      Instituto Gramsci, Archivio Storico

UNITED STATES
   New York
      New York Public Library Archives
   Washington, DC
      Library of Congress, Periodicals Section
      National Archives and Records Administration

Primary Sources

Amendola, Giorgio. *Lettere a Milano. Ricordi e documenti, 1939–1945*. Rome: Riuniti, 1974.

Andreotti, Giulio. *De Gasperi e il suo tempo: Trento-Vienna-Roma*. Milan: Rizzoli, 1956.

Andreotti, Giulio. *De Gasperi visto da vicino*. Milan: Rizzoli, 1986.

Andreotti, Giulio. *I nonni della Repubblica*. Milan: Rizzoli, 2002.

Andreotti, Giulio. *Intervista su De Gasperi*. Edited by Antonio Gambino. Bari: Laterza, 1977.

Andreotti, Giulio. "La continuità dell'opera di De Gasperi." In *De Gasperi: Storia-Memoria-Attualità*, edited by Ammos Ciabattoni and Armando Tarullo. Soveria Mannelli: Rubbettino, 2004.

Andreotti, Giulio. "Montini e la politica italiana," *30 Giorni*. June 6, 1999.

Andreotti, Giulio. *Visti da vicino*. Milan: Rizzoli, 1986.

Aristotle. *Nichomachean Ethics*. Translated and edited by Martin Oswald. Indianapolis: Bobbs-Merrill, 1962.

Ascoli, Max. "Political Reconstruction in Italy." *The Journal of Politics* 8:3 (August 1946): 319–328.

Atkinson, Rick. *The Day of Battle. The War in Sicily and in Italy, 1943–1944*. New York: Henry Holt, 2007.

Benedetti, A. "Ecco la settimana elettoriale dei milanesi." *Risorgimento Liberale*. April 5, 1946.

Bertelli, S. *La Segreteria di Togliatti. Memorie di N. Bocenina*. Florence: Le Monnier, 1973.

Biagi, Enzo. *Io c'ero: un grande gionalista racconta l'Italia del dopoguerra*. Milan: Rizzoli, 2008.

Bonomi, Ivanoe. *Diario di un anno (2 giugno 1943–10 giugno 1944)*. Milan: Garzanti, 1947.

Bracci, Mario. "Storia di una settimana (7–12 giugno 1946)." *Il Ponte* II 7–8 (July–August 1946): 607.

Calamandrei, Piero. "Il Miracolo della Ragione." *Il Nuovo Corriere della Sera*. June 9, 1946. In *1946: La nascita della Repubblica*, edited by Maurizio Ridolfi and Nicola Tranfaglia, 219–221. Bari: Laterza, 1996.

Catti De Gasperi. M.R. *See De Gasperi, M.R.*

Cicero. *On the Commonwealth*. Translated and edited by G. H. Sabine and S. B. Smith, Columbus: Ohio State University Press, 1992.

Cicero. "Treatise on Friendship." In *Of Friendship: Philosophic Selections on a Perennial Concern*, edited by Marshell Carl Bradley and Philip Blosser, 86–101. Wolfeboro, NH: Longwood, 1989.

Cortesi, Arnaldo. "Italy's 'Indispensable' Premier: A Portrait of Alcide De Gasperi." *New York Times*. September 16, 1951.

Croce, Benedetto. *Filosofia e storiografia. Saggi*. Bari: Laterza, 1947.

Croce, Benedetto. "Il partito come giudizio e pregiudizio." In *Cultura e Vita Morale. Intermezzi polemici*, 191–198. Bari: Laterza, 1955.

De Feo, Italo. *Diario politico, 1943–1948*. Milan: Rusconi, 1973.

De Feo, Italo. *Tre anni con Togliatti*. Milan: Mursia, 1970.

De Gasperi, Alcide. *Cara Francesca. Lettere*. Edited by Maria Romano De Gasperi. Brescia: Morcelliana, 1999.

De Gasperi, Alcide. *De Gasperi scrive. Corrispondenza con capi di stato, cardinali, uomini politici, giornalisti, diplomatici*. 2 vols. Edited by Maria Romana De Gasperi. Brescia: Morcelliana, 1974.

De Gasperi, Alcide. "Discorso al conferenza di pace di Parigi" (August 10, 1945). In *I discorsi che hanno cambiato l'Italia*, edited by Antonello Capurso, 193–204. Milan: Mondadori, 2008.

De Gasperi, Alcide. "Intervento al forum di Cleveland" (January 10, 1947). In *I discorsi che hanno cambiato l'Italia*, edited by Antonello Capurso, 205–216. Milan: Mondadori, 2008.

De Gasperi, Alcide. "La dichiarazione Della Presidenza Del Consiglio." *L'Italia Libera*, June 14, 1946. In *1946: La nascita della Repubblica*, edited by Maurizio Ridolfi and Nicola Tranfaglia, 219–221. Bari: Laterza, 1996.

De Gasperi, Alcide. "Le basi morali della democrazia." In *De Gasperi e l'Europa*, edited by Maria Romana De Gasperi, 55–71, Brescia: Morcelliana, 1979.

De Gasperi, Alcide. *Scritti e discorsi politici*. Edited by Paolo Pombeni and Giuliana Nobile Schiera, 4 tomes (10 vols.). Bologna: Il Mulino, 2006–2009.

De Gasperi, Alcide. *Scritti politici di Alcide De Gasperi*. Edited by P. G. Zunnino. Milan: Feltrinelli, 1979.

De Gasperi, Cecilia. *Cecilia De Gasperi racconta*. Istituto Luigi Sturzo Website. December 2005–January 2006.

De Gasperi, Lucia. *Appunti spirituali e lettere al padre*. Brescia: Morcelliana, 1968.

De Gasperi, Maria Romana. Introduction to *Alcide De Gasperi*, vol. 1. Soveria Mannelli: Rubbettino, 2009.

De Gasperi, Maria Romana. *De Gasperi, uomo solo*. Milan: Mondadori, 1964.

De Ruggiero, Guido. "Questo popolo. Gli intelletuali." *La nuova Europa* 13 (April 1, 1945).

Fallaci, Oriana. *Interview with History*. Translated by John Shepley. Boston, MA: Houghton Mifflin, 1977. Reprint of March 1971 interview with Senator Nenni in the periodical *Europeo*.

Fanello-Marcucci, Gabriela. *Alle origini della Democrazia Cristiana 1929–1944. Dal carteggio Spataro-De Gasperi*. Brescia: Morcelliana, 1982.

Ferrara, Marcella and Maurizio Ferrara. *Conversando con Togliatti*. Rome: Riuniti, 1953.

Ferri, Mauro. "Un leader amato." In *Nenni dieci anni dopo*, edited by Giuseppe Tamburrano, 77–90. Rome: Lucarini, 1990.

Foa, Vittorio. *Il cavallo e la torre: reflessioni su una vita*. Turin: Einaudi, 1991.

Gabrielli, Patrizia. *Il 1946, le donne e la repubblica*. Rome: Donizelli, 2009.

Garofalo, Franco. *Un anno al Quirinale*. Milan: Garzanti, 1977.

Gayre, George Robert. *Italy in Transition: Extracts from the Private Journal of G. R. Gayre*. London: Faber and Faber, 1946.

Gedda, Luigi. *18 aprile 1948. Memorie inedite dell'artefice della sconfitta del fronte popolare*. Milan: Mondadori, 1998.

Gonella, Guido. *Con De Gasperi nella fondazione della Democrazia Cristiana*. Rome: Cinque lune, 1978.

Gramsci, Antonio. *The Modern Prince and Other Writings*. Translated by Lewis Marks, New York: International Publishers, 1957.

Guareschi, Giovanni. *Comrade Don Camillo*. Translated by Frances Frenaye. New York: Farrar, Straus, 1964.

Guareschi, Giovanni. "Il Ta-pum del Cecchino." *Candido*. January 4, 1953.

Hauser, Ernest. "The Strangest Strong Man in Europe." *Saturday Evening Post*. September 4, 1948, 26–27, 113–114.

La Malfa, Ugo. "The Socialist Alternative in Italy." *Foreign Affairs* 35:2 (January 1957): 311–319.
Levi, Carlo. *Christ Stopped at Eboli*. Translated by Frances Frenaye. New York: Farrar, Straus and Giroux, 1947.
Levi, Carlo. *The Watch (listed in Fiction section below)*.
Lombardi, Riccardo. "L'Italia a Maria: Il discorso di padre Lombardi a Napoli." *Bollettino bimestrale del Santuario della Madonna di Divino Amore*. April 11, 1948, 3–4.
Machiavelli, Niccolò. *The Prince*, Norton Critical Edition. New York: Norton, 1992.
Matteotti, Matteo. "I 'giovani turchi.'" In *Nenni dieci anni dopo*, edited by Giuseppe Tamburrano, 56–60. Rome: Lucarini, 1990.
Melchionni, Maria Grazia. "De Gasperi che persona era? Una conversazione con Maria Romana De Gasperi." *Il Risorgimento* 55:1 (2003): 5–68.
Montanelli, Indro. *Incontri italiani*. Milan: Rizzoli, 1982.
Murphy, Robert. *Diplomat among Warriors*. New York: Doubleday, 1964.
Nenni, Pietro. *Discorsi parlamentari 1946–1979*. Rome: Camera Dei Deputati, 1983.
Nenni, Pietro. *Gli anni del centro-sinistra. Diari 1957–1966*. Milan: SugarCo, 1982.
Nenni, Pietro. *Intervista sul socialismo italiano*. Edited by Giuseppe Tamburrano. Bari: Laterza, 1977.
Nenni, Pietro. *Tempo di Guerra Fredda. Diari 1943–1956*. Milan: SugarCo, 1981.
Nenni, Pietro. *Vento del Nord: giugno 1944–guigno 1945*. Turin: Einaudi, 1978.
Nenni, Pietro. "Where the Italian Socialists Stand." *Foreign Affairs* (January 1962). http://www.foreignafffairs.com/articles/23370/pietro-nenni/wheree-the-Italian-socialists-stand, accessed March 6, 2018.
Origo, Iris. *War in the Val D'Orcia: A War Diary, 1943–1944*. Boston, MA: David Godine, 1947.
Orlando, Federico. *I 45 giorni di Badoglio*. Rome: Bonacci, 1993.
Pacciardi, Randolfo. "Democracy Lives in Italy." *Foreign Affairs* 32:3 (April 1954): 14–23.
Pacciardi, Randolfo. "Il ricordo di un amico mazziniano." In *Nenni dieci anni dopo*, edited by Giuseppe Tamburrano, 16–24. Rome: Lucarini, 1990.
Parri, Ferruccio. "In memoria di Palmiro Togliatti." *Il Movimento di Liberazione in Italia* 76: 87–89.
Parri, Ferruccio. *Scritti 1915–1975*. Milan: Feltrinelli, 1976.
Pius XII. *Discorsi e radiomessaggi*, vol. 13. Vatican City: Tipografia poliglotta vaticana, 1953.
Pugliese, Stanislao, ed. *Fascism, Anti-Fascism and the Resistance in Italy*. Lanham, MD: Rowan & Littlefield, 2004.
Ravera, Camilla. *Dario di trent'anni, 1913–1943*. Rome: Riuniti, 1973.
Ricci, A. G., ed. *I verbali del Consiglio dei Ministri*. Rome: Archivio Centrale dello Stato, 1992–1993.

Ridolfi, Maurizio and Nicola Tranfaglia, eds. *1946; La nascita della Repubblica*. Bari: Laterza, 1976.

Rodd Lord, Rennell of. "Allied Military Government in Occupied Territory," *International Affairs*. Oxford: Oxford University Press. 20:3 (July 1944): 307–316.

Rossi, Mario. "De Gasperi vs. Catholic Action." *The Nation*. October 14, 1950, 338–341.

Rossi, Mario. "Queste generazioni nuove." *Gioventù* (1953): 154.

Salvadori, Massimo. *Brief History of the Patriot Movement in Italy, 1943–1945*. Chicago, IL: University of Chicago Press, 1954.

Salvemini, Gaetano. "La guerra per bande." Reproduced in *Aspetti della Resistenza in Piemonte*, edited by Giorgio Agosti, 7–11. Turin: Bookstore, 1977.

Scalfari, Eugenio. *Interviste ai potenti*. Milan: Mondadori, 1979.

Silone, Ignazio. "La repubblica dei poveri." *Avanti!* June 9, 1946. In *1946: La nascita della Repubblica*, edited by Maurizio Ridolfi and Nicola Tranfaglia. 222–223. Bari: Laterza, 1996.

Spadolini, Giovanni. *Nenni sul filo della memoria 1949–1980*. Florence: Le Monnier, 1982.

Spadolini, Giovanni. *Padri della Repubblica*. Florence: Passigli, 1985.

Spataro, Giuseppe. "Le giornate della clandestinità." In *Processo a De Gasperi 211 testimonianze*, edited by Giovanni Di Capua, 875–877. Roma: EBE, 1976.

Spataro, Giuseppe. *Passioni di un decennio*. Milan: Garzanti, 1986.

Stalin, Joseph. "*Yugoslav Record of Conversation of I. V. Stalin and the Yugoslav Delegation Headed by J. Broz Tito, 27–28 May 1946.*" Wilson Center Digital Archive. http://digitalarchive.wilsoncenter.org/document/117099, accessed October 28, 2018.

Tardini, Cardinal Domenico. *Memories of Pius XII*. Westminster: Stackpole Press, 1961.

Togliatti, Palmiro. *De Gasperi il restauratore: È possibile un giudizio equanime sull'opera di Alcide De Gasperi?* Edited by Fabio Silvestri. Rome: Gaffi, 2004.

Togliatti, Palmiro. *Discorsi parlamentari*, I. Rome: Riuniti, 1984.

Togliatti, Palmiro. *Lineamenti di una politica*. Milan: Sera Editrice, 1948.

Togliatti, Palmiro. "Ma come sono cretini!" '*L'Unità*." May 7, 1947, 20.

Togliatti, Palmiro. *Opere*, I. Edited by Ernesto Ragionieri. Rome: Riuniti, 1967.

Togliatti, Palmiro. *Opere*. IV, V, VI. Edited by Franco Andreucci and Paolo Spriano. Rome: Riuniti, 1967–1984.

Togliatti, Palmiro. *Opere scelte*. Edited by Gianpasquale Santomassimo. Rome: Riuniti, 1974.

Togliatti, Palmiro. "Rapporto ai quadri communisti di Napoli." (April 11, 1944). In *I discorsi che hannno cambiato l'Italia*, edited by Antonello Capurso, 141–176. Milan: Mondadori, 2008.

Trabucco, Carlo. *La prigionia di Roma. Diario dei 268 giorni dell'occupazione tedesca*. Rome: S.E.L.I, 1947.

Tupini, Giorgio. *De Gasperi: una testimonianza*. Bologna: Il Mulino, 1992.

Umberto II. "Il Proclama di Umberto II agli Italiani." *L'Italia Libera*, June 14, 1946. In *1946: La nascita della Repubblica*, edited by Maurizio Ridolfi and Nicola Tranfaglia, 222–223. Bari: Laterza, 1996.

Valiani, Leo. *L'avvento di De Gasperi*. Turin: De Silva, 1949.

Valiani, Leo. *L'Italia di De Gasperi*. Florence: Le Monnier, 1982.

Vasili, Turi. "Altro che spot e sondaggi." *30 Giorni* 3 (March 1998): 43.

Vessolo, Arthur. "Italy: Education under Allied Military Government." *Yearbook of Education* (1948): 578–591.

Vittorini, Elio. "Repubblica, con 'altro' al potere." *Il Politecnico*, June 30, 1946. In *1946: La nascita della Repubblica*, edited by Maurizio Ridolfi and Nicola Tranfaglia, 230–232. Bari: Laterza, 1996.

Washburne, Carleton. "Education under Allied Military Government." *The Educational Record* XXVI:10 (October 1945): 261–272.

Weber, Max. "The Profession and Vocation of Politics." In *Political Writings*, edited by Peter Lassman and Ronald Spies, 309–369. Cambridge: Cambridge University Press, 1994.

Wiskemann, Elizabeth. *Italy since 1945*. Published posthumously. London: Macmillan, 1971.

Wiskemann, Elizabeth. "Socialism and Communism in Italy." *Foreign Affairs* 24:3 (April 1946): 484–493.

Interviews

Bartolotta, Francesco. Interviewed by author, June 29, 1994.
De Gasperi, Maria Romana. Interviewed by author, July 27, 1999.
De Gasperi, Maria Romana. Interviewed by author, April 10, 2006.
Ferguson, Harvey. Interviewed by author, July 18, 1997.
Hughes, H. Stuart. Interviewed by author, September 24, 1999.

Fiction

Burns, John Horne. *The Gallery*. New York: Harper & Brothers, 1947.

Calvino, Italo. *La giornata d'uno scrutatore*. Milan: Mondadori, 1963. Translated as *The Watcher* by William Weaver, 1971.

Guareschi, Giovanni. *Mondo Piccolo: Il Compagno Don Camillo*. Milan: Rizzoli, 1963. Translated as *Comrade Don Camillo* by Frances Frenaye. New York: Farrar, Straus & Young, 1964.

Hersey, John. *A Bell for Adano*. New York: Knopf, 1944.

Levi, Carlo. *L'orologio*. Turin: Einaudi, 1950. Translated as *The Watch*. New York: Farrar, Straus & Young, 1951.

Morante, Elsa. *Storia*. Turin: Einaudi, 1974. Translated as *History: A Novel* by William Weaver. Philadelphia: The Franklin Library, 1977.

Pavese, Cesare. *Il diavolo sulle colline*. Turin: Einaudi, 1948.

Secondary Sources

Acanfora, Paolo. "Myths and the Political Use of Religion in Christian Democratic Culture." *Journal of Modern Italian Studies* 12:3 (2007): 307–338.

Agarossi, Elena and Victor Zaslavsky. *Stalin and Togliatti: Italy and the Origins of the Cold War*. Washington, DC: Woodrow Wilson Center Press, 2011.

Agosti, Aldo. *Palmiro Togliatti: A Biography*. London: I.B. Taurus, 2008.

Ajello, Mario. "La destra divora Machiavelli, la sinistra Cavour." *Il Messagero*. June 5, 1995, 13.

Ajello, Mario. "Luigi Gedda: l'ultimo dei crociati." *La Repubblica*. September 28, 2000.

Ajello, Nello. *PCI e intellettuali, 1944–1958*. Bari: Laterza, 1979.

ALCIDE digitized platform. http://alcidedigitale.fbk.eu.

Andreucci, Franco. *Falce e Martello: Identità e linguaggi dei communisti italiani fra stalinismo e guerra fredda*. Bologna: Bononia University Press, 2005.

Arendt, Hannah. *The Human Condition*. New York: Vintage Books, 1958.

Arendt, Hannah. *Men in Dark Times*. New York: Harcourt, Brace, Jovanovich, 1968.

Arfè Gaetano, ed. *De Gasperi e Togliatti, politiche a confronto*. Rimini: Maggioli, 1985.

Baget-Bozzo, Gianni. *Il partito cristiano al potere*. 2 vols. Florence: Le Monnier, 1974.

Ballini, Pier Luigi. *Alcide De Gasperi. Vol. III. Dalla costruzione della democrazia alla "nostra patria Europa" (1948–1954)*. Soveria Mannelli: Rubbettino, 2009.

Barbagallo, Francesco. *Storia dell'Italia repubblicana: La costruzione della democrazia dalla caduta del fascismo agli anni cinquanta*. Turin: Einaudi, 1994.

Barzini, Luigi. *I communisti non hanno vinto*. Milan: Mondadori, 1955.

Barbanti, Marco. "Funzioni stratigiche dell'anti-communismo nell'età del centrismo degasperiano." *Italia contemporanea* 40:1 (1988): 39–69.

Battini, Michele. "Una debole religione politica civica: il patriottismo costituzionale." In *1945–1946. Le origini della Repubblica*, vol. II, edited by Giancarlo Monina, 229–238. Soveria Mannelli: Rubbettino, 2007.

Battista Re, Giovanni. "Alcide De Gasperi tra radici religiose e impegno politico." In *Alcide De Gasperi, vol. 1. Dal Trentino all'esilio in patria (1883–1943)*, edited by Alfredo Canavero et. al., 3–176. Soveria Mannelli: Rubbettino, 2009.

Behan, Tom. "'Going Further': The Aborted Italian Insurrection of July, 1948." *Left History* 3:2 & 4: 1 (Fall 1995–Spring 1996): 168–203.

Belco, Victoria. *War, Massacre and Recovery in Central Italy, 1943–1948*. Toronto: Toronto University Press, 2010.

Bellasai, Sandro. *La morale communista pubblico e privato nella representazione del PCI (1947–1956)*. Rome: Carocci, 2000.

Benvenuto, Giorgio. "Quello che gli dobbiamo ancora oggi." In *Nenni dieci anni dopo*, edited by Giuseppe Tamburrano, 172–175. Rome: Lucarini, 1990.

Binchy, Daniel F. *Church and State in Fascist Italy*. London: Oxford University Press, 1970.

Blackmer, Donald. *Unity in Diversity: Italian Communism and the Communist World*. Cambridge, MA: MIT Press, 1968.

Bobbio, Norberto. *Dal fascismo alla democrazia. I regimi, le ideologie, le figure e le culture politiche*. Milan: Baldini & Castoldi, 1997.

Bocca, Giorgio. *Togliatti*. Milan: Feltrinelli (first published in Bari: Laterza, 1972), 2014.

Bondanella, Peter. *Italian Cinema from Neo-realism to the Present*. New York: Unger, 1983.

Bonomelli, Emilio. "Il senso della sua autonomia politica." article published in *Concretezza*, August 16, 1964, reproduced in *Processo a De Gasperi*, edited by Giovanni Di Capua, 192–199. Rome: EBE, 1976.

Bosworth, Richard. *The Italian Dictatorship: Problems and Perspectives in the Interpretation of Mussolini and Fascism*. London: Arnold, 1998.

Braschi, Angelo. *Mussolini e De Gasperi: vite divergenti*. Bologna: Cappelli, 1983.

Braschi, Danilo. "Le forme di anti-communismo alle origini della repubblica." In *1945–1946. Le origini della Repubblica*, vol. II, edited by Giancarlo Monina, 304. Soveria Mannelli: Rubbettino, 2007.

Brogi, Alessandro. *A Question of Self-Esteem. The United States and the Cold War Choices in France and Italy, 1944–1988*. Westport: Praeger, 2002.

Buchanan, Tom and Martin Conway, eds. *Political Catholicism in Europe 1918–1968*. New York: Oxford University Press, 1996.

Bull, Anna Cento. "Social and Political Cultures in Italy from the 1860s to the Present Day." In *The Cambridge Companion to Modern Italian Culture*, edited by Zygmunt Baranski and Rebecca West, 35–62. Cambridge: Cambridge University Press, 2001.

Canavero, Alfredo. *Alcide De Gasperi: Cristiano, democratico, europeo*. Soveria Mannelli: Rubbettino, 2003.

Capperucci, Vera. Introduction to *Alcide De Gasperi scritti e discorsi politici*, III, I. Bologna: Il Mulino, 2008, 156.

Caprara, Massimo. "Strategie togliattiane." In *Dovuto a De Gasperi: testimonianze & documenti nel 50. anniversario della morte*, edited by Nicola Guiso, 78–87. Milano: Ares, 2004.

Capua, Giovanni. *L'anno della grande svolte: Maggio 1947–aprile 1948: L'Italia di Alcide De Gasperi*. Soveria Mannelli: Rubbettino, 2007.

Capua, Giovanni, ed. *Processo a De Gasperi*. Rome: EBE, 1976.

Capurso, Antonello, ed. *I discorsi che hanno cambiato l'Italia*. Milan: Mondadori, 2007.

Carbone, Maurizio, ed. *Italy in the Post-Cold War Order: Adaptation, Bipartisanship, Visibility*. Lanham, MD: Lexington Books, 2011.

Carocci, Giampiero. "Togliatti e la Resistenza." *Nuovi argomenti* 53–54 (1961–1962): 123–155.

Carrillo, Elisa. *Alcide De Gasperi: The Long Apprenticeship*. Notre Dame, IN: Notre Dame University Press, 1965.

Casula, Carlo Felice. "L'impegno sociale di Vittorino Veronese." In *Vittorino Veronese dal dopoguerra al Concilio: un laico nella Chiesa e nel mondo*, Atti del convegno di studi Roma, 7–8 maggio. 65–77. Rome: A.V.E, 1993.

Cau, Maurizio. "Alcide De Gasperi: A Political Thinker or a Thinking Politician?" *Modern Italy* 14:4 (November 2009): 433–444.

Cau, Maurizio. "Il discorso politico degasperiano. Nuove prospetive di ricerca." In *Parole sovrane. Communicazione politica e storia contemporanea in Italia e Germania*, edited by S. Cavazza and F. Triola, 159–182. Bologna: Il Mulino, 2017.

Cavazza, Stefano and F. Triola. *Communicazione politica e storia contemporanea in Italia e Germania*. Bologna: Il Mulino, 2017.

Cavazza, Stefano and F. Triola. "Suspicious Brothers: Reflections on Political History and Social Sciences." *Ricerche di Storia Politica*. Special Issue, 2017, 53–70.

Ciabattoni, Amos and Armando Tarullo, eds. *De Gasperi: Storia-Memoria-Attualità*. Sovenia Mannelli: Rubbetino, 2004.

Clark, Martin. *Modern Italy, 1871–1982*. London: Longman, 1984.

Colarizi, Simona. *Storia dei partiti nell'Italia repubblicana*. Bari: Laterza, 1996.

Coles, Henry L. and Albert K. Weinberg. *Civil Affairs: Soldiers Become Governors*. Center of Military History, United States Army in World War II: Special Studies. Washington, DC: Department of the Army, 1964.

Conley, Thomas. *Rhetoric in the European Tradition*. White Plains, NY: Longman, 1990.

Constantin, Cornelia. "'Great Friends'; Creating Legacies, Networks And Policies That Perpetuated the Memory of the Fathers of Europe." *International Politics* 48:1: 112–128.

Cook, Paul. *Ugo La Malfa*. Bologna: Il Mulino, 1999.

Corbi, Gianni. *Nilde*. Milan: Rizzoli, 1993.

Cousins, Norman. *The Improbable Triumvirate: John F. Kennedy, Pope John, Nikita Khrushchev*. New York: Norton, 1972.

Craveri, Piero. *La repubblica dal 1958 al 1992*. Turin: UTET, 1995.

Craveri, Piero. *De Gasperi*. Bologna: Il Mulino, 2006.

Cruciani, Sante. "L'immagine di Palmiro Togliatti nel communismo italiano." *Memoria e Ricerca* 34 (May–August 2004): 129–135.

D'Angelo, Augusto. *De Gasperi le destre e l'"Operazione Sturzo"*. Rome: Studium, 2002.

D'Angelo Bigelli, Maria Grazia. *Pietro Nenni dalle barrecate a Palazzo Madama*. Milan: Giorgio Giannini, 1970.

Davis, John. "Dalla Gran Bretagna." In *L'Italia contemporanea e la storiografia internazionale*, edited by Filippo Mazzonis, 93–114. Venice: Marsilio, 1995.

De Conde, Alexander. *Half Bitter, Half Sweet: An Excursion into Italian-American History*. New York: Scribners, 1971.

De Grand, Alexander. *The Hunchback's Tailor: Giovanni Giolitti and Liberal Italy from the Challenge of Mass Politics to the Rise of Fascism, 1882-1922*. Westport, CT: Greenwood, 2000.

De Grand, Alexander. "Review of *Renewing Italian Socialism: Nenni to Craxi*, by Spencer Di Scala." *Journal of Modern History* 66:2 (June 1994): 411-412.

De Grand, Alexander. "To Learn Nothing and to Forget Nothing: Italian Socialism and the Experience of Exile Politics, 1935-1945." *Contemporary European History* 14: 539-558.

De Grazia, Victoria. "Dagli Stati Uniti D'America." In *L'Italia contemporanea e la storiografia internazionale*, edited by Filippo Mazzonis, 283-300. Venice: Marsilio, 1995.

De Grazia, Victoria. *How Fascism Ruled Women: Italy 1922-194*. Berkeley: University of California Press, 1992.

Del Pero, Mario. "American Pressures and Their Containment in Italy during the Ambassadorship of Clare Boothe Luce, 1953-1956." *Diplomatic History* 28:3 (2004): 407-439.

Del Pero, Mario. *L'alleato scomodo. Gli Usa e la DC negli anni del Centrismo, 1948-1955*. Rome: Carocci, 2001.

Del Pero, Mario. "The United States and 'Psychological Warfare' in Italia, 1948-1955." *The Journal of American History* (March 2001): 1304-1334.

Delzell, Charles. "Adolfo Omodeo: Historian of the 'Religion of Freedom.'" In *Historians of Modern Europe*, edited by Hans A. Schmitt, 123-150. Baton Rouge: Louisiana State University, 1971.

Delzell, Charles. *Mussolini's Enemies: The Italian Anti-Fascist Resistance*. Princeton, NJ: Princeton University Press, 1969.

Delzell, Charles. "The Italian Anti-Fascist Resistance in Retrospect. Three Decades of Historiography." *Journal of Modern History* 47: 66-96.

Di Capua, Giovanni, ed. *Processo a De Gasperi. 211 testimonianze raccolte da Giovanni Di Capua*. Rome: Ebe, 1976.

Di Nolfo, Ennio, ed. *Vaticano e Stati Uniti, 1939-1952: dalle carte di Myron C. Taylor*. Milan: Angeli, 1978.

Di Scala, Spencer. *Italy from Revolution to Republic, 1700 to the Present*. 3rd edn. Boulder, CO: Westview, 2004.

Di Scala, Spencer. *Renewing Italian Socialism: Nenni to Craxi*. New York: Oxford University Press. 1988.

Di Scala, Spencer. *Il socialismo italiano visto dagli USA*. Milan: SugarCo, 1991.

Diggins, John. *Mussolini and Fascism: The View from America*. Princeton, NJ: Princeton University Press, 1972.

Disch, L. J. "On Friendship in 'Dark Times.'" In *Feminist Interpretations of Hannah Arendt*, edited by B. Honig, 285-311. University Park: Penn State University Press, 1995.

Domenico, Roy. *Italian Fascists on Trial*. Chapel Hill: University of North Carolina Press, 1991.

Domenico, Roy. *Remaking Italy in the Twentieth Century*. Lanham, MD: Rowan & Littlefield, 2002.

Dorigo, Wladimiro. *Polemiche sull'integrismo*. Vicenza: La Locusta, 1962.

Duggan, Christopher. *The Force of Destiny: A History of Italy since 1796*. Boston, MA: Houghton Mifflin, 2008,

Durand, Jean-Dominique. "Alcide De Gasperi ovvero la politica ispirata." *Storia contemporanea* 15:4 (1984): 545–592.

Earl, Donald. *The Moral and Political Tradition of Rome*. London: Thames and Hudson, 1976.

Eisenberg, Deborah. "The Driest Eye" (review of three books by Natalia Ginzburg). *New York Review of Books* LXVI:12 (July 18, 2019): 12–14.

Elia, Leopoldo. "De Gasperi e la questione istituzionale." In *1945–1946: le origini della Repubblica*, edited by Giancarlo Monina, 19–49. Soveria Mannelli: Rubbettino, 2007.

Elia, Leopoldo. *Lectio 2005: Alcide De Gasperi e l'Assemblea Costituente*. Rome: Luigi Sturzo, 2005.

Ellis, Joseph J. *American Creation. Triumphs and Tragedies at the Founding of the American Republic*. New York: Knopf, 2007.

Ellis, Joseph J. *Founding Brothers: The Revolutionary Generation*. New York: Knopf, 2000.

Ellwood, David. *L'alleato nemico: la politica dell'occupazione anglo-americana in Italia, 1943–1946*. Milan: Feltrinelli, 1977.

Emiliani, Vittorio. "Il talento del grande giornalista." In *Nenni dieci anni dopo*, edited by Giuseppe Tamburrano, 149–159. Rome: Lucarini, 1990.

Esposito, Roberto. *Living Thought: The Origins and Actuality of Italian Philosophy*. Translated by Zakiya Hanafi. Stanford, CA: Stanford University Press, 2012.

Evangelista, Rhiannon. "The Particular Kindness of Friends: Ex-Fascists, Clientage and the Transition to Democracy in Italy, 1945–1960." *Modern Italy* 20:4 (November 2015): 411–425.

Faenza, Roberto and Marco Fini. *Gli Americani in Italia*. Milan: Feltrinelli, 1976.

Fanello-Marcucci, Gabriela. *Giuseppe Spataro: lineamenti per una biografia*. Rome: Cinque Lune, 1982.

Fanello-Marcucci, Gabriela. *Il primo governo De Gasperi (dicembre 1945–giugno 1946) sei mesi decisive per la democrazia in Italia*. Soveria Mannelli: Rubbettino, 2004.

Fantoni, Gianluca. "After the Fall: Politics, the Public Use of History and the Historiography of the Italian Communist Party, 1991–2011." *Journal of Contemporary History* 49:4 (2014): 815–830.

Fisher, Thomas R. "Allied Military Government in Italy." *Annals of the America Academy of Political and Social Science* 267 (1950): 114–122.

Flynn, George Q. *Roosevelt and Romanism. Catholics and American Diplomacy, 1937–1945*. Westport, CT: Greenwood, 1976.

Forlenza, Rosario. *Le elezioni amministrative della Prima Repubblica. Politica e propaganda locale nell'Italia del secondo dopoguerra (1946–1956)*. Rome: Donizelli, 2008.

Forlenza, Rosario and Bjorn Thomassen. *Italian Modernities: Competing Narratives of Nationhood*. New York: Macmillan, 2016.
Formigoni, Guido. *La Democrazia Cristiana e l'Alleanza Occidentale 1943–1953*. Bologna: II Mulino, 1996.
Formigoni, Guido. "De Gasperi e l'America tra storia e storiografia." *Studi Trentini di Scienze Storiche* LXXXIV1:2 (Supplemento 2005): 317–333.
Formigoni, Guido. Introductory Essay to De Gasperi. *Scritti e discorsi politici* Ill:I Bologna: Il Mulino 2006. 11–147, 35.
Formigoni, Guido. *Storia d'Italia nella Guerra Fredda (1943–1978)*. Bologna: Il Mulino, 2016.
Franco, Massimo. *Andreotti visto da vicino*. Milan: Mondadori, 1993.
Freeden, Michael. *Ideologies and Political Theory: A Conceptual Approach*. Oxford: Clarendon, 1996.
Freeden, Michael. "Ideology and Political Theory." *Journal of Political Ideologies* 11:1 (2006): 3–22.
Frei, Matt. *Italy: The Unfinished Revolution*. New York: NY Times Books, 1995.
Galli, Giorgio. *Fanfani*. Milan: Feltrinelli, 1975.
Galli, Giorgio. *Storia della Democrazia Cristiana*. Bari: Laterza, 1978.
Gambino, Antonio. *Storia del dopoguerra dalla liberazione al potere DC*. Bari: Laterza, 1988.
Gatta, Bruno. *De Gasperi politico, De Gasperi con la folla, De Gasperi con se stesso*. Naples: Edizioni Scientifiche Italiane: 1983.
Gilbert, Mark. "Biography in Modern Italian Studies: A Conversation with Carole Angier, Richard Bosworth and Christopher Duggan." *Modern Italy* 8:2 (November 2003): 223–241.
Gilbert, Mark. *The Italian Revolution: The End of Politics, Italian Style?* Boulder, CO: Westview Press, 1995.
Ginsborg, Paul. *A History of Contemporary Italy: Society and Politics 1943–1988*. New York: Penguin, 1990.
Ginsborg, Paul. *Italy and Its Discontents: Family, Civil Society, State 1980–2001*. New York: Palgrave Macmillan, 2003.
Ginsborg, Paul. *Silvio Berlusconi: Television, Power and Patrimony*. London: Verso, 2004.
Giovagnoli, Agostino. *La cultura democristiana: fra chiesa cattolica e identità italiana 1918–1948*. Rome: Laterza, 1991.
Gnocchi, Alessandro. *Giovanni Guareschi: Una storia italiana*. Milan: Rizzoli, 1998.
Goodwin, Doris Kearns. *Team of Rivals: The Political Genius of Abraham Lincoln*. New York: Simon and Schuster, 2005.
Goretti, Leo. "Truman's Bombs and De Gasperi's Hooked Nose: Images of the Enemy in the Communist Press for Young People after April 18, 1948." *Modern Italy* 16:2 (May 2011): 159–178.
Gorresio, Vittorio. *I carissimi nemici*. Milan: Longanesi, 1977.
Grayling, A.C. *Friendship*. New Haven, CT: Yale University Press, 2013.

Grimal, Pierre. *La civiltà dell'antica Roma.* Rome: Newton Compton, 2006.
Grindrod, Muriel. *The Rebuilding of Italy: Politics and Economics, 1945–1955.* Westwood, MA: Greenwood Press, 1977.
Guaiani, Yuri. *Il Tempo della Repubblica: le feste in Italia (1943–1949).* Milan: Unicopli, 2007.
Gualtieri, Robert. "La nascita della repubblica. Dibattito politico e transizione istituzionale." In *1945–1946, Le origini della repubblica*, vol. II, edited by Giancarlo Monina, 101–103. Soveria Mannelli: Rubbettino, 2007.
Gualtieri, Robert, ed. *Togliatti nel suo tempo.* Rome: Carocci, 2007.
Guiso, Nicola, ed. *Dovuto a De Gasperi: testimonianze & documenti nel 50 anniversario della morte.* Milan: Ares, 2004.
Harper, John L. *America and the Reconstruction of Italy, 1945–1948.* Cambridge: Cambridge University Press, 1986.
Harris, Charles R. S. *Allied Military Administration of Italy.* London: H.M. Stationery Office, 1957.
Hebblethwaite, Peter. *Paul VI. The First Modern Pope.* New York: Paulist Press, 1993.
Holmes, J. Derek. "Pope Pius XII: Impressions of a Pontificate." *Clergy Review* LXI (1976): 434–435.
Huebner, Andrew J. *Warrior Image: Soldiers in American Culture from the Second World War to the Vietnam Era.* Chapel Hill: University of North Carolina Press, 2008.
Hughes, Stuart H. *Consciousness and Society: The Reorientation of European Social Thought 1890–1930.* New York: Knopf, 1958.
Hughes, Stuart H. *The United States and Italy.* Cambridge, MA: Harvard University Press, 1979.
Innocenti, Marco. "I socialisti." In *1945–1946; le origini della Repubblica*, vol II, edited by Giancarlo Monina, 207. Soveria Mannelli: Rubbettino, 2007.
Innocenti, Marco. *L'Italia del 1948: Quando De Gasperi battè Togliatti.* Milan: Mursia, 1997.
Iuso, Pasquale. *Lezioni sul secondo dopoguerra 1945–1960.* Rome: Gangemi, 1994.
Joll, James. *Antonio Gramsci.* New York: Penguin Books, 1977.
Judt, Tony. *Postwar: A History of Europe since 1945.* New York: Penguin Press. 2005.
Kalyvas, Stathis N. *The Rise of Christian Democracy in Europe.* Ithaca, NY: Cornell University Press, 1996.
Kertzer, David. *Ritual, Politics and Power.* New Haven, CT: Yale University Press, 1988.
Killinger, Charles. *Gaetano Salvemini.* Westport, CO: Praeger, 2002.
Kogan, Norman. *A Political History of Postwar Italy.* New York: Praeger, 1966.
Kogan, Norman. *La politica estera italiana.* Milan: Lerici, 1965.
Korner, Alex. *America in Italy: The United States in the Political Thought and Imagination of the Risorgimento, 1763–1865.* Princeton, NJ: Princeton University Press, 2017.
Kselman, Thomas and Buttigieg, Joseph, eds. *European Christian Democracy in Historical and Comparative Perspective.* Notre Dame, IN: Notre Dame University Press, 2003.

Labriola, Silvano, ed. *Valori principi del regime repubblicano*, vol. 3. *Legalità e garanzie*. Bari: Laterza, 2002.

Lanaro, Silvio. *Storia dell'Italia repubblicana: dalla fine della guerra agli anni novanta*. Venice: Marsilio, 1992.

LaPalombara, Joseph. *Democracy Italian Style*. New Haven, CT: Yale University Press, 1987.

Leeden, M. *Lo zio Sam e l'elefante rosso*. Milan: SugarCo, 1987.

Lepre, Aurelio. *Storia della prima repubblica. L'Italia dal 1942 all 1992*. Bologna: II Mulino, 1994.

Logan, Oliver. "*Pius XII*, Romanità, Prophesy and Charisma." *Modern Italy* 3:2 (1998): 237–247.

Lovett, Clara. *Giuseppe Garibaldi, 1805–1882; A Biographical Essay and Selective List of Reading Materials*. Washington, DC: The Library of Congress, 1982.

Mack Smith, Dennis. *Italy: A Modern History*. Ann Arbor: University of Michigan Press, 1969.

Mack Smith, Dennis. *Italy and Its Monarchy*. New Haven, CT: Yale University Press, 1989.

Mafai, Miriam. "Que due carissimi nemici nell'Italia che nasceva." *La Repubblica* (August 19, 1984).

Magister, Sandro. *La politica vaticana in Italia 1943–1948*. Rome: Studium, 1979.

Malgeri, Francesco. *Alcide De Gasperi, vol. II: Dal Fascismo alla democrazia (1943–1947)*. Soveria Mannelli: Rubbettino, 2009.

Malgeri, Francesco. "La presenza di Vittorino Veronese nel ACI e la rinascita democratica del dopoguerra." In *Vittorino Veronese un laico nella chiesa e nel mondo*, 15–46. Rome: Ave, 1994.

Marchi, Michele. "La DC, la Chiesa e il centro-sinistra: Fanfani e l'asse vaticano, 1959–1962." *Mondo contemporaneo* 2 (2008): 39–90.

Mariuzzo, Andrea. *Divergenze parallele. Communismo e anti-communismo alle origini del linguaggio politico dell'Italia repubblicana*, Soveria Mannelli: Rubbettino, 2010.

Marsili, Marzia. "De Gasperi and Togliatti: Political Leadership and Personality Cults in Post-war Italy." *Modern Italy* 3:2 (1998): 249–261.

Martinelli, Renzo. "La politica del Pci nel period costituente. Il rapporto di Palmiro Togliatti al Comitato centrale del 18-19 settembre 1946." *Studi storici* 32:2 (April–June 1991): 487–494.

Marrou, Henri. *The Meaning of History*. Baltimore, MD: Helicon, 1966.

Mattera, Paolo. "Dopo il 18 aprile: La crisi e la 'seconda rifondazione' del PSI." *Studi Storici* 43:4: 1147–1179.

McCarthy, Patrick. *The Crisis of the Italian State: From the Origins of the Cold War to the Fall of Berlusconi and Beyond*. New York: St. Martins, 1996.

Messeri, Marco. "Decennali parallele. De Gasperi e Togliatti nella stampa italiana." *Ventunesimo Secolo*. aprile 7, 2005, 141–181.

Miller, James E. "Carlo Sforza e l'evoluzione della politica americana verso l'Italia, 1940–1943." *Storia contemporanea* 7 (December 1976): 825–854.

Miller, James E. *The United States and Italy 1940–1950: The Politics and Diplomacy of Stabilization*. Chapel Hill: University of North Carolina Press, 1986.

Mistry, Kaeten. "The Dynamics of Postwar US-Italian Relations, American Interventionism & the Role of James C. Dunn." Paper delivered at Society for Historians of American Foreign Relations Meeting. Madison, June 26, 2010.

Mistry, Kaeten. "Re-Thinking American Intervention in the 1948 Italian Elections: Beyond a Success-Failure Dichotomy." *Modern Italy*. April 2011, 179–194.

Mola, Aldo. *Declino e crollo della monarchia in Italia: i Savoia dall'Unità al referendum del 2 giugno 1946*. Milan: Mondadori, 2006.

Monina, Giancarlo, ed. *1945–1946: le origini della Repubblica*. 2 vols. Soveria Mannelli: Rubbettino, 2007.

Moro, Renato. *La Chiesa e lo sterminio degli ebrei*. Bologna: Il Mulino, 2002.

Morris, Sylvia Jukes. *Rage for Fame: The Honorable Clare Boothe Luce*. New York: Random House, 2014.

Mowat, Charles Loch. *Britain between the Wars 1918–1940*. Boston, MA: Beacon Press, 1955.

Nassi, Enrico. *Alcide De Gasperi: L'utopia del centro*. Florence: Comunia, 1997.

Natoli, Claudio. "Togliatti nella storia del Novecento." *Studi Storici* 38:4 (October–December 1997): 1170–1193.

Natta, Alessandro. *Togliatti in parlamento*. Rome: Riuniti, 1988.

Neri Serneri, Simone. "In margini ai dairi di Pietro Nenni." *Il Ponte* 38:11/12 (1982): 1238–1248.

Nichols, Peter. "On the Italian Crisis," *Foreign Affairs* 54 (April 1976): 511–526.

Nuti, Leopoldo. "Security and Perceptions of Threat in Italy in the Early Cold War Years, 1945–1953." In *The Soviet Union and Europe in the Cold War, 1943–1953*, edited by Francesco Gori and Silvio Pons, 412–429. London: Palgrave Macmillan, 1996.

Nuti, Leopoldo. *Stati Uniti e la apertura a sinistra: l'importanza e limiti della presenza americana in Italia*. Bari: Laterza, 1999.

Orfei, Ruggero. *L'occupazione del potere. I democristiani '45–'75* Milan: Longanesi, 1976.

Ornaghi, Lorenzo. "I progetti di stato (1945–1948)." In *Cultura politica e partiti nell'età della Costituente*, vol. 1, edited by Roberto Ruffili, 39–102. Bologna: Il Mulino, 1979.

Ottone, Piero. *De Gasperi*. Milan: Mondadori, 1968.

Pace, Enzo. *L'unità dei cattolici in Italia: Origini e decadenza di un mito collettivo*. Milan: Guerini, 1995.

Pakaluk, Michael. "Political Friendship." In *The Changing Face of Friendship*, edited by Leroy S. Rouner, 197–213. Notre Dame, IN: Notre Dame University Press, 1944.

Painter, Borden. "Historicizing Nenni." In *Italian Socialism between Politics and History*, edited by Spencer Di Scala, 73–79. Amherst: University of Massachusetts Press, 1996.

Pavan, Mons. Pietro. "Colloquio con Alcide De Gasperi sul mandato di Sua Eccellenza Tardini a nome del Santo Padre." In *Pio XII e Alcide De Gasperi: una storia segreta*, edited by Andrea Riccardi, 71-79. Bari: Laterza, 2003.

Pavone, Claudio. *A Civil War: History of the Italian Resistance*. London: Verso, 2013.

Pavone, Claudio. "The General Problem of the Continuity of the State." In *After the War: Violence, Justice, Continuity and Renewal in Italian Society*, edited by Jonathan Dunnage, 5-19. Leicester: Troubador, 1996.

Pavone, Claudio. "Italy: Trends and Problems" *Journal of Contemporary History* 2:1 (January 1967): 49-77.

Pavone, Claudio. "Sulla continuità dello Stato. Instituzioni e uomini." In *Italia 1945-1948. Le origini della Repubblica*, edited by Giancarlo Monina, 172-205. Soveria Mannelli: Rubbettino, 2007.

Piombino, Giancarlo. "Attualità di De Gasperi." *Civitas* XLVI:1 (January-March 1995): 11-24.

Pombeni, Paulo. "De Gasperi costituente." *Quaderni Degasperiani*, I (2009): 55-124.

Pombeni, Paulo. *Il primo De Gasperi: La formazione di un leader politico*. Bologna: Il Mulino, 2007.

Pombeni, Paulo. *Partiti e sistemi politici nella storia contemporanea (1830-1968)*. Bologna: Il Mulino, 1985.

Pombeni, Paulo. "Sul retroterra politico di Palmiro Togliatti. Note in margine alla formazione di un leader." In *Togliatti nel suo tempo*, edited by Roberto Gualtieri et. al., 183-192. Rome: Carocci, 2007.

Pons, Silvio and Robert Service, eds. "Introduzione." In *Dizionario del communismo nel XX secolo*. Turin: Einaudi, 2006.

Popoff, Gabrielle Elissa. "'Once upon a Time There Was an S.S. Officer': The Holocaust between History and Fiction in Elsa Morante's *La Storia*." *Journal of Modern Jewish Studies* 11:1 (2012): 25-38.

Procacci, Giuliano. *History of the Italian People*. Translated by Anthony Paul. New York: Harper & Row, 1970.

"'La proposta politica di De Gasperi' di Pietro Scoppola. Lettura di Francesco Margiotta Broglio e Claudio Pavone con una replica dell'autore." *Italia Contemporanea* XXX:130 (January-March 1978): 93-110.

Putnam, Robert. "Attegiamenti politici dell'alta burocrazia nell'Europa occidentale." *Rivista Italiana di Scienza Politica* III:1 (1973): 145-186.

Putnam, Robert. *The Beliefs of Politicians. Ideology, Conflict and Democracy in Britain and Italy*. New Haven, CT: Yale University Press, 1973.

Putnam, Robert. *Making Democracy Work: Civic Traditions in Modern Italy*. Princeton, NJ: Princeton University Press, 1993.

Ragionieri, Ernesto. *Palmiro Togliatti*. Rome: Riuniti, 1973.

Ragionieri, Ernesto. *Palmiro Togliatti. Per una biografia politica e intellettuale*. Rome: Riuniti, 1976.

Rapone, Leonardo. "Il socialismo italiano dall'antifascismo alla repubblica in alcuni studi recenti." *Studi storici* 31:1 (January–March 1990): 213–234.
Rawlins, William K. *The Compass of Friendship: Narratives, Identities, Dialogues*. Los Angeles, CA: Sage, 2009.
Reisman, John. *Anatomy of Friendship*. North Stratford, NH: Irvington, 1979.
Riall, Lucy. *Garibaldi: Invention of a Hero*. New Haven, CT: Yale University Press, 2007.
Riall, Lucy. "The Shallow End of History? The Substance and Future of Political Biography." *Journal of Interdisciplinary History* XL:3 (2010): 375–397.
Ricci, Aldo. *Aspettando la Republica: I governi di transizione, 1943–1946*. Rome: Donizelli, 1996.
Ricci, Aldo. *La breve età degasperiana, 1948–1953*. Rome: Istituto Sturzo, 2010.
Riccardi, Andrea. "*Roma, 'citta sacrá?' Dalla Conciliazione all'operazione Sturzo*. Milan: Vita e Pensiero, 1979.
Riccardi, Andrea. *Pio XII e Alcide De Gasperi: una storia secreta*. Bari: Laterza, 2003.
Ridley, Jasper. *Garibaldi*. Stanford, CA: Hoover Institution Press, 1974.
Ridolfi, Maurizio and Nicola Tranfeglia, eds. *1946: La nascita della Repubblica*. Bari: Laterza, 1996.
Riosa, Alceo. *Biografia e storiografia*. Milan: Franco Angeli, 1983.
Roberts, David. "Benedetto Croce and the Dilemmas of Liberal Restoration." *Review of Politics* 44 (April 1982): 214–241.
Roberts, David. *Benedetto Croce and the Uses of Historicism*. Berkeley: University of California Press, 1986.
Romano, Sergio. "Considerazioni sulla biografia storica." *Storia della storiografia* 3 (1983): 113–123.
Rouner, Leroy S. ed. *The Changing Face of Friendship*. Notre Dame, IN: Notre Dame University Press, 1994.
Ruffili, Roberto, ed. *Culture politica e partiti nell'età della Costituente*. 2 vols. Bologna: Il Mulino, 1979.
Sale, Giovanni. *Dalla monarchia alla repubblica, 1943–1946. Santa Sede, Cattolici italiani e referendum*. Milan: Jaca Book, 2003.
Sale, Giovanni. "De Gasperi e la Costituzione italiana." *La Civiltà Cattolica* (2008): 324–337.
Sale, Giovanni. *De Gasperi, gli USA e il Vaticano all'inizio della guerra fredda*. Milan: Jaca Book, 2005.
Salvi, Luca. "Togliatti and the Hotel Lux." *World Affairs* 154:3 (Winter 1992).
Santarelli, Enzo. *Dalla monarchia alla repubblica 1943–1946*. Rome: Riuniti, 1974.
Santarelli, Enzo. *Pietro Nenni*. Turin: UTET, 1988.
Sassoon, Donald. *The Strategy of the Italian Communist Party*. New York: St. Martin's, 1981.
Schmitt, Hans, ed. *Historians of Modern Europe*. Baton Rouge: University of Louisiana Press, 1971.

Schmitt, Hans. *Quakers and Nazis: The Inner Light in the Outer Darkness.* Columbia: University of Missouri Press, 1997.
Scoppola, Pietro. *La Nuova Cristianità perduta.* Rome: Stadium, 1985.
Scoppola, Pietro. *La proposta politica di De Gasperi.* Bologna: Il Mulino, 1978.
Scoppola, Pietro. *La repubblica dei partiti. Profilo storico della democrazia in Italia, 1945–1990.* Bologna: Il Mulino, 1991.
Scoppola, Pietro. "Tessuto etico, forze politiche, istituzioni." In *Interpretazioni della Repubblica*, edited by Agostino Giovagnoli, 17–32. Bologna: Il Mulino, 1998.
Settembrini, Domenico. *La Chiesa nella politica italiana (1944–1963).* 2nd edn. Milan: Rizzoli, 1977.
Settembrini, Domenico. "The Divided Left: After Fascism, What?" In *Italian Socialism between Politics and History*, edited by Spencer Di Scala, 107–120. Amherst: University of Massachusetts Press, 1996.
Sigmund, Paul E. "The Catholic Tradition and Modern Democracy." *The Review of Politics* 49:4 (Autumn 1967): 530–548.
Silverman, Sydel. *Three Bells of Civilization: the Life of a Tuscan Hill Town.* New York: Columbia University Press, 1975.
Silvestri, Fabio. Introduction to *Palmiro Togliatti, De Gasperi il restauratore*, 3, followed by the full text of the *Rinascità* articles appearing from October of 1955 to June of 1956.
Slaughter, Jane. *Women in the Italian Resistance, 1943–1945.* Denver, CO: Arden Press, 1997.
Spriano, Paolo. "De Gasperi e Togliatti: protagonisti e antagonisti." In *De Gasperi e Togliatti: politiche a confronto*, edited by Gaetano Arfè, 25–32. Rimini: Maggioli, 1985.
Spriano, Paolo. *Le passioni di un decennio.* Milan: Garzanti, 1986.
Spriano, Paolo. *Storia del Partito communista italiano, vol. V, La Resistenza, Togliatti e il Partito Nuovo*, Turin: Einaudi, 1985.
Sylos Labini, Paolo. *Saggio sulle classi sociali.* Bari: Laterza, 1975.
Tamburrano, Giuseppe, ed. *Nenni dieci anni dopo.* Rome: Lucarini, 1990.
Tamburrano, Giuseppe. *Pietro Nenni.* Bari: Laterza, 1986.
Tamburrano, Giuseppe. *Pietro Nenni: una vita per la democrazia e per il socialismo.* Rome: Laicata: 2005.
Tannenbaum, Edward. *The Fascist Experience: Italian Society and Culture 1922–1945.* New York: Basic Books, 1972.
Taylor, Barbara. "Separations of Soul: Solitude, Biography, History." *American Historical Review* 114:3 (June 2009): 640–651.
Taylor, Charles. *Modern Social Imaginaries.* Durham, NC: Duke University Press, 2004.
Tenaglia, Aldo. *Religione e politica in Alcide De Gasperi.* Reggio Emilia: Pozzi, 2001.
Terzuolo, Eric. "The Uncongenial Realism of Palmero Togliatti." Paper delivered at Society for Italian Historical Studies Annual Meeting. Washington DC, January 2018.

Tobia, Simona. *Advertising America: The United States Information Service in Italy 1945–1956*. Milan: LED Edizioni Universitarie, 2008.
Truffelli, Matteo. "L'antipolitica." In *1945–1946, Le origini della repubblica*, vol. II, edited by Giancarlo Monina, 341–372. Soveria Mannelli: Rubbettino, 2007.
Ulam, Adam. *Stalin: The Man and His Era*. Expanded edition. Boston, MA: Beacon, 1989.
Urban, Joan. *Moscow and the Italian Communist Party*. Ithaca, NY: Cornell University Press, 1986.
Urbinati, Nadia. "Liberalism in the Cold War: Norberto Bobbio and the Dialogue with the PCI." *Journal of Modern Italian Studies* 8:4 (2003): 578–603.
Vaillancourt, Jean Guy. *Papal Power: A Study of Vatican Control over Lay Catholic Elites*. Berkeley: University of California Press, 1980.
Valota, Bianca. *Storia e Biografia*. Milan: Franco Angeli, 1981.
Van Dijk, Teun. "Ideology and Discourse Analysis." *Journal of Political Ideologies* 11:2 (2006): 115–140.
Vansan, Piersandro. "Alcide De Gasperi, un grande statista." *La Civiltà Cattolica* 16 (August 7–21, 2010): 270–278.
Vatalaro, Giuseppe. "Togliatti's Conception of the Italian Road to Socialism: Hegemony or Pragmatism?" *The Italianist* 31 (2011): 79–98.
Venneri, Giulio. "Man of Faith and Political Commitment: Alcide De Gasperi." *Journal of Modern Italian Studies* 13:1 (March 2008): 89–92.
Ventresca, Robert. *From Fascism to Democracy: Culture and Politics in the Italian Election of 1948*. Toronto: University of Toronto Press, 2004.
Ventrone, Angelo. *La cittidinanza repubblicana: forma-partito e identità nazionale alle origini della democrazia italiana (1943–1948)*. Bologna: Il Mulino, 1996.
Vercellone, P. "The Italian Constitution of 1947–48." In *The Rebirth of Italy*, edited by Stuart J. Woolf, 121–134. New York: Humanities Press, 1972.
Vian, Francesca. *Resistere in piedi. Le parole di Pietro Nenni*. Viterbo: Stampa Alternativa, 2016.
Volterra, Sara. *La costituzione italiana e modelli anglosassoni con particolare sguardo agli Stati Uniti*. Bologna: Il Mulino, 1950.
Von Heyking, John and Richard Avramenko, eds. *Friendship and Politics: Essays in Political Thought*. Notre Dame, IN: Notre Dame University Press, 2008.
Ward, David. *Anti-Fascisms: Cultural Politics in Italy, 1943–1946*. Teaneck, NJ: Fairleigh Dickinson University Press, 1996.
Warner, Carolyn. *Confessions of an Interest Group: The Catholic Church and Political Parties in Europe*. Princeton, NJ: Princeton University Press, 2000.
White, Steven F. "Amici-nemici: Catholic-Communist Encounter in Post-Fascist Italy." Paper delivered at American Catholic Historic Association Annual Meeting. Emmitsburg, MD, April 14, 2018.
White, Steven F. "Anti-Communist Duet: Alcide De Gasperi and James Clement Dunn." Paper delivered at Workshop on European Christian Democracy. Leuven, Belgium November 14–15, 2013.

White, Steven F. "Christian Democracy or Pacellian Populism? Rival Forms of Postwar Italian Political Catholicism." In *European Christian Democracy: Historical Legacies and Comparative Perspectives*, edited by Thomas Kselman and Joseph Buttigieg, 199–227. Notre Dame, IN: Notre Dame University Press. 2003.

White, Steven F. "De Gasperi through American Eyes: Media and Public Opinion, 1945–1953." *Italian Politics and Society* 61 (Fall/Winter 2005): 11–21.

White, Steven F. "Deconstructing Berlusconi: Another De Gasperi?" Paper delivered at the American Association for Italian Studies Conference. Eugene, OR, April 11, 2013.

White, Steven F. "Gentleman Rebel: H. Stuart Hughes, the OSS and the Resistance." *Journal of Modern Italian Studies* 4:1 (s, 1999): 64–67.

White, Steven F. "Italy's Odd Couple: Alcide De Gasperi and Pietro Nenni as Founders of the Italian Republic." Paper delivered at Society for Italian Historical Studies Annual Meeting. Washington, DC, January 7, 2018.

White, Steven F. "Liberal Antipodes: Omodeo, Smith and the Struggle over Schooling, Naples and Salerno 1944." In *Italy and America 1943–1944. Italian, American and Italian American Experiences of the Liberation of the Italian Mezzogiorno*, 479–500. Naples: Città del Sole (for the Istituto Italiano per gli Studi Filosofici), 1997.

White, Steven F. "Like Father, Like Sons? Alcide De Gasperi's Search for Christian Democratic Heirs." Paper delivered at American Catholic Historical Association Semi-Annual Meeting, Princeton, NJ. 2010.

White, Steven F. "A Modern Schism: Alcide De Gasperi, Pius XII and the Meaning of Christian Democracy." Paper delivered at American Historical Association Annual Meeting, Washington. DC, January 9, 1999.

White, Steven F. "The Politics of Psychology in Post-Fascist Italy." Paper delivered at American Historical Association Annual Meeting, December 29, 1990.

White, Steven F. "The Retrospective Cult of De Gasperi." Paper delivered at Association for the Study of Modern Italy Conference: Charisma and Personality Cults in Modern Italy. London, November 3, 1996.

White, Steven F. *Progressive Renaissance: America and the Reconstruction of Italian Education, 1943–1962*. New York: Garland 1991.

White, Steven F. "In Search of Alcide De Gasperi: Innovations in Italian Scholarship since 2003." *Journal of Modern Italian Studies* 15:3 (2010): 462–470.

White, Steven F. "Soft on Catholicism: Secular-Clerical Rapprochement and American Policy in Italy, 1943–1948." Paper delivered at Society for Historians of American Foreign Relations meeting. Charlottesville, VA, March 23, 1993.

White, Steven F. "Visual Politics in Italy from Mussolini to Berlusconi." *The International Journal of Civic, Political and Community Studies* 11 (2014): n.p.

Wood, Neal. *Cicero's Social and Political Thought*. Berkeley: University of California Press, 1988.

Wood, Sharon. "Excursus as Narrative Technique in 'La Storia.'" In *Elsa Morante's Politics of Writing: Rethinking Subjectivity, History and the Power of Art*, edited by Stefania Lucamante, 75–86. Lantham, MD: Rowan and Littlefield, 2015.

Woolf, Stuart, ed. *L'Italia repubblicana vista da fuori 1945–2000*. Bologna: Il Mulino, 2007.

Zizola, Giancarlo. *Il microfono di Dio: Pio XII, padre Lombardi e i cattolici italiani*. Milan: Mondadori, 1990.

Zunino, Pier Giorgio. *La Repubblica e il suo passato*. Bologna: Il Mulino, 1982.

Zunino, Pier Giorgio. *Profilo di De Gasperi*. Turin: Giappichelli, 1978.

Index

Acerbo Law (1923) 184
Action Party 4, 56, 72–4, 80, 89–92, 93
　n.4, 93 n.7, 101, 103–4, 108, 130,
　133, 149
Adenauer, Konrad 169
administrative elections 103–8, 182–4
　centrist victories 108
　eligible voters 105
　June 2 108–16, 130, 139
　open election 107
　procedures 104
　women's suffrage 103, 106–7
Africa 47–8, 50–1, 77, 140
Agarossi, Elena 9, 212–13 n.25
Agosti, Aldo 9, 94 n.12, 97 n.88, 198
Ajello, Mario 10
Allied Control Commission (ACC) 52,
　109
Allied invasion of Sicily 45
Allied Military Government (AMG) 46–7,
　49, 52–3, 64 n.3, 85
Allied Occupation policy 46–51
　Administrative Instruction Order
　　No. 1 48
　American/British officials 46–7
　Amlire currency 49
　"epuration" (*epurazione* policy) 47–8,
　　85–7
　indirect control policy 47
　training for civil affairs officers 49–50
Allied Powers 59, 100, 132, 139
Amendola, Giorgio 33, 80–1, 83, 133,
　200–1
American Federation of Labor (AFL) 150
American imperialism 199
American Office of War Information 61
Andreotti, Giulio 9, 193 n.45, 194 n.53,
　207, 212 n.10, 212 n.12, 214 n.54
　and De Gasperi 22, 27, 32, 36, 111,
　　131, 162, 199–200
　De Gasperi's apparent *dauphin* 199
　interview 209

launch of journal 199
memo to Pope 179
Anglo-Americans 36, 45, 52, 84, 156
　and occupation policies 46–51
Anselmi, Tina 117 n.27
anti-clericalism 10, 20, 27, 34–5, 51, 55,
　57–9, 172
anti-communism/anti-communist 8, 150,
　155, 157, 170–1, 178, 187, 197–9,
　201, 207
anti-Fascism/anti-Fascist 3, 8, 55, 59, 78,
　81, 172, 180, 187
　coalition 151, 198, 207
　De Gasperi's conception of 75
　end of alliance 148–51, 154
　exiles 11, 51, 55
　ideologies 7, 132
　parties 30, 35, 46, 62, 71–7, 82–3, 88–9,
　　102, 105, 129, 134
　Resistance and 11, 35, 63, 71–7, 88, 147
　and women's suffrage 107
anti-Semitic 60, 63
Antonini, Luigi 150
Arendt, Hannah 20, 23
Aristotle/Aristotelian 20–1, 23, 38–9, 215
　n.69
Armistice (September Armistice)
　agreement 31, 45–6, 51, 64 n.3, 72,
　　78–9, 84, 86, 109
Ascoli, Max 90

Badoglio, Pietro 45, 76, 82–3, 96 n.60
　armistice agreement 79, 84
　commitments on Fascism 78–9
　letter from Gedda 79
Bakunin, Mikhail 205
Barbagallo, Francesco 143 n.8
Bari Congress 1944 102–3
Bartelotta, Francesco 42 n.46
Battini, Michele 118 n.31
Bellonzi, Fortunato 163
Berlinguer, Enrico 9, 207

Berlinguer, Mario 86
Berlusconi, Silvio 8, 16 n.28, 89, 209–10
Biagi, Enzo 15 n.18
Binchy, D. A. 51, 54
Bobbio, Norberto 93 n.5
Bocca, Giorgio 35, 212 n.25
Bologna 203
Bondanella, Peter 69 n.79
Boniface VIII 176–7
Bonomelli, Emilio 22, 178–9, 194 n.53
Bonomi, Ivanoe 36, 46, 75, 77, 80–1, 86, 88, 139
  conduct 80
  fall of government 85
  leaders meeting 84
  reaffirmation of authority 102
Bracci, Mario 114
Braschi, Angelo 26
Brigante, Saverio 115
Brosi, Manlio 101
Bunker, Ellsworth 170
Burns, John Horne 49, 65 n.20
Buttiglione, Rocco 16 n.28
Byrnes, James 140

Calamandrei, Piero 71–2, 74, 134, 144 n.27, 145 n.49, 184
Calvino, Italo 163
Canavero, Alfred 9
Carrillo, Elisa 23, 27
Carter, Bonham 189
Catholic Action 58, 74–5, 79, 139, 158, 160, 173–5, 177–80, 182, 199
Catholicism/Christianity 34, 132, 140, 152, 162–3, 172, 199
  Camaldoli Code 160
  Catholics 6, 23–6, 57, 59, 68 n.55, 74–5, 147, 156, 159, 166 n.47, 172, 179–80, 200
  Church 11, 25–7, 31, 38, 50–1, 55–60, 76, 80, 83, 93, 108–9, 137–8, 142, 151, 158, 160, 162, 169, 174–8, 183, 203–4, 207, 210
  instruction in religion 137
  political 2–3, 11, 74, 156, 158, 172, 181
  Protestantism 27, 156
  Veronese's role in Italy 159
Cattani, Leone 80, 101, 113
Catti De Gasperi, M. R. See De Gasperi, M. R.

Cau, Maurizio 41 n.33
Cavour, Camillo De 10–11, 132
centrism/centrist 25, 108, 169, 172, 175–7, 179–83
Cervantes, Miguel 208
Charles, Noel 113
Christian Democratic Party 1, 8, 12, 22, 24, 31, 72, 75, 77, 80–2, 84, 86–7, 89, 91–2, 100–1, 104, 106, 109, 111, 129–30, 135, 147, 149, 151, 154, 156, 158–63, 170–1, 173–4, 177–9, 183–4, 189, 197–9, 207, 209. See also De Gasperi, Alcide
Churchill, Winston 61, 84
Cianca, Alberto 138
Cicero 20–1, 23
Cingolani, Angela Guidi 106–7
Cingolani, Mario 86
Civic Committees 158–63, 173, 199
civitas/civiltà/civile 40 n.6, 142, 215 n.69
Clark, Martin 12
Clean Hands Inquest 209
clericalism 12, 27, 60, 171–2, 174, 198, 202–3
  clerico-Fascism/-Fascist 26, 51
co-belligerent Italian government 46, 51, 106
Code of Camaldoli 159–60
Coles, Henry L. 64 n.3
Cominform 147, 170
Comintern (Communist Information Bureau) 30–1, 33, 35, 170, 210
Comitato di Liberazione Nazionale di Alta Italia (CLNAI) 73
comizi (popular assemblies) 105–6
Committee of Anti-Fascist Currents 72, 77–8
Committee of National Liberation (CLN) 31, 37, 73–4, 79–80, 82–4, 85, 91–2, 100, 102–3, 129
Common Man's Front. See Uomo Qualunque
Communism/Communists 2–4, 19, 31–6, 57–8, 60, 73, 76–7, 81, 83, 99, 101–2, 104, 109, 113, 129, 133–4, 140, 148–50, 152–3, 155–6, 162, 169–72, 176–9, 182–4, 187–8, 198, 203, 207, 209
Communist Refoundation Party 209
Concordat of 1929 26, 58, 67 n.54, 83, 158

Conley, Thomas 15 n.16
Constituent Assembly (*Costituente*) 87,
    99, 101–3, 108, 110, 113, 129, 142,
    158, 160
  articles 134–9
  De Nicola's inaugural address to 131
  drafting of republican constitution
    135–6
  election and outcome 129–30
  nomination for Head of State 130–1
  prime minister's address to 132–3
  principles of 134–5
  selection of president 130
Constitutional Court 135, 138–9
Constitution of the Republic of Italy 6–7,
    12, 110, 133, 136, 138–9, 148
conventio ad excludendum 198, 203
Corbi, Gianni 31
Corbino, Epicarmo 102, 130, 133
Costantini, Celso 81
coup d'etat 91, 113–14, 116
Court of Cassation 112–15, 138
Craxi, Bettino 9
  corruption 208–9
  eulogy to Nenni 208
  Nenni's apparent *dauphin* 208
Cristina, Maria 29
Croce, Benedetto 10–11, 13, 32, 61, 74–5,
    89, 142
  anti-clericalism 10
  view of Fascism as "parenthesis" 74–5
Czech Communist Party 157

D'Alema, Massimo 16 n.28
D'Angelo, Augusto 176
D'Angelo Bigelli, Maria Grazia 38
Dante Alighieri 190
Davis, John 14, 18 n.47
De Gasperi, Alcide 1–3, 5–12, 19–21,
    34–9, 57–9, 73, 79–81, 107–12,
    115, 128–9, 150, 162, 169–71,
    186–8, 197–9, 205, 209–11. *See also*
    Christian Democratic Party
  addresses/speeches of 84, 116, 131–3,
    136–7, 141–2, 173
  ancestry 23
  Andreotti as *dauphin* 199
  attitude toward Americans 141–2, 188
  attitudes toward social class 25, 162
  Byrnes' gesture 140

cause for canonization 210
charisma 3
and Christianity/Catholics 24–7, 134,
    191 n.18, 207
on Communist involvement 77
comparison with Abraham Lincoln 6,
    42 n.46
conception of anti-Fascism 75
conflict with Sturzo 184–5
death of 190, 206
drafting of republican constitution
    131–4
Dunn's confidence in 156–7
early life and education 23–4
employment in Vatican Library 26–7,
    72
ethos 39
faith 5, 25
fall of 188–90
family ties and marriage 22
first government 99–103
    governing coalitions 3, 100–1, 130,
        147–8, 151
gravitas 211
imprisonment 3, 25–6
"I would rather argue with you (Nenni)
    than agree with Togliatti" 7
journalistic vocation 24 ("*mestieraccio*")
Levi's description of 91–2
meeting with leaders 84, 111, 114–15,
    143, 148, 176–9, 182, 188
party leadership 189
and peace treaty 140–3
personal appearance 19, 39 n.3
and Pius XII 28, 38, 114, 152, 163,
    172–4, 181
political suffering 20, 26, 141
political vocation 24–5, 38
realism 23, 111
relationship with Nenni 1–3, 5–8, 10,
    19, 34–7, 72, 75, 80–1, 89–90, 100–1,
    107, 109–11, 115–16, 129–30,
    132–3, 135–6, 140, 148, 150, 153–5,
    171, 182, 188–90, 197, 208, 211
relationship with Togliatti 1–3, 5–8,
    10, 14 n.4, 19, 28, 31–2, 34, 37,
    39 nn.2–3, 72, 75, 90, 100, 107,
    115, 129–30, 132–3, 135, 137, 140,
    150–5, 165 n.28, 169, 171–2, 198–9,
    208–11

reservations about Catholic integralism 190, 200, 207
reservations about 1929 Concordat when signed 26
restoration of the State 76, 92–3, 132
rhetoric and oratory 25, 28, 37, 89, 173, 188, 199
skepticism about Nenni's leadership ability 110
skepticism about Parri's leadership ability 90
"sphinx" 5
support for Article 7 in Constitution 137
and Umberto II 112–16
trust 21–2
visit to the United States 141–2
women's suffrage 99, 106
De Gasperi, Francesca 22, 25, 27, 178, 181
De Gasperi, Lucia 181, 194 n.54
De Gasperi, Maria Romana 4–5, 111, 141, 177, 181, 194 nn.53–4, 207
De Gasperi, M. R. 193 n.46, 194 n.53
De Grand, Alexander 37
De Grazia, Victoria 16 n.21, 17 nn.40–1
Della Torre, Count 83
Del Pero, Mario 187
democracy 26, 38, 49, 55, 58–60, 74, 82, 92, 107, 110, 129, 132, 134–6, 186, 191 n.4
Democracy of Labor Party 72, 75, 77, 80, 100–2, 129–30
Democratic Party of the Left 209
Democrazia Cristiana (DC). *See* Christian Democratic Party
De Nicola, Enrico 124, 130, 142–3
 inaugural address to *Costituente* 131
 Nenni's conversation with 165 n.32
 Toscano and 143
De Ruggiero, Guido 56
Dewey, John 52
Diggins, John 47, 65 n.21, 67 n.43
Dilthey, Wilhelm 14
Dini, Lamberto 16 n.28
Di Nolfo, Ennio 166 n.43
Di Scala, Spencer 149–50
Disch, L. J. 23
Dolfuss, Engelbert 1

Domenico, Roy 208
doppio gioco 4, 163
Dorigo, Wladimiro 180, 193 n.51
Dossetti, Giuseppe 111, 134
Duca, Borgognoni 118 n.54
Dulles, John Foster 170
Dunn, James 147, 155–7, 170, 186–7

Earl, Donald 21
Education in Italy 51–8
 Allied-approved textbooks 54
 Allied Education Subcommission's mission of 52
 damage of schools 52–3
 educational directors/officials 52, 56
 educational involvement of Church 58
 educational reforms of 1960s 205
 "moral and civic education" 52–3
 PWE handbook 54
 status of teachers 53–5
Einaudi, Luigi 126, 147–8, 154
Eisenhower, Dwight 170, 195 n.71
elections 104, 113, 131, 163, 173, 179, 189
 administrative (*see* administrative elections)
 Costituente 130
 law 183
 municipal (*see* municipal elections)
 parliamentary (*see* national parliamentary elections)
 results of Sicily's regional 149
Elia, Leopoldo 109
Ellis, Joseph 6
Engels, Friedrich 205
Eurocommunism 207
Evangelista, Rhiannon 15 n.17

Faenza, Roberto 143 n.1
Fallaci, Orianna 37, 210
Fanello-Marcucci, Gabriela 94 n.18, 97 n.86
Fanfani, Amintore 9, 111, 177, 186, 189–90, 199–200, 203
Fascism/Fascist 9, 12, 15 n.17, 19, 36, 45, 47, 51, 57, 59, 75, 78, 107, 132, 139, 184, 186, 200
 Fascist regime 3, 25–6, 58, 60, 75, 77, 137
 Grand Council 45

High Commission for Sanctions against 86
Republic of Salò 35, 87
slogans of 33
against women's suffrage 107
FDR. *See* Roosevelt, Franklin D. (FDR)
Fellini, Federico 204
feminism 185
Ferretti, Gino 55
Ferri, Enrico 205
Fini, Marco 143 n.1
First World War 25, 34, 50, 61, 77–8, 81, 186
Fisher, Thomas R. 66 n.23
Foa, Vittorio 72, 91, 97 n.91
Fogazzaro, Antonio 24
Forlenza, Rosario 63
Franco, Massimo 31, 34, 58, 212 n.13
Freeden, Michael 14 n.7
French Revolution 58, 110, 153

Gabrielli, Patrizia 107
Galeazzi, Enrico 109, 178
Galli, Giorgio 193 n.51
Gambino, Antonio 85, 115
"Garibaldi Brigades" 11, 34, 73
Garibaldi, Giuseppe ("The Hero of Two Worlds") 10–11, 16 n.31, 34
Garofalo, Franco 101
Gayre, George Robert 52, 54, 66 n.41
Gedda, Luigi 79, 158–63, 173–6, 178, 180–1, 194 n.57
  Civic Committees 158–63, 173, 199
  De Gasperi's secret summit with 179
Gemeinschaft 39 n.5
Gemelli, Agostino 57
Germany 16 n.21, 27, 45, 73, 78, 82, 142, 169
Gesellschaft 39 n.5
Gianinni, Guglielmo 108
Giannini, Amadeo 86–8
Ginsborg, Paul 12, 64 n.1
Ginzburg, Natalia 93 n.5
Giolitti, Giovanni 9
Giovagnoli, Agostino 12
Gioventù Italiana Azione Cattolica (GIAC) 79, 158, 179–80
  Pius XII's address to 160
Gonella, Guido 27, 57–8, 110, 115, 133, 136, 174, 177, 179–80, 189, 212 n.10

Goodwin, Doris Kearns 6, 42 n.46
Gorresio, Vittorio 19, 33, 153
Gramsci, Antonio 29–32, 38, 93 n.3, 200, 212 n.17
Great Britain 9–10, 16 n.21, 50, 110, 156
Grindrod, Muriel 12, 184
Gronchi, Giovanni 28, 80, 183
Guareschi, Giovannino 189–90, 199
Gullo, Fausto 101

Harper, John 5, 155
Hersey, John 49, 55, 65 n.21
historicism 9–10, 14–15, 16 n.20
Huebner, Andrew J. 65 n.20
Hughes, H. Stuart 19, 39 n.3, 55–6, 67 n.44, 67 n.46
Hugo, Victor 34
Hull, Cordell 103
humanism/humanistic 6, 10–11, 13, 20, 29, 33, 37, 140, 142, 172, 215 n.69

ideology/ideologies
  closed 14 n.7
  concrete 14 n.7
Ingrao, Pietro 200–1
institutional referendum. *See* referendum
Iotti, Nilde 4, 19, 33, 201, 209
Istituto Cattolico di Attività Sociale (ICAS) 159
Italian Communist Party 1, 3, 30, 32, 80, 130, 151–3, 162–3, 169–70, 197–9, 202–4, 207, 210
  "*doppio gioco*" 4, 163
  "Hour X" 4
  "new party" patriotic force 82
Italian Liberal Party 72, 75, 77, 80, 100–2, 104, 113, 129–30, 133, 172, 182–4
Italian Popular Party 25–6, 59, 72, 81, 176, 178
Italian Socialist Party 1, 35–6, 80, 130, 147, 149–50, 197, 207
Italian Social Movement 176, 182

Jemolo, Carlo Arturo 184
John XXIII 203–4
Judt, Tony 32

Kalyvas, Stathis 12
Kennedy, John 204

Kertzer, David 107, 144 n.18
Khrushchev, Nikita 200–1, 204
"King's Italy" 45–6, 64 n.3
Kirk, Alexander 103
Knights of Columbus 57
Kogan, Norman 12, 108, 143 n.1
koinonia (sharing) 20
Korner, Alex 66 n.22
Krommer, Ernst 24

La Malfa, Ugo 74, 80, 101–2, 150, 203, 213 n.31
Lanaro, Silvio 27
LaPalombara, Joseph 12
La Pira, Giorgio 180
Lateran Treaty of 1929 26, 58, 83, 133, 138, 148, 158, 175, 181
Lebedeva, Elena 33
Left-wing parties 25, 55, 72, 82, 85, 89, 101, 104, 107–8, 130, 133–6, 151, 163, 169, 176, 181–3, 185, 200, 202–3, 206, 209
Lenin, Vladimir 31, 205
Leopardi, Giacomo 34
Leo XIII 24
Levi, Carlo 62, 66 n.22, 73–4, 91–2, 94 n.13, 203
liberalism 23, 56, 58, 132, 155
Liberal Monarchy 74, 137
Liberal Party *See* Italian Liberal Party
Lincoln, Abraham 6, 42 n.46
Lippman, Walter 141, 204
Lombardi, Riccardo ("The Microphone of God") 162, 173, 177–8, 180, 182, 194 n.57
Longo, Luigi 90
Luce, Clare Boothe 170, 185–6, 195 n.71
Luce, Henry 141, 185–6
Luciano, Lucky 65 n.11
Lucifero, Falcone 101
    meeting with De Gasperi 111, 114–15

Machiavelli, Niccolo 10, 13, 16 n.28, 29, 71, 91, 190
Mack Smith, Denis 116
Mafai, Miriam 28, 209
Mani puliti ("Clean Hands Inquest") 209
Mao Zedong 205
Marcuse, Herbert 205
Mario, Luigi 24

Marshall, George 187
Marshall Plan 157, 170–1
Marsili, Marzia 200
Martinelli, Renzo 144 n.32
Martin, Jim 7
Marx, Karl 152, 205
Marxism/Marxist 2–3, 7, 11–12, 28, 33, 35–7, 60, 72, 76, 107, 130, 152–3, 162, 170, 174, 204, 209
"Mary, Jesus and Joseph Agency" 161
Mazzini, Giuseppe 10–11, 34, 64, 74, 90, 132, 134, 140, 210
McCormick, Anne O'Hare 141
Messineo, Antonio 182
Miller, James 56, 140, 149, 155, 164 n.9, 165 n.33
miseria 61–4, 173
Missiroli, Mario 193 n.51
Molè, Enrico 102
Molotov–Ribbentropp Non-Aggression Pact of 1939 83
monarchy/monarchism/monarchists 60–1, 83, 88, 99–100, 108–11, 113–14, 116, 129–30, 170, 176–7, 180, 182–3
    Liberal Monarchy 74, 137
    liberal supporters of 102
    monarchist regime 46, 115
    Savoyard Monarchy 3, 31, 50, 60–1, 74–5, 82, 88, 101, 109–10, 116
Montgomery, Bernard 170
Montagnana, Rita 33
Montanelli, Indro 4, 28, 37, 205
Montini, Giovanni Battista 38, 159, 174, 178, 193 n.47, 200
Morante, Elsa 63–4, 69 n.76
More, Thomas 10, 16 n.28
Moro, Aldo 202–3
    "convergent parallels" 202
    kidnapping and murder 207
    legitimation of Nennian socialism 202
Movimento Sociale Italiano (MSI) 170, 182
municipal elections 180–2, 200
    of 1946 160
    of 1951–1952 170, 175–7
Murphy, Robert 57
Murri, Romolo 24
Mussolini, Benito 3, 7, 11, 26, 51, 58–9, 62, 73, 76, 83, 85, 92, 107
    Badoglio's commitment to 78

degradation of women 106
execution of 46
fall from power in Rome 45, 71–2, 77
and Pius XI 58, 137
protests against 79
regime 3, 26, 59, 62, 73, 75–6, 138
Republic of Salò 35, 87
totalitarianism 50–1
Victor Emmanuel III's affiliation with 60–1

Naples 31, 48–9, 73, 82, 115, 182
damage of schools 52–3
Neapolitans 13, 31, 49, 75
National Bloc of Freedom 129–30
national parliamentary elections 68 n.55, 134, 147, 149, 157, 171, 173, 182–3, 185, 188, 194 n.52, 200, 205
National Socialism. *See* Nazi/Nazism
NATO 171, 188, 202, 207
Nazi/Nazism 3, 26, 35, 45, 52, 59–60, 62–3, 71, 79–81, 142
"The Nenni Law" 86
Nenni, Carmen 205
Nenni, Pietro 1–3, 5–12, 19–21, 31, 39, 73–4, 81, 83–5, 100–1, 103, 110–11, 115–16, 125, 129–30, 133, 140, 148–9, 151, 153, 164 n.9, 184, 209
anarchism 34, 43 n.75, 205
ancestry 34
anti-clericalism 20, 34, 89, 213 n.36
aphorisms 37, 43 n.75, 89, 96 n.80
against Badoglio 78
charisma 3
Craxi as *dauphin* 208
"(De Gasperi) always had his foot on the brake, mine (Nenni's) on the accelerator" 7
death of 208
diary entries of 38, 80, 102, 109, 132, 171, 190, 197, 203
disappointment at De Gasperi address to Constituent Assembly 132
drafting of republican constitution 135–6
early life 34
education 34
"Excellency" 84
exile in France 35, 72
family ties and marriage 38, 205
friendships 38

honor 206
interview with 210–11
journalistic vocation 35, 89, 206
magnitudo animi 211
meeting with leaders 84, 148, 154, 165 n.32, 171, 182, 188
opposition to Article 7 138
pathos 39
and peace treaty 140
political reincarnation 202
politique d'abord 38
radicalism 34, 149
relationship with De Gasperi 1–3, 5–8, 10, 19, 34–7, 72, 75, 80–1, 89–90, 100–1, 107, 109–11, 115–16, 129–30, 132–3, 135–6, 140, 148, 150, 153–5, 171, 182, 188–90, 197, 208, 211
relationship with Togliatti 1–3, 5–8, 10, 31, 34–6, 72, 76, 83–4, 89–90, 103, 105, 107, 111, 115, 129–30, 132–3, 135, 140, 148, 150, 202–3, 208, 211
republicanism 3, 11, 34, 113, 211
return to Rome in 1943 35
rhetoric and oratory 37, 105, 164 n.9, 165 n.32, 206
sentimentalism 31
socialism 34, 202
and Spanish Civil War 35, 38, 210
Stalin Peace Prize (1951) 171, 202
stanza dei bottoni 202
student protest 205
temperament 31, 34
Valiani on 89
women's suffrage 107
Nenni, Victoria 38
neo-Fascism/neo-Fascist 45, 72–3, 154, 156, 170, 177, 180, 182–3, 200
Niccolini, Mosi 29
Nitti, Francesco Saverio 34, 135, 176

Occhiocupo, Nicola 134, 144 n.28
Ogliati, Monsignor 57
Omodeo, Adolfo 56, 67 n.47
"Opening to the Left" 202–3
Orlando, Vittorio Emmanuele 9, 99, 142
Ottaviani, Alfredo 169, 191 n.2

Pacciardi, Randolfo 34, 38, 150, 154, 210
paese legale/paese reale 7, 197

Pagano, Giuseppe 114–15
Paganuzzi, Quirino 179
Pajetta, Gian Carlo 184
Pakaluk, Michael 15 n.17
Paris Peace Conference 129, 131
Paronetto, Sergio 75
Parri, Ferruccio ("Maurizio") 74, 84, 87–8, 90–2, 97 n.88, 135, 184
   De Gasperi and 90, 156
   exit from power 99–100
   partitocrazia 12
   personal austerity 90
   view of Togliatti 97 n.88, 135
partisans. *See* Resistance (Italian)
Partito Communista Italiano (PCI). *See* Italian Communist Party
Partito Liberale Italiano (PLI). *See* Italian Liberal Party
Partito Socialista Italiano (PSI). *See* Italian Socialist Party
Paul VI 159, 174, 200, 203
Pavan, Pietro 176, 192 n.31
Pavese, Cesare 63
Pavone, Caudio 9
peace treaty 92, 104, 109, 129, 139, 141–2, 143 n.1, 148
Pertini, Sandro 80, 101
Petacci, Clara 46
Piedmont/Piedmontese 96 n.60, 131, 135
Pignedoli, Don Sergio 174
Pius XI 26–7, 57, 59, 191 n.16
   acclamation of Mussolini 58, 137
Pius XII 2, 11, 34, 60, 79, 147, 158–63, 169, 174–5, 176–8, 180–2, 187, 189, 194 n.53, 195 n.71, 203, 207
   addresses/speeches of 108–9, 160
   Andreotti's memo to 179
   charisma/cult of personality 11
   Christmas Message of December 1944 59
   and De Gasperi 28, 38, 114, 152, 163, 172–4, 181
   distaste for Christian Democracy 170
   Easter notes of 162
   Episcopal Jubilee Year 166 n.47
   and La Pira 180
   letter from Ogliati 57
   response to Holocaust 60
Plutarch 10, 16 n.28

Poletti, Charles 48
political biography 9–14
political Catholicism 2–3, 11, 74, 156, 158, 172, 181
political friendship 20–3
   fidelity to friendship 38
   friendships of pleasure 21–2
   friendships of utility 21, 23
   friendships of virtue 21, 38
   sharing community of 20
   trust 21–2
political parties
   constitutional role of 131, 134–5
   in Italy in comparison with the United States 6
political religion 107, 118 n.31
Political Warfare Executive (PWE) 54
polycentrism 201
Pope, Generoso 157
Popular Front 100, 147, 149, 158, 161, 169–71, 197, 201
Popular Unity Party 184
Purdy, William 180
Putnam, Robert 12, 214 n.40

Quazza, Guido 94 n.12

Raggioneri, Ernesto 13
Ravaioli, Domenico 109
Ravera, Camilla 152
Rawlins, William 20, 41 n.25
Reale, Eugenio 33
Red Brigades 206–7
referendum 3, 8, 60, 99, 102–3, 108, 110–16, 139, 206, 211
reformists 34, 47, 56–7, 77, 149, 203
Rennell of Rodd, Lord 47, 54
   Administrative Instruction Order No. 1 48
republicanism 3, 11, 34, 58, 60, 100, 211
Republican Party 36–7, 42 n.46, 87, 129–30, 150, 172, 182–4, 203, 208, 210
Resistance (Italian) 35, 37, 62, 64, 71, 85, 91, 106, 134, 141, 147, 208
   and anti-Fascist parties 11, 46, 72–7
   female participation 107
   Resistance Movement 88, 104
Revelli, Nuno 79
revolution 31, 37, 92

French Revolution 58, 110, 153
  proletarian 82
Right-wing parties 1, 72, 82, 88, 100, 107–8, 133–4, 154, 170, 176, 179, 181–3, 185, 187, 189, 200, 206, 209
Riosa, Alceo 17 n.42
Risorgimento 9–10, 64, 72, 74, 90, 131–2, 187, 199
Roberts, David 13, 16 n.20
"rollback" doctrine 155, 170, 186
Romagna, Romagnuol 20, 34, 36, 81, 111
Romano, Francesca 22
Romano, Sergio 9–10
Rome/Roman 10, 22, 46, 63, 71–2, 77–8, 83, 90, 139, 152, 161–3, 172, 188–9
  bureaucracy 50, 74, 85
  CLN in 73
  Episcopal Jubilee Year of Pope 166 n.47
  Façade of Montecitorio palace 128
  military violation of 59
  miseria 62
  municipal elections 170, 175–7, 179–82, 200
  Mussolini's fall from power in 45
  Nazi occupation of 3, 35, 80–1
  Pope's visit to damaged Church 59
  romanità (Catholic) 59
  Roman Republic 13, 21
Romita, Giuseppe 77, 80, 100–1, 104, 111–12, 116
  accusation against 113
  on referendum vote 112
Ronca, Roberto 81, 95 n.48, 176
Roosevelt, Franklin D. (FDR) 49, 61, 84, 156
Rossellini, Roberto 69 n.79
Rossi, Mario 200
Rowell, Henry 53–4
Royal Italian Armed Forces 79
Ruini, Meuccio 75, 80, 100–1
Rumor, Mariano 189, 205–6
Russia. *See* Soviet Union

Sale, Giovanni 111
Salerno Turn 31, 36, 52–3, 76, 82–5, 198
Sallust 13
Salvemini, Gaetano 13, 55, 64, 72
  contadini 69 n.78
  return to Italy 163 n.1

view of Resistance as "second Risorgimento" 64, 72
Santarelli, Enzo 13
Saragat, Giuseppe 80, 130–1, 147, 149–50, 164 n.8, 202, 204
Scelba, Mario 1, 89, 126, 183–4, 198
Schmitt, Hans 18 n.45
Scoccimarro, Mauro 80–1, 86, 148
Scoppola, Pietro 6, 12–13, 94 n.15, 143 n.1, 197, 206–7
Second World War 3, 20, 23, 27, 36, 38, 45, 50, 59, 61, 76, 79, 155, 187, 189, 203
Sereni, Emilio 107
Settembrini, Domenico 193 n.48, 209–10
Sforza, Carlo 56, 67 n.46, 85–6, 100, 143, 147, 154, 156–7
Shakespeare, William 154
Sicily 60, 115. *See also* Allied Occupation policy
  Allied invasion of Sicily 45
  liberation of 47–8
  results of regional elections 149
  Sicily landings 48, 51, 54, 73
Silverman, Sydel 40 n.6, 215 n.69
Smith, Thomas Vernor 52, 56, 65 n.7, 67 n.47
Social Democratic Party 172, 182–4, 202, 204
socialism/socialists 2–3, 5–6, 23, 30–1, 34–7, 58, 60, 76–7, 81, 83, 85, 87, 99–101, 104, 129–30, 133–4, 136, 148, 150, 153, 169, 171–2, 176, 183–4, 187, 198
Soviet Communist Party 30, 200–1, 210, 212 n.20
Soviet Union 2, 31, 72, 76–7, 83, 139–40, 163, 169–70, 198, 201, 204, 210
Spadolini, Giovanni 206, 208, 210
Spain 2, 31, 34, 58, 110
Spataro, Giuseppe 21–2, 77, 80–1
Spellman, Francis 142
Stalin, Joseph 2, 4, 9, 30–2, 35–6, 43 n.64, 61, 76, 82–3, 161, 163, 170, 199–203, 207, 210
Stangone, F. S. 86
St. Augustine 40 n.6
Stirner, Max 205
St. John Lateran Seminary 35, 72, 80–1, 171
Stone, Ellery 86, 109, 111, 148

Stricht, Samuel 142
Sturzo, Luigi 25, 55, 72, 176, 180, 184–5
   view of Resistance as "second Risorgimento" 72
   opposition to Swindle Law 184–5
Sturzo Operation (1952) 95 n.48, 158, 170, 175–82, 200
Svolta di Salerno. See Salerno Turn
Swindle Law 182–5

Tamburrano, Giuseppe 13, 37
Tangentopoli ("Bribesville scandal") 209
Tarchiani, Alberto 142, 185
Tardini, Domenico 28, 42 n.44, 156, 176, 180
Taylor, Myron 156
Terracini, Umberto 126, 130, 135
Terzuolo, Eric 29
Thommasen, Bjorn 63
Tito, J. Broz 30, 43 n.64, 163
Tittman, Harold 156
Togliatti, Aldo 33
Togliatti, Maria Cristina 29
Togliatti, Palmiro 2, 6–12, 19–21, 34, 36, 38, 48, 73, 89, 96 n.60, 97 n.88, 103, 111, 113–14, 116, 129, 133, 197, 209–10, 212 n.25
   addresses/speeches of 82, 132, 135
   amnesty decree 3
   ancestry 29
   on anti-Fascist coalition 198
   aphorism 144 n.30
   arrival in Rome 35
   assassination attempt 1
   and Badoglio 82, 84, 95 n.52
   charisma/cult of personality 3, 32, 200
   constantia 211
   death of 201, 203, 206
   drafting of republican constitution 135–6
   dress and manners 32
   education 23–4, 29
   "Ercole" 31, 83, 200
   exile in Moscow 30, 72, 81, 83, 200
   family ties and marriage 33
   "half Croce, half Stalin" 32
   intelligence 28–9
   as justice minister 3, 87, 101–2, 115
   letter to Longo 90–1

logos 39
   Parri's view of 97 n.88, 135
   and peace treaty 142
   personal appearance 19
   realism 29–31
   respect for Catholicism 31, 138
   relationship with De Gasperi 1–3, 5–8, 10, 14 n.4, 19, 28, 31–2, 34, 37, 39 nn.2–3, 72, 75, 90, 100, 107, 115, 129–30, 132–3, 135, 137, 140, 148, 150–5, 165 n.28, 169, 171–2, 198–9, 208–11
   relationship with Nenni 1–3, 5–8, 31, 34–6, 72, 76, 83–4, 89–90, 103, 105, 107, 111, 115, 129–30, 132–3, 135, 140, 148, 150, 202–3, 208, 211
   rhetoric and oratory 28, 31, 105
   support for article 7 138
   temperament 28–33
   vision of 211
   and women's suffrage 107
   Yalta Testament 201
Tonnies, Ferdinand 39 n.5
Toscano, Mario 143, 146 n.66
Trentine/Trentino 20, 23–5, 36, 38, 77, 81, 110–11, 162, 173, 190, 200, 210
Trieste 60, 140–1
Trotsky, Leon 30
Truman, Harry 142
trust 3, 21–2, 79, 100, 136, 141
Tupini, Umberto 109

Umberto II 61, 83, 85, 99, 106, 108–9, 111–15
   denunciation of Republic 116
   Portuguese exile 115
Union for the Catholic Women of Italy 106
Unità Popolare. See Popular Unity Party
Unitary Socialist Party (PSU) 204–5
The United Nations 140, 206
United Nations Relief and Rehabilitation Administration (UNRRA) 148
The United States 2–3, 9–10, 14, 49, 51–2, 139, 141, 147, 150, 154, 169–70, 204
   American economic aid 129, 155
   American Federation of Labor (AFL) 150
   Office of War Information 61

American-style consumerism 204
De Gasperi's visit to 141
Italian-American relations 155–7,
    185–8
School of Military Government 49
Uomo Qualunque 87–8, 100, 108, 129
USSR. *See* Soviet Union

Valiani, Leo 4, 73, 92, 163
    view of Nenni 89
    view of De Gasperi 92–3
Vatican 2–3, 26, 34, 46, 59, 72, 75, 77, 81,
    93, 112, 137, 147, 151, 155–9, 163,
    171, 176, 178–80, 189, 204
    De Gasperi's government and 114, 134,
        169–70, 187
    Gonella in 58
    opposition to American liberal
        reformers 57
    Pope's disappointment in De Gasperi
        173–5
    Popular Party abandoned by 25
    right-wing sources 183
    support for monarchy 60
Veronese, Vittorino 158–60, 174–5

Vessolo, Arthur 57
Vico, Giambattista 9, 13
Victor Emmanuel III 45, 59–61, 83,
    161
virtù 4, 71

Warner, Carolyn 12
Warsaw Pact 201
Washburne, Carleton 52, 54–5, 65 n.7
Weber, Max 39 n.5, 97 n.90
Welles, Sumner 150
White, Steven F. 15 n.17, 66 n.29, 165 n.42,
    191 n.14, 211 n.9
Wind from the North 85, 104
Wiskemann, Elizabeth 92

Yalta Testament 201
Years of Lead 37, 206
Young Men of Catholic Action. *See*
    Gioventù Italiana Azione Cattolica
    (GIAC)

Zaslavsky, Victor 9, 212–13 n.25
Zola, Emile 34

www.ingramcontent.com/pod-product-compliance
Lightning Source LLC
Chambersburg PA
CBHW072137290426
44111CB00012B/1901